# the communism of mao tse-tung

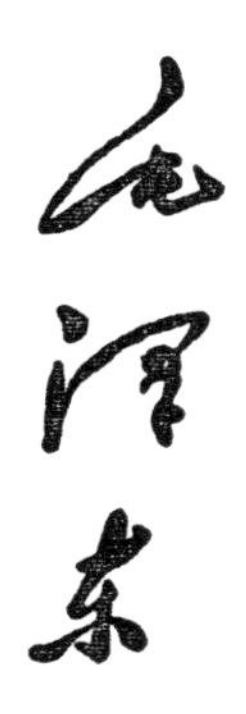

# the communism of mao tse-tung

Arthur A. Cohen

THE UNIVERSITY OF CHICAGO PRESS
CHICAGO & LONDON

*Library of Congress Catalog Card Number: 64-23420*

THE UNIVERSITY OF CHICAGO PRESS, CHICAGO & LONDON

THE UNIVERITY OF TORONTO PRESS, TORONTO 5, CANADA


*Published 1964*

PRINTED IN THE UNITED STATES OF AMERICA

to my co-workers

# Preface

This appraisal of Mao Tse-tung attempts to distinguish between those of his ideas and actions which justifiably may be described as unique in the history of the world Communist movement and those which may not. In an effort to reduce the perplexities of certain doctrinal issues, I have tried to make the plainest statement of the point in question, recognizing that perfectly clear and precise meanings nevertheless may not always be the result.

In the course of my research, I have found nourishment in several articles written by Professor Benjamin I. Schwartz and Professor Karl A. Wittfogel. I owe a debt of gratitude to my good friend Leonard Jaffe for his assistance with the Soviet aspects of chapters 2, 3, and 4. I wish respectfully to thank my colleagues for their ideas and penetrating comments on the manuscript and Mary Patzer for her translations from certain Russian texts.

In this and other work, I have been greatly inspired by my wife, Phyllis.

# Contents

Introduction — 1

1
Mao as Philosopher — 7

2
Mao and Revolution — 29

3
Mao and the State Form — 74

4
The "Transition to Socialism" — 105

5
"Contradictions" in a "Socialist Society" — 139

6
The "Transition to Communism": "People's Communes" — 168

Conclusion — 188

Index — 207

# Introduction

Although doctrine would have it otherwise, belief in the great man as maker of history seems to be a characteristic of many orthodox Communists. For them, the history of Communist thought has been remarkably simple: it has been the history of four hero thinkers.

First in the field was Marx, who by all accounts was one of the most brilliant thinkers of the nineteenth century. Marx's contribution to nineteenth-century political theory was his view that material conditions (production) determine the life of the community. Changes in the mode of production rather than man's ideas of eternal truth or law and justice determine all social change.[1] He also held that "class struggle" did not end with the rise to power of the bourgeoisie but with the rise to power of the proletariat, the establishment of the dictatorship by revolution, and the abolition of all classes in a future Communist society. As for the capitalist economy, its disappearance was a "scientific" certainty. His contribution to epistemology was his restatement

[1] In 1859, Marx wrote, "I was led by my studies to the conclusion that legal relations as well as forms of state could neither be understood by themselves, nor explained by the so-called general progress of the human mind, but that they are rooted in the material conditions of life. . . ." Preface to his *Contribution to the Critique of Political Economy* (1859), English translation (Chicago: Charles H. Kerr, 1904).

of the view that knowledge is inseparably bound up with action or practice, that only action can really complete the process of knowing. On the matter of moral consciousness, Marx taught that the ethical system of a society always reflects the interests of the dominant class. And Engels, the man with whom he collaborated and who expanded his views, wrote in 1877 that "all former moral theories are the product, in the last anlysis, of the economic stage which society had reached at that particular epoch. And as society has hitherto moved in class antagonisms, morality was always a class morality. . . ."[2] From this view it was only one step to building the basis of a political teaching that would justify a policy of violence against men. Lenin took that step, and Stalin was among his students.

Lenin as a philosopher was below the level of Marx and Engels. In his major theoretical work, *Materialism and Empirio-Criticism* (1909), he did little more than follow the latter's ideas on the knowing process. More important, he *imposed* this philosophy on all Communists. Lenin showed greater originality on more practical matters, which are given by R. N. Carew Hunt as his ideas on the strategy and tactics of revolution, his version of Marx's dictatorship of the proletariat, his view of the Communist party as "the vanguard of the proletariat," his ideas on how world revolution could be carried out by various Communist parties, and his theory of capitalist imperialism as the "final stage of capitalism" which opened a new revolutionary phase.[3] These contributions to Marxism — his version of Marx and Engels — were uniquely expressed in terms of blood and iron, power and terror. This was particularly so on the matter of building the party into a fighting unit. When, at the 1903 Congress of the Russian Social-Democratic Labor party, a delegate urged that the Central Committee should become the "omnipresent and

[2] Engels, *Anti-Dühring*, in *A Handbook of Marxism*, ed. E. Burns (New York: International Publishers, 1935), pp. 109–10.

[3] R. N. Carew Hunt, *The Theory and Practice of Communism* (rev. ed.; New York: Macmillan Co., 1952), pp. 135–68.

one," the all-pervasive, all-informing, and all-uniting "spirit," Lenin cried out from his seat: "Ne dukh, a kulak!" ("Not spirit, but fist!")[4] Men such as Plekhanov showed greater excellence in philosophy, but Lenin had no master in the theory and practice of making a party and a revolution.

As for Stalin, he was intellectually inferior to Marx, Engels, and Lenin. His contribution to Marxist philosophy is insignificant, consisting in large part of mere paraphrases or small elaborations on ideas of his mentors. Stalin had a stable of philosophers who performed the donkey-labor of linking philosophy to the needs of the Communist party and whose ideas he often used as his own. In the 1930's these men made of Stalin a theorist of "infallible" rank, which he was not, but thereafter most certainly pretended to be. On practical matters he showed considerable shrewdness but there is no theoretical originality in the justifications he devised for his policies. His "contributions" consist primarily in distortions or deviations from the views of Marx and Engels. Stalin departed from the view of Marx by stressing the supremacy of the superstructure and politics over the base and economics, and he says in *Dialectical and Historical Materialism* (1938) that once new social "ideas and theories" arise, they become "a most potent force" which facilitates social progress. But this position is merely a revival of Lenin's attack on the Economists, who saw the economic factor alone as the determinant of the historical process. Stalin was not the first or the most enlightened to discuss the "national question." As for the doctrine of "socialism in one country," it too was not original with the Soviet leader. It was a matter of how much emphasis should be given to world revolution and how much to building "socialism" in Russia. By 1924–25 many Bolsheviks in addition to Stalin were prepared to stress the latter.

Marx and Engels are the great theorists of Communism. But

[4] Quoted from Bertram D. Wolfe's excellent article, "The Durability of Soviet Despotism," *Commentary*, August, 1957.

neither man had the opportunity to carry out, to apply the totalitarian political theory he had helped create. The crucial step toward the realization of this theory was made by Lenin. As Karl A. Wittfogel puts it, Lenin "through the introduction of new operational methods of total organization and total demagoguery became the true father of modern Communist totalitarianism."[5] It was characteristic of Stalin that he used new methods to wrench authority from his peers in the party, making it total authority, and to silence the voices of those Bolsheviks whose intellectual merit exceeded his own.

Yet many Communist historians and revolutionary leaders for many years have linked the names of Lenin and Stalin with those of Marx and Engels as the "unique theorists" of Communist doctrine. For the orthodox, of course, men like Trotsky do not belong in this elite group of hero thinkers. But neither does the less vilified Plekhanov: it is no easy matter to join the group. And in Khrushchev's view, Stalin should not belong and never really did.

Nevertheless, a bid has been entered for a new and controversial figure: the Chinese leader, Mao Tse-tung (b. 1893). The Chinese Communists believe that just as Germany had its Marx and Engels and Russia had its Lenin and Stalin, so China has its genius for all Communists to acknowledge. The ideas of Marx and Engels rule the late nineteenth century, followed by those of Lenin and Stalin in the first half of the twentieth century. The death of Stalin in 1953, the Chinese feel, marked the end of the great Russian thinkers and opened the field to Mao—the only great thinker in the second half of the century. As one Chinese writer put it: "Comrade Mao Tse-tung is the most outstanding representative of the proletariat in China and the greatest and most outstanding revolutionary leader, statesman, and theorist of Marxism-Leninism in the modern era." Moscow disagrees with

[5] "The Operational Ideas of the Communist Doctrine," *Problems of Communism* (Washington), September–October, 1956, p. 32.

this immodest claim and attacks the Chinese separatism which flows from it. Thus the evaluation of Mao's "contributions" to doctrine and revolutionary practice is and will continue to be an issue in the bitter Sino-Soviet dispute.

The purpose of this book is to delineate Mao's view of Communism. Chinese claims for him as an innovator will be examined to see at what point his Communism becomes different, because of a new strategem or idea, from the "classical" tradition. The Chinese writers will be permitted to state their case for Mao, before that case is examined. It should be said at once that Chinese spokesmen see many more "contributions" to doctrine than do others, as it is their duty to do so. At one time generous with Mao, Soviet spokesmen now see no contribution, and they would have all men see the matter in this way.

The Chinese, who had recognized that Soviet Premier Krushchev's assault in 1956 on Stalin's cult was also partly an implicit assault on Mao's enormous doctrinal pretensions, apparently had anticipated an open attack for several years. In the summer of 1963, following the signing of the tripartite nuclear test ban treaty, the Soviet leaders began to move toward open denunciation of Mao and his personality cult. An article in the organ of the Central Committee of the Soviet Communist party, *Kommunist*, of July 31, 1963, complained that the Chinese leaders are trying to create their "own" Marxism and to impose it on "everyone else as the real truth." Aiming its shaft at Mao, the article goes on to conjecture:

> Perhaps they would like to return the world Communist movement to the stage in which a single man could rise above the people, like a god, and resolve the major problems in the activities of all Communist parties.

This seems to be, with some slight exaggeration, the Chinese Communist goal, and claims for Mao's genius are intended to provide the motive force for advancing toward that goal.

In their effort to build the image of Mao, the Chinese are

using language carefully in order to insure uniqueness for his works. In Communist China today, the ideas found in Mao's writings are referred to not as "Maoism," but as the "thought of Mao Tse-tung." This phrase is intended to set his ideas off from those of all other Marxist-Leninists. It is a rejection of the 1947 Chinese use of "ism," namely, "Mao Tse-tungism," because the Chinese do not want to refer to the entire doctrine as Marxism-Leninism-Maoism: to the Chinese Communists, the "thought of Mao Tse-tung" represents a distinctive non-European cultural ethos which is peculiarly Chinese. As such, they have referred to it on occasion as "Marxism-Leninism sinicized" or "Chinese Marxism." They contend, moreover, that the "thought of Mao Tse-tung" is not only the practical application of European Marxism-Leninism to conditions in China but also a further development of the basic theoretical principles of the "classical" doctrine. In appraising the claims for Mao as an innovator, we will center our attention primarily on this contention in order to see in what sense Mao has or has not made a real contribution.

To lend precision to our effort, we will quote extensively from the most detailed and relevant claims made by his eulogists and then discuss these claims in the context of what the important leaders and theorists in the Communist movement had written earlier on the subject in question. The reader may well find the discussion tiresome at times, but in our view a less rigorous treatment would lead to a superficial and fruitless exercise. The essential features of Mao's thought could certainly have been set out more concisely and without occasional reference to historical context or the political reality he confronted. Any such compression, however, would leave the reader asking if there were not something more to Mao; after all, he is acclaimed internationally by many Communists as being beyond doubt a great theorist. Only a more thorough account of his doctrinal views, the claims for them, and their validity when seen against the "classical" background will permit us to determine if there is any merit in this international acclamation.

# 1

# Mao as Philosopher

In the history of the Chinese people the decisive victories of Mao Tse-tung's party and field armies in 1949–50 mark the beginning of a new type of imposed emperor worship: worship of the genius philosopher. Sun Yat-sen, who had abolished the imperial throne, was revered by most Chinese, but he did not pretend, as Mao was to pretend, to semidivine insight. He rejected the idea that as leader he should be held in awe just as the emperors had been in the dynastic period. But Mao's ego was more demanding than Sun's, and he soon tried to become a *total* genius.

Now the Mao whose name was on everyone's lips in 1950 was the Mao of the Long March, party-building in Yenan, "tiger" hunting—that is, hunting Chiang Kai-shek's armies—in the central plains, and finally building the "people's democratic dictatorship" in Peking. Mao was master organizer and leader. His plan for victory had been written down in many of his works since 1926, and for most of the faithful these works on political and military tactics were their only contact with Mao's thinking.

Mao Tse-tung was a "genius" military and political thinker until December 18, 1950. On that date he became a "genius" philosopher as well.

In his enterprise of increasing his prestige, Mao in 1950 seems to have revived his plan to join the ranks of Marx, Engels, Lenin, and Stalin. Starting from the premise that to all Communists these men were not just great political thinkers but also masters of philosophy, Mao probably concluded that he could receive no honor more decisive for his name than the publication of a treatise on Marxist-Leninist philosophy. He had tried his hand at this in 1940 and, as will be demonstrated below, failed miserably. In 1950 he apparently decided to try again.

Stalin undoubtedly encouraged and aided Mao in his enterprise in 1950, as the Soviet leader at last felt compelled to act to gain Mao's goodwill after years of subordinating the interests of the Chinese Communist party (CCP) and its leader to the larger interests of the Communist party of the Soviet Union (CPSU) and its leader. On December 18, 1950, *Pravda* for the first time appraised one of Mao's works as creative in that it "develops basic concepts of Marxism-Leninism on dialectical materialism."

### *"On Practice"*

The *Pravda* review was referring to *On Practice*, which the Chinese claim was written in July, 1937, but which actually was fully publicized in 1950. The *Pravda* tribute, probably sanctioned by Stalin himself, was in a short time surpassed by Chinese Communist praise.

Li Ta, chairman of the Scientific Association for Philosophy, termed the essay "a development of the Marxist-Leninist theory of practice." [1] This and other Chinese claims went beyond the more modest and accurate view that *On Practice* had "summed up" existing theory and doctrinal tradition, but the Soviet theorists were soon content to rest on their oars.

[1] Li Ta, "*On Practice* — the Philosophical Foundation of Mao Tse-tung's Ideology," in *Selected Essays for the Study of "On Practice"* (Hankow: Chung-nan Jen-min Ch'u-pan She, 1951), p. 72. (This article was originally printed in Peking *Jen-min Jih-pao*, February 1, 1951.)

In his article, Li Ta approaches the role of practice in the knowing-process by citing a passage from Lenin's *Philosophical Notebooks*: "From living intuition to abstract thought and from thence to practice — that is the dialectical road to knowledge of the truth, to knowledge of objective reality." But Mao, he claims, has "developed" this principle of Lenin by drawing a penetrating distinction between two stages in the knowing-process: that is, "from perception (intuition) to thought and from thought to practice." Mao pointed out that the "perception" of the first stage is a low stage of knowledge, while the "thought" of the second stage is a high stage of knowledge.

It is difficult to grant validity to Li's claim on the grounds he chooses for it. For Lenin's above-mentioned remark clearly posits two stages in the knowing-process, and other statements made by him indicate that it was precisely with this process that he dealt. The theory of knowledge, he wrote, must study "the origin and development of cognition, the transition from *non*-consciousness to consciousness" (Lenin's emphasis here and hereafter)[2] "We must not regard our knowledge as ready made . . . but must determine how *knowledge* emerges from *ignorance*, how incomplete, inexact knowledge becomes more complete and more exact."[3] "Sensation [psychological perception] is the transformation of the energy of external excitation into a state of consciousness [thought]."[4] But how this transition from physical to mental occurs in the concrete and exactly through what mechanism, Lenin never actually informs us, and neither does Mao.

Lenin repeatedly makes the point, which Mao merely reiterates in *On Practice*, that knowledge moves upward, ascends in stages. Lenin's view is that knowledge must not be regarded as

[2] Lenin, *The Teachings of Karl Marx* (New York: International Publishers, 1930), p. 14.

[3] Lenin, *Materialism and Empirio-Criticism* (English language version, Moscow, 1952), p. 65.

[4] *Ibid.*, p. 39.

a passive, "immediate" reflection of reality, but as a process in which the knowing subject takes an active part, ascending by abstraction from sensations to higher products of knowledge, that is, as a process occurring by stages. He says, "Knowledge is the reflection of Nature on the part of man. This reflection, however, is by no means a simple, immediate, total affair, but rather a process involving a series of abstractions, formulations, the framing of concepts, laws, etc."[5] "In ascending from the concrete to the abstract, thought — provided it is *correct* — does not get farther away from truth, but comes closer to it . . . *all* scientific abstractions present a deeper, more faithful, *more complete* reflection of Nature."[6] "The movement of knowledge *towards* its object must always take place in a dialectical fashion. . . ."[7] "Truth is a process. Man advances from subjective idea to objective truth by way of 'practice' (and technology)."[8] "Man is unable to grasp-reflect-copy Nature as a *whole*, a complete thing, in its 'immediate totality'; he can only approach *eternally* closer to it, by creating abstractions, concepts, laws, a scientific world-picture, and so on, and so forth."[9]

Lenin's emphasis in these passages stems from his effort to strike a contrast to the sensationalist views of materialists such as Mach. He insists, throughout the working-out of the "dialectical" transition from the sensory to the "logical" stages of knowledge, on preserving an essential distinction between the two. He thereby acknowledges the basic impossibility of assimulating intellectual cognition to sensory activity. When, therefore, Mao, discussing two stages in the process of gaining knowledge, states, "Conception (thought) is not only quantitatively but also qualitatively different from perception (sensory activity)"[10] he is at-

[5] Lenin, *Philosophical Notebooks* (1914–18) (Moscow, 1947), p. 156.
[6] *Ibid.*, p. 146.
[7] *Ibid.*, p. 261.
[8] *Ibid.*, p. 174.
[9] *Ibid.*, p. 157.
[10] Mao, *Selected Works*, I (1961), 274. Citations from Mao's selected works will be made from the following Chinese language editions: (1) *Mao Tse-tung*

tacking the sensationalist dragons precisely from Lenin's position.

Chinese theorists also advanced claims of philosophical uniqueness for *On Practice* in connection with the Marxist theory of truth. Ai Ssu-ch'i, deputy chairman of the Scientific Association for Philosophy, who has been writing on the methodology of thought since at least 1936,[11] states that Mao "clarifies and develops Engels' and Lenin's famous principle on absolute and relative truth."[12] Ai seems to have abstracted a statement in *Pravda*, December 18, 1950, which had reviewed Mao's essay. His case appears to rest primarily on the following statement of Mao's:

> A Marxist recognizes that the development of the total process of the universe is absolute, whereas the development of each particular process in this total process is relative. Hence in the great river of absolute truth, man's knowledge of a particular process in each given stage of development is only relatively true. Absolute truth is compounded of a sum-total of relative truths.[13]

Actually, this is merely a paraphrase, not a development, of Lenin's remarks in *Materialism and Empirio-Criticism* (1909):

---

*Hsüan-chi*, Vol. II, published in the border area of Shansi-Chahar-Hopei in March, 1945, hereafter cited as Mao, *Selected Works*, II (1945). (2) *Mao Tse-tung Hsüan-chi*, published in Dairen in November, 1947, hereafter cited as Mao, *Selected Works* (1947). (3) *Mao Tse-tung Hsüan-chi*, Supplement, published in the Shansi-Chahar-Hopei border area in December, 1947, hereafter cited as Mao, *Selected Works*, Supplement (1947). (4) *Mao Tse-tung Hsüan-chi*, Vol. I, published in Peking in October, 1951, hereafter cited as Mao, *Selected Works*, I (1951). (5) *Mao Tse-tung Hsüan-chi*, Vol. II, published in Peking in April, 1952, hereafter cited as Mao, *Selected Works*, II (1952). (6) *Mao Tse-tung Hsüan-chi*, Vols. I–IV, published in Peking in January, 1961, hereafter cited as Mao, *Selected Works*, I, II, III, or IV (1961). Editions 1–5 will be cited primarily to discuss the matter of Mao's falsification of dates and revisions of his texts. Edition 6 will be used primarily to discuss various doctrinal concepts. All these editions contain works by Mao written prior to 1950, although some include footnotes commenting on Mao's post-1950 ideas. Reference will be made to individual journals, pamphlets, or newspapers for Mao's 1950 and post-1950 writings.

[11] Ai Ssu-ch'i, *On the Methodology of Thought* (Sheng-huo Shu-tien, no place, 1936), 161 pp. Other early articles discuss "philosophy for the masses."

[12] Ai Ssu-ch'i, "Comrade Mao Tse-tung Develops the Theory of Truth," in *Selected Essays for the Study of "On Practice,"* p. 56.

[13] Mao, *Selected Works*, I (1961), 284.

> Human reason in its nature is capable of yielding and does yield the absolute truth which is composed of the sum-total of relative truths. Each step in the development of science adds new fragments of truth, and from this absolute truth is constituted, but the limits of the truth of each scientific statement are relative.[14]

And indeed, Lenin was merely repeating Engels' argument in *Anti-Dühring* (1877), where he discusses "eternal truths" and states that "the knowledge which has an unconditional claim to truth is realized in a series of relative errors."

Another argument used by Ai Ssu-ch'i, which on first consideration appears pertinent to the claim for Mao's uniqueness, is that Mao "proved the necessity of the uninterrupted development of true knowledge."[15] That is, that all "truths" must be corrected without interruption. This is an important point, and the manner in which Ai underscores it indicates that this is the philosophical rationalization for any reversal of line by a revolutionary leader; it may be used as a club against those who are reluctant to change course ("dogmatists, die-hards"). Thus Mao says, "A true revolutionary leader must be adept at correcting his ideas, theories, plans, or programs when they are mistaken. . . . If the cognition of revolutionaries does not change quickly with a situation, they cannot lead the revolution towards victory."[16]

While Mao was well advised in making this practical point, his eulogists are not justified in stressing its novelty. For, among other things, Engels in *Anti-Dühring* states, "Truth and error, like all concepts which are expressed in polar opposites, have absolute validity only in an extremely limited field." And Lenin, more concretely, tells Gorky that "there is nothing either sacred or holy about theories or hypotheses; they serve us only as instru-

[14] Lenin, *Materialism and Empirio-Criticism*, p. 122.

[15] Ai Ssu-ch'i, "Comrade Mao Tse-tung Develops the Theory of Truth," *op. cit.*, p. 66.

[16] Mao, *Selected Works*, I (1961), 283.

ments."[17] Finally, Lenin again: Above all, we "must take account of real life, of the exact facts of reality, and not hang on to the tails of the theories of yesterday, which . . . do not come near enough to the complexities of life."[18]

As in Mao's discussion of (*a*) the two stages of the knowing-process and (*b*) relative truth, his (*c*) distinction betwen appearance and essence, in the matter of cognition, is also part of the already organized Marxist doctrine. Mao has nothing to add to Engels' and Lenin's ideas on appearance and essence, or to (*d*) Marx's critical reformulation of "the primacy of practice in knowledge"[19] as elaborated in the writtings of Engels, Lenin, and Stalin.

Thus, nowhere in *On Practice* does Mao introduce a genuinely novel idea or make a constructive contribution to dialectical materialist doctrine on practice. Indeed, in a rather unusual commentary on Mao's treatise, published in a Chinese Communist journal, Professor Feng Yu-lan, perhaps the greatest living historian of Chinese philosophical thought, acknowledges in effect that even pre-modern Chinese philosophers — particularly Mo Ti, Wang Ch'ung, and Wang Chuan-shan — had anticipated all of Mao's ideas on the role of practice in the knowing-process.[20]

[17] Maxim Gorky, *Days with Lenin* (New York: International Publishers, 1932), p. 45.

[18] Lenin, *Revolutionary Lessons* (London: Modern Books, 1929), p. 14. Lenin's remark, made in 1917, was intended to justify "pushing" the revolution despite the orthodox dictum that the bourgeois revolution must first be completed.

[19] Karl Marx, "Theses on Feuerbach, II" in *Ludwig Feuerbach*, by Friedrich Engels (New York: International Publishers, 1941), p. 82.

[20] Feng Yu-lan, "Mao Tse-tung's *On Practice* and Chinese Philosophy," *People's China* (Peking), November 16, 1951. Although Feng seems compelled to end his article routinely by saying that Mao "successfully solved a problem which has claimed the attention of so many brillant minds through the centuries," what his argument actually reveals is that Mao's views were anticipated centuries before by these "brilliant minds." See Leo Strauss, *Persecution and the Art of Writing* (Glencoe, Ill.: Free Press, 1952), p. 24. Professor Strauss argues convincingly that "persecution cannot prevent even public expression of the heterodox truth" by an intelligent writer (such as Feng) — one who has developed "a peculiar technique of writing . . . writing between the lines."

Mao's great attack upon the fortress of originality in 1950 appears, therefore, to have failed. Few observers would then have predicted that almost two years later the onslaught would be renewed on a different front, with added power, and with results generally similar.

### *"On Contradiction"*

The Chinese case with respect to the second of Mao's philosophical essays, *On Contradiction* (published in Peking *Jen-min Jih-pao*, April 1, 1952), is similarly exaggerated, but perhaps a shade stronger.

The first official Peking commentary on the essay states that Mao "develops the dialectical materialism of Marx, Engels, Lenin, and Stalin . . . deeply expounds every phase of the law of the unity of opposites . . . and in particular, he expounds the particularity of contradiction."[21] Ai Ssu-ch'i is also precise as he states, with his usual clarity, that *On Contradiction* "further develops Lenin's brilliant idea that 'Dialectic, briefly defined, is the theory of the unity of opposites'"[22] and that Mao "further defined the correct relationship between internal contradiction and external causation in the development of things."[23]

To complete this sketch of claims, we note that in the various Chinese tributes to *On Contradiction*, no Soviet praise is cited. This is in sharp contrast to Soviet eulogies for *On Practice* in 1950 and the publication of a Russian translation of it in the Soviet Union on January 13, 1951. We have conjectured that, at that time (1950–51), Stalin was anxious to prove his friendship and respect for Mao, sanctioning the publication of *On Practice*

[21] Peking *Jen-min Jih-pao*, April 9, 1952. Cf. Shen Chih-yüan, *Explanation of "On Contradiction," Wen-hui Pao*, Shanghai, August, 1952, p. 34. Shen says that Mao "greatly deepened and developed the law of the unity of opposites."

[22] Ai Ssu-ch'i, "Comprehend and Use the Dialectic from the Aspect of *On Contradiction*," in *Study "On Contradiction"* (Peking: Hsin Chien-she Ch'u-pan She, 1952), p. 5.

[23] *Ibid.*, p. 7.

in *Bol'shevik* and Soviet praise for it. Following the initial (1950–51) Soviet and Chinese claims that *On Practice* was a creative "development" of the theory of cognition, Moscow apparently decided to avoid the effusive tributes to Mao, probably from concern that the Chinese leader had started to rise to Stalin's level as a theorist in the world Communist movement. By 1952 it was clear that Stalin had no intention of further enhancing Mao's prestige, and in reviewing the first volume of the *Selected Works of Mao Tse-tung* (published in Peking, October 12, 1951), Soviet theorists attempted to show Mao's complete theoretical dependence on Lenin's views on national-colonial revolutions and, particularly, on Stalin's analysis of the peculiarities and developmental stages of the Chinese revolution.[24] Chinese reviewers, on the other hand, often assigned an independent value to Mao's revolutionary strategy.[25] Somewhat more Soviet praise was accorded Mao immediately following Stalin's death, as Stalin's heirs in 1953 and 1954 sought to establish a friendly working relationship with Mao and the Chinese leadership.

Returning to Ai Ssu-ch'i's claims, the second seems worthy of being discussed first, as it concerns Mao's definition of the "correct relationship between internal contradiction and external

[24] P. Yudin, for example, first cites Stalin's remarks on the agrarian movement in China and says that Stalin has "armed the Chinese Communists with a true understanding of the development of the agrarian movement." He then refers to Mao as a leader having been directed by "Leninist-Stalinist theory" in his analysis of the revolution in China. Thus by careful arrangement of his material, Yudin seeks to show Mao's dependence on Stalin, but does not make it clear that the statement of Stalin which he cites was made in April, 1927, whereas Mao's analysis of the peasant movement appeared one month earlier. See P. Yudin, "Volume I of the *Selected Works of Mao Tse-tung*," *Pravda*, August 26, 1952.

[25] Shen Chih-yüan, for example, first insists that in the 1924–27 period, the works of Lenin and Stalin "had been disseminated in China only to a very small extent." He then says, "Yet Chairman Mao had already in this very period, and even somewhat earlier, finished his *Analysis of the Various Classes of Chinese Society* (March, 1926) and *Report of an Investigation Into the Peasant Movement in Hunan* (March, 1927) . . . exercising independent powers of reflection." See Shen Chih-yüan, *Study the "Selected Works of Mao-Tse-tung, Volume I"* (Peking: Hsin Chien-she Ch'u-pan She, 1952), pp. 19, 25, and 26.

causation." In *On Contradiction*, Mao stresses from the start that the "contradiction within a thing is the basic cause of its development, while the interconnection of a thing with, and its interaction upon, other things are secondary causes of its development," and then goes on to repeat this view, stating that external causes are the "condition" of change while internal causes are the "basis" of change.[26] History is invoked to instance the point: the October Revolution in Russia influenced, from the outside, changes in all countries, but such changes arose according to an "inner necessity" within those countries as well as in China.

It is not true that these statements "further define" the philosophical idea of causation, for they in no manner advance from the Marxist "necessary self-movement" of things which Hegel's *Logic* had fathered. Thus Hegel states in his *Logic* that "contradiction is the root of all movement and life, and it is only in so far as it contains a contradiction that anything moves . . . ," and Lenin repeats that "development as a unity of opposites [in contradiction] . . . furnishes a key to the 'self-movement' of everything in existence."[27] Lenin rejects any source of motion lying outside things — that is, any Prime Mover — and Mao follows his lead by criticizing "motion by external forces" as a metaphysical concept.[28] Engels, too, had contrasted the "metaphysical mode of thought" with the dialectical materialist position, which maintains that "contradiction is precisly what motion is."[29]

The first of Ai's claims — that Mao further develops Lenin's views on the unity of opposites — can be analyzed with the precision it deserves only if we assume that there are two claims here: concerning (*a*) unity and (*b*) struggle of opposites.

After listing a handful of synonyms for "unity," Mao informs

[26] Mao, *Selected Works*, I (1961), 290–91.
[27] Lenin, *Philosophical Notebooks*, p. 328.
[28] Mao, *Selected Works*, I (1961), 290.
[29] Friedrich Engels: *Anti-Dühring*, in *Handbook of Marxism*, (London: Gollanz, 1936), pp. 256–57.

us that there are two conditions of unity. "First, two aspects of every contradiction in the process of development of a thing find the presupposition of their existence each in its opposite aspect and both coexist in an entity. Second, the two contradictory aspects according to given conditions, tend to transform themselves each into its opposite aspect."[30]

Mao appears to be merely compressing three of sixteen elements which Lenin describes as constituting the essence of dialectics: ". . . the totality of this thing's manifold *inter-connections* with other things . . ."; "Everything (phenomenon, process, etc) is bound up with every other"; and ". . . not only unity of opposites, but *transformation* of *every* degree, quality, feature, aspect, trait into *every* other (into its opposite)"[31] (Lenin's emphasis). Mao's interesting gloss, that without the contradictory aspect which is opposed to it "each aspect loses the condition of its existence," is a logical deduction from Lenin's element mentioned second above.

The unity of opposites had a practical significance, of course, at the time Ai Ssu-ch'i discussed it in 1952 shortly after the April 1 publication of *On Contradiction*. He says that, although "conditional and relative"—Lenin's phrase—this unity could be observed in the "coexistence of two opposite classes in New China: the working class and the bourgeoisie, which together form part of the people's democratic united front."[32] The publication of *On Contradiction* had marked the beginning of a shift of the CCP to a relatively soft line on the national bourgeoisie and appears to have been part of Mao's effort to call a halt to the "5-anti's,"[33]

[30] Mao, *Selected Works*, I (1961), 315.

[31] Lenin, *Philosophical Notebooks*, pp. 192 ff.

[32] Ai Ssu-ch'i, "Comprehend and Use the Dialectic from the Aspect of *On Contradiction*," p. 26.

[33] Theorists who had followed dutifully the party's "hard" line on the patriotic capitalists in writing for *Hsüeh-hsi* (Study) were made scapegoats, as the line changed in April. In the February 10, 1952, issue of *Hsüeh-hsi*, Yu Kuang-yüan and Hu Sheng had declared that the capitalists should be counterattacked, as

inasmuch as the capitalists had been given a thorough lesson in political power.[34]

Mao seems anxious to view the unity of opposites as being not only inevitable but also, at times, desirable. What appears to be crucial for him is that this aspect of contradiction gives a revolutionary leader *carte blanche* to change the line and even compromise temporarily with an "enemy" without transgressing on doctrine.[35] He is in effect attempting to make criticism of politburo policy from the party ranks virtually impossible. Thus in explaining the CCP's united front with the Kuomintang (KMT), his theoretical justification is, "Contradictory things change into one another; therein is contained a certain identity."[36]

As for struggle, Mao informs us that "the struggle within a

---

they had launched "a ferocious attack" on the workers, and Ai Ssu-ch'i himself as late as March 16 had written in *Hsüeh-hsi* on the "reactionary nature" of the capitalists. When, therefore, on April 10 the publication of *Hsüeh-hsi* was suspended until June, the editorial board stated: "In several recent issues [i.e., spring, 1952], some articles on the question of the bourgeoisie made the mistake of onesidedness, which is also related to dogmatism. . . . The republication [*sic*] of Comrade Mao Tse-tung's *On Contradiction* awakens us and makes us feel the need to adopt an extremely sober attitude and quickly correct these shortcomings and mistakes. The editorial board is now conducting a penetrating investigation and will inform our readers of the results."

Scapegoats were also found in the party's Central Committee. In documents connected with his case, Hu Feng informs us that even Lu Ting-i, chief of the party's propaganda department, made a "self-criticism" in April, 1952. During the shakeup period, apparently Ch'en Po-ta, politburo alternate and chief eulogizer of Mao, carried the burden of the propaganda department's activity. In a Peking *Jen-min Jih-pao* article on May 13, he praises Mao for his correct understanding of the "transformation" of the contradiction between the workers and capitalists.

[34] The Peking *Jen-min Jih-pao* on April 21, 1952, made the revealing statement that now the "bourgeoisie will be afraid to break the law" and that the policy of the CCP is now "to unite with the bourgeoisie, not to liquidate its economy."

[35] Lenin is more candid: "Of course, in politics, in which sometimes extremely complicated — national and international — relationships between classes and parties have to be dealt with . . it would be absurd to concoct a recipe or general rule . . . that would serve in all cases. One must have the brains to analyze the situation in each separate case." (*Left-Wing Communism*, [New York: International Publishers, 1940], Chap. 8).

[36] Mao, *Selected Works*, I (1961), 317.

contradiction runs throughout a process from beginning to end and causes one process to transform itself into another, and as the struggle within the contradiction is present everywhere, we say the struggle within the contradiction is unconditional, absolute."[37]

This accords precisely with Lenin's view. For Lenin, it is struggle, not unity, which is primary in a contradiction. The unity of opposites is relative, temporary, transient; but the struggle between mutually exclusive opposites is "absolute, just as development and motion are absolute."[38] In summing up, Mao demonstrates just how faithful he really is as a disciple of Lenin: "Conditional, relative unity, combined with unconditional, absolute struggle, constitutes the movement in opposites in all things."[39] In *Dialectical and Historical Materialism* (1938), Stalin, too, informs us that "struggle" constitutes the "internal content of the process of development" and that "struggle" arises on the basis of all contradictions.

A practical application of this view of contradiction to the situation in China is made by Ai, who not surprisingly says that the "relationship of bourgeoisie–working class coexistence inevitably will pass through a definite struggle."[40] The struggle against the national bourgeoisie, however, will be waged, Ai says, "economically . . . legally . . . ideologically; that is, in the form of education and reform," inasmuch as—here he quotes Mao—"Contradictions and struggle are universal, absolute, but the methods for solving contradictions, that is, the forms of struggle, differ according to differences in the nature of the contradictions."[41]

In other words, the national bourgeoisie who remain responsive

[37] *Ibid.*, p. 321.

[38] Lenin, *Philosophical Notebooks*, p. 328.

[39] Mao, *Selected Works*, I (1961), 321.

[40] Ai Ssu-ch'i, "Comprehend and Use the Dialectic from the Aspect of *On Contradiction*," pp. 27–28.

[41] *Ibid.*, p. 28.

to Mao's policies will not be physically eliminated but will be permitted to exist as a class.

Ai goes on to discuss "Mao Tse-tung's" distinction between "antagonistic and non-antagonistic" contradictions [42] and, though insisting that this is "based on certain basic ideas of Lenin," he gives no statement of Lenin to support the distinction directly. The question arises: Is Mao here making an original contribution?

It appears that he is not. Soviet writers had begun to develop the theory of "non-antagonistic" contradictions as early as 1935 and this theory had subsequently been elaborated on by M. Rozenthal, P. Yudin, A. A. Zhdanov, B. Kedrov, and Ts. Stepanyan.[43]

To return to the first official Peking commentary on the essay, Mao is said to have "expounded the particularity of contradiction." The "particularity of contradiction" is the idea discussed most fully not only in Ai's article but also in that of other important theorists, including Shen Chih-yüan [44] and Li Ta.[45] Mao's discussion of the idea is thus given considerable emphasis. This emphasis, it appears, results from Mao's own instruction: "The particularity of contradiction should be studied with special attention." Following his discussion of the "universality of contradiction," which is merely a thematic treatment of Engels' and Lenin's view that contradictions appear everywhere and in everything, Mao asserts that "if we do not study the particularity of contradiction, we can in no way determine the particular quality of a thing." [46] Taken by itself, this is tautological.

But it soon emerges from Mao's discussion that he is anxious to stress, not general propositions, but rather "concrete things" —

[42] *Ibid.*, p. 29.

[43] The Soviet theory of "non-antagonistic" contradictions will be discussed in chapter 5.

[44] Shen Chih-yüan, "*On Contradiction* and the Science of Economics," in *Study "On Contradiction,"* pp. 73–96.

[45] Li Ta, "*On Contradiction* — the Guide to Revolutionary Action and Scientific Research," in *Study "On Contradiction,"* pp. 1–25.

[46] Mao, *Selected Works*, I (1961), 297.

"concrete things" which "our dogmatists" refuse to study. "Our dogmatists do not observe the principle" of using different methods to solve different contradictions.[47] Mao concludes on a practical note: because of certain conditions, "an alliance of the KMT and CCP is brought about at one time, and at another time a struggle."[48]

This is crude dialectics. It is below the level of Marx, Engels, and Lenin. It resembles Stalin's clumsy thinking and style.

We can see how thus far Mao's discussion of particularity qualifies the "law" of universality, introduces ifs and buts, and in this way reduces its effectiveness as a general rule of *philosophy*. But at the same time, it obviously makes the "law" of universality less of a hindrance to a revolutionary leader, who must frequently change course in actual *practice*. As for its novelty, none seems to exist, not even the term "particularity." The *Short Philosophical Dictionary* (1939), edited by M. Rozenthal and P. Yudin, quotes Engels and Lenin on the matter of particularity, and Mao himself says that Stalin analyzed the "particularity of the imperialism of tsarist Russia" and his analysis "serves us as a model."[49]

### *Mao's Contribution to Dialectical Materialism*

In his discussion of particularity, Mao makes a distinction which appears to have been made by no Communist theorist before him. Of two contradictory aspects in any contradiction, one must be the principal and the other the secondary. "The quality of a thing is mainly determined by the principal aspect of the contradiction that has won the dominant position." It follows — and this is crucial — that the "quality of a thing changes . . . when the principal aspect of the contradiction undergoes a change."[50]

[47] *Ibid.*, p. 298
[48] *Ibid.*, p. 305.
[49] *Ibid.*, p. 307.
[50] *Ibid.*, pp. 310–11.

Mao seems to have hit upon a new way to *describe* the laws of the Transformation of Quantity into Quality and the Negation of the Negation. It is his way of commenting on the "supercession of the old by the new." We can agree with Shen Chih-yüan's statement that "the point at which Mao Tse-tung was especially creative is in his thesis on the principal contradiction and the principal aspect of contradiction." [51]

Mao's description of qualitative change seems to be the extent of his originality as a Marxist dialectical materialist. *On Contradiction*, which is more elaborate and more pretentious than *On Practice*, is a work in which Mao tries to make platitudes appear as profundities. H. B. Acton points out that upon only a little reflection one can see that Mao's way of illustrating the transformation of opposites into each other is not a great philosophical achievement. Mao notes the passage of war to peace and peace to war, and gravely informs the reader that "as everybody knows, war and peace transform themselves into each other. War is transformed into peace: for example, the First World War was transformed into the post-war peace. . . ." This sort of thing, says Acton, is nothing but dressing up commonplaces ("the First World War came to an end") into apparent profundities ("it transformed itself into its opposite"). Acton gives another example of Mao's verbalisms: to demonstrate that contradictory aspects are things which presuppose one another, Mao cites above and below. "Now of course," Acton concludes, " 'above' and 'below' are logically connected so that if A is above B, B is below A." [52]

## *Chinese Publication Dates*

Quite apart from the question of the substantive value of *On Practice* and *On Contradiction* as contributions to Marxist philos-

[51] Shen Chih-yüan, "*On Contradiction* and the Science of Economics," in *Study "On Contradiction,"* p. 88.

[52] H. B. Acton, "Remarks on J. and M. Miller's Review of *The Illusion of the Epoch*," *Soviet Studies*, VII (April, 1956), 410.

ophy, there is also the question whether the two essays were, in fact, "written" by Mao in *substantially their present form* in 1937, as the Chinese Communists claim. For, every Chinese theorist who has discussed the essays explicitly or implicitly (mostly, explicitly) asks the reader to assume that they were written in *substantially their present form* in 1937. This does not appear to be true.

When, on the basis of his unique description of the Negation of the Negation, Mao makes the deduction that even the predominant productive forces (base) become subordinated to elements in the superstructure, which manifest themselves in the "principal and decisive role," he denies one of Marx's most consistently held views: that is, the view that the productive forces are decisive in determining the superstructural relations of production. "Political and cultural reforms," Mao says, "become the principal and decisive factors." [53] But this is precisely a restatement of Stalin's departure from Marx's view. In *Dialectical and Historical Materialism* (actually the work of several scholars), Stalin states that "new social ideas and theories" become a "most potent force . . . which facilitates the progress of society." This is part of the theoretical base on which Stalin erected his doctrine of "revolution from above." Later, in *Marxism in Linguistics* (1950), Stalin again assigns an almost decisive role to the superstructure: "The superstructure, having emerged . . . becomes a great active force, actively helping its foundation to take shape and gain strength, takes all measures in order to help the new system finish off and destroy the old foundation and old classes." And the Communist party in power is, of course, the most active force in the superstructure.

We now ask: Did Mao anticipate Stalin's revision of Marx? Stalin's *Dialectical and Historical Materialism* was published in October, 1938, but Chinese theorists claim, as we have said, that Mao's *On Contradiction* "was written in August, 1937."

[53] Mao, *Selected Works*, I (1961), 314.

We must state flatly that the Chinese claim appears to be fraudulent. There is considerable evidence for the view that neither *On Practice* nor *On Contradiction* was written in 1937, but rather in the period from 1950 to 1952 and that Mao copied Stalin's abovementioned revision of Marx. It may be worthwhile to summarize the available facts.

To begin with, as far as can be determined, *On Practice* was fully publicized in China for the first time in the central party organ Peking *Jen-min Jih-pao* on December 29, 1950 (it was also published in the Soviet journal *Bol'shevik*, No. 23, December, 1950, and commented on in *Pravda*, December 18, 1950); and *On Contradiction* first appeared in print in China, also in Peking *Jen-min Jih-pao*, on April 1, 1952. Although earlier collections of Mao's major writings to date had been published in the mid-1940's, they did not include either of these essays. A comparatively early edition of Mao's selected works in the Hoover Library's extensive Chinese Collection (Stanford, California), dated 1945, includes essays written in the period from May, 1937, to December, 1944, but makes no mention of either of Mao's philosophical essays.[54] This holds true also for another edition of Mao's selected works in the Hoover Library, dated December, 1947.[55]

Moreover, in a philosophical article published in May, 1941, the Communist theorist Hsiao Chou specifically discussed the theory of "practice" without making any reference to Mao's purported essay on the same subject.[56]

The *Cheng-feng Wen-hsien* (Party Reform Documents) used in the CCP's 1942–44 "rectification" campaign—the effort to tighten up party organization by Stalinist indoctrination and the effort to adapt doctrine to conditions in China — contains no ref-

[54] Mao, *Selected Works*, II (1945).

[55] Mao, *Selected Works*, Supplement (1947).

[56] Hsiao Chou, "Study Theory and Practice," in *Ch'ün-chung* (The Masses), IV (May 20, 1941), 397–400.

erences to the essays.[57] In fact, *no* CCP document available at the Hoover Library mentions *On Contradiction*, prior to April, 1952.

It is also curious that Volume I of Mao's *Selected Works*, as published in 1951, included *On Practice* but not *On Contradiction*, and that the latter appeared out of proper chronological sequence in Volume II, published in April, 1952, just after the essay had come out for the first time in Peking *Jen-min Jih-pao*. A statement by the Committee on Publication of Mao's Works, appearing on the flyleaf of Volume II, offered no explanation of this curious fact, merely noting that *On Contradiction* "should have been in Volume I to accord with the author's chronology" and would be transferred there in a later reprinting of the volume.[58] This strongly suggests that *On Contradiction* had not been ready for publication even at late as October, 1951, when Volume I appeared.

There is additional evidence for the view that *On Contradiction* was not available for publication as late as 1951. *Thirty Years of the CCP*, at one time the standard history of the CCP, written by Hu Ch'iao-mu and published in July, 1951, refers specifically to *On Practice* but does not mention *On Contradiction*. *On Practice* is described as a "renowned philosophical treatise" which Mao "wrote in the summer of 1937."[59] In discussing the month of August, 1937, when *On Contradiction* allegedly was written, Hu mentions only the fact that the Lo-ch'uan conference of the Central Committee adopted a "Ten-Point Program for National Salvation."[60]

Still further reason for doubting the Chinese version is furnished by the sharp contrast in caliber of Marxist thinking be-

[57] *Cheng-feng Wen-hsien* (Party Reform Documents) (Yenan: Chieh-fang She, 1944).

[58] Mao, *Selected Works*, II (1952).

[59] Hu Ch'iao-mu, *Thirty Years of the CCP* (Peking: Foreign Languages Press, 1954), p. 43.

[60] *Ibid.*, p. 51.

tween *On Practice* and *On Contradiction*, as published in 1950 and 1952, and another example of philosophical writing by Mao dating back, in actual fact, to 1940. The latter — part of an essay on dialectical materialism printed in a Shanghai magazine in March, 1940 [61] — appears to be the only sample of Mao's writing on Marxist philosophy to have been fully publicized prior to 1950, and it sheds revealing light on his incompetence as a philosopher. Mao's remarks on concepts indicate his ignorance in 1940 of the Marxist views that (1) abstract concepts present a deeper and more complete reflection of nature, (2) sensation and concept are distinct stages in the knowing-process, (3) matter is self-motivated, and (4) concepts mirror or copy nature. He commits a major blunder in attributing to pre-Marxists the view that "thought . . . is the mirror that reflects nature"— a view in fact held by Engels and Lenin. Small wonder that his 1940 essay was not included in any edition of his selected works: it was proscribed. Even Mao's lieutenants apparently regarded the essay as a catastrophe. According to General Sheng Shih-ts'ai, the one-time warlord of Sinkiang Province, the Yenan Communist Fang Lin refused to show him the essay in 1940 with the remark, "You had better not read it. From the theoretical point of view, Chairman Mao's 'Dialectics' is full of errors." [62]

If this was the caliber of Mao's philosophical thinking in 1940, it is difficult to believe that any lectures he may have prepared and given at Yenan in 1937 on the Marxist theories of practice and contradiction could have been anything but equally primitive and philosophically erroneous. By contrast, however, *On Practice* and *On Contradiction* in the form in which they were published in 1950 and 1952 clearly show the hand of a theorist who, if not original in his thinking, at least develops his arguments

[61] Mao Tse-tung, "Pien-cheng Wei-wu-lun" (Dialectical Materialism), Part II, in *Min-chu* (Democracy). Vol. I, No. 2, Shanghai, March, 1940.

[62] Allen S. Whiting and General Sheng Shih-ts'ai, *Singkiang — Pawn or Pivot?* (East Lansing: Michigan State University Press, 1958), pp. 229–31.

along well-schooled and correct Marxist-Leninist lines. It therefore seems reasonable to conclude that the published versions either were written at a much later date than the Chinese claim or represent such drastic revisions of Mao's purported 1937 lectures as to be altogether different from them.

To sum up, the claims for Mao as a contributor to the theory of dialectical materialism are largely spurious. His only contribution seems to be the extensive discussion of contradiction — a discussion rather dubious as philosophy — in which he has hit upon a new way *to describe* the process of qualitative change in things. Other than this, he is indeed tedious and unoriginal, and although the terminology of his philosophical essays is technical and the ideas abstract, the descriptions of processes they contain are childish and platitudinous.

Yet, Mao's prestige in China as a "philosopher" remains high, as it does not depend on the *credibility* of his essays as real philosophy, but rather on the image of him as a "philosopher" they have helped to create. This is an image of the 1950's. As early as 1936, Edgar Snow described Mao as "an ardent student of philosophy." To support this contention, Snow says only that Mao showed intense interest in philosophy, avoiding the issue of whether Mao had any real competence as a philosopher.[63] In fact, Snow stresses the pragmatic character of Mao's thinking — "his judgments were reached, I believe, on the basis of reason and necessity"[64] — and goes on to speak of Mao's "philosophy" as the dialectics of the long-term view in which "the preciousness of human life is only relative."[65] To discuss Mao as a philosopher in this way is to avoid the question of competence and to stress the obvious, namely, that Mao in 1936 was certain that the Marxist-Leninist doctrine teaches the truth and therefore that human life may be taken in the name of that truth.

[63] Edgar Snow, *Red Star over China* (New York: Modern Library, 1944), p. 77.
[64] *Ibid.*, pp. 77–78.
[65] *Ibid.*, p. 78.

The publication of *On Practice* and *On Contradiction* "in 1937" was intended, Chinese writers tell us, to combat dogmatists and the pretentiousness of their theories. Actually, the publication of these essays in 1950 and 1952, respectively, was intended as the first major move to transform the image of Mao as a revolutionary guerrilla leader into that of Mao as an erudite philosopher. Mao's motives in this move stemmed partly from the need to strengthen his authority as leader of the party and partly from his desire to gain influence for the CCP in Communist parties elsewhere in Asia. It may be confidently surmised, however, that the deeper motive was personal vanity.

# 2

# Mao and Revolution

In the summer of 1920, the year in which Lenin laid it down at the Second Congress of the Communist International (Comintern) that peasants' soviets should be established everywhere, backward countries and colonies included, Mao Tse-tung became a Marxist.[1] Soon thereafter, in May, 1921, at the founding meeting of the CCP[2] — a date which orthodox CCP historians now say should be July 1, 1921[3] — he became a Communist party member.

A large part of the preparatory work for the establishment of a Communist party in China had been carried out in the seven-man cells organized in Shanghai primarily by Ch'en Tu-hsiu in early 1920, following his contacts with the Comintern in 1919. Similar cells were established in the fall of 1920 in Peking and Canton as well as in Hunan, Hupeh, and Honan provinces, and

[1] The date is Mao's: "By the summer of 1920, I had become, in theory and to some extent in action, a Marxist, and from this time on I considered myself a Marxist." Quoted by Edgar Snow, *Red Star over China* (New York: Modern Library, 1944), p. 155.

[2] *Ibid.*, p. 157.

[3] Hu Ch'iao-mu, *Thirty Years of the CCP* (Peking: *Foreign Languages Press,* 1954), pp. 6–7. See also Peking *Jen-min Jih-pao* on the fortieth anniversary of the CCP, July 1, 1961, as well as the interview with politiburo member Tung Pi-wu, in *Chung-kuo Ch'ing-nien* (China Youth), Nos. 13–14 (combined), July 5, 1961.

among the Chinese students in Tokyo and Paris.[4] At first, Mao was active in organizing workers. Within four years, he, along with five other Chinese Communists, had been elected an alternate member of the KMT's Central Executive Committee at the First Congress of the KMT in Canton in January, 1924. At the Second Congress, which met in Canton, two years later, in January, 1926, Mao was elected acting head of the KMT's Propaganda Department. Following the May 30 Incident (1925), Mao began a rural organization campaign in Hunan which was similar to the fully developed campaign in Kwangtung, and by early 1926 he took charge of training at the KMT's Peasant Movement Training Institute (Nung-min Yün-tung Chiang-hsi So). It was in connection with activities in the Training Institute that Mao wrote his first Marxist treatises on revolution.

Marx and Engels had discussed revolution with primary emphasis on the way in which the material production of goods is organized, the relations between the classes producing them, and the fatal contradiction between the capitalist class and the proletariat. Proletarian revolution would occur almost spontaneously and according to the dialectical "law" of history as the inevitable stages of class struggle developed.

Lenin and Stalin shifted the emphasis slightly but decisively, concentrating in their works more on the tactics of revolution and less on the modes of production. That is, as actual leaders as well as "theorists," they constantly attempted to gauge the strength of political and military forces and the possibilities of "pushing the revolution forward," relegating theoretical analysis of economic factors in any country to a secondary position. Thus Lenin says, "We Marxists have always been proud of the fact that by a strict analysis of the mass forces and mutual class relations we have

[4] According to Teng T'o, formerly chief editor of the Peking *Jen-min Jih-pao*, the cells of the "Marxist Society" — forerunner of the CCP — were also established in Anwhei, Shantung, and Chekiang provinces in 1920. Cf. *Chung-kuo Ch'ing-nien*, May 7, 1959.

been able to determine the expediency of this or that form of mass struggle."[5] The same is true of Mao Tse-tung, who, in his first Marxist-Leninist work, *Analysis of the Various Classes in Chinese Society*[6] of March, 1926, centers his attention on estimating the revolutionary potential of social classes in China.

## *Claims of Mao's Originality*

Chinese Communist writers have agreed with Soviet writers that Mao Tse-tung used Lenin's and Stalin's ideas in his analysis of the Chinese revolution. Thus Chang Ju-hsin states in 1953 that in the period of the First Revolutionary Civil War (1924–27), "Comrade Mao Tse-tung . . . the faithful student and comrade-in-arms of Stalin, upheld the standpoint of Lenin and Stalin on problems of the revolution in China."[7]

But Chang, who was writing one month after Stalin's death, implies that there was an element of originality in Mao's analysis: "In 1926 (the time of the publication of Stalin's *Prospects of the*

[5] Lenin, "On the Revolutionary Phase," *Pravda*, February 21, 1918. Stalin's emphasis in the conclusion of the *History of the Communist Party of the Soviet Union (B), Short Course* is similar: "Mastering Marxist-Leninist theory means assimilating the *substance* of this theory and learning to use it in the solution of the practical problems of the revolutionary movement under the varying conditions of the class struggle of the proletariat" (Stalin's emphasis). Cf. *History of the Communist Party of the Soviet Union (B), Short Course* (October, 1938) (New York: International Publishers, 1939), p. 355.

[6] Hereafter cited as *Analysis*. Actually, *Analysis of the Various Classes [sic] among the Chinese Peasants and Their Attitude toward the Revolution* appears to be Mao's first Marxist-Leninist work. This essay, which was published in the January 1, 1926, issue of *Chung-kuo Nung-min* (China Peasant), is not discussed separately here, as it was incorporated into the larger essay, *Analysis of the Various Classes in Chinese Society*, which appeared in *Chung-kuo Nung-min* (Canton), No. 2, February 1, 1926 — a publication of the KMT Central Executive Committee, Peasant Department. The current CCP date for *Analysis* is March, 1926 — the date of its publication in *Chung-kuo Ch'ing-nien* (China Youth).

[7] Chang Ju-hsin, "Stalin's Great Theoretical Contributions to the Chinese Revolution," Peking *Jen-min Jih-pao*, April 3, 1953. Because he had quoted Lenin and Stalin on Chinese revolutionary problems too often, at times depicting Mao as merely following their lead, Chang was denounced five years later as the CCP turned away from "learning from the Soviet Union." See Wang Tzu-yeh's critique in *Che-hsüeh Yen-chiu* (Philosophical Research), No. 3, June 15, 1958.

*Chinese Revolution*), Comrade Mao Tse-tung published his *Analysis,* in which he used as a basis the theories of Lenin and Stalin to arrive at a similar conclusion with that of Stalin on the fundamental problems of the Chinese revolution."[8] That is, Chang seems to feel that any careful Communist reader will know that Mao's *Analysis* was written before Stalin's *Prospects,* as these works were published in March and November, 1926, respectively.

Chang's implied claim that Mao was an independent thinker on the Chinese revolution in early 1926 is enlarged by politburo alternate Ch'en Po-ta, who insists:

> Both in 1927 . . . and afterwards . . . opportunists . . . obstructed the dissemination inside the Chinese party of Stalin's many works on the Chinese question. There were also language difficulties and the counter-revolutionary blockade. For these reasons, many comrades in our party who were actually leading the Chinese revolution did not have an opportunity to make a systematic study of Stalin's many works on China. . . . Comrade Mao Tse-tung was also one of them. It was only after the *cheng-feng* movement in 1942 that Stalin's works on China were systematically edited by our party . . . but despite these obstacles in dissemination, Comrade Mao Tse-tung has been able to reach the same conclusions as Stalin on many fundamental problems through his independent thinking.[9]

Another writer says that only Stalin's *Problems of the Chinese Revolution* of April, 1927, was "published and circulated" in China at some unspecified date between 1927 and 1936 "under conditions of bitter fighting and White terror."[10]

But neither Chang nor Ch'en makes any reference to the fact

[8] *Ibid.*

[9] Ch'en Po-ta, "Stalin and the Chinese Revolution," *Chung-su Yu-hao* (Sino-Soviet Friendship), December 15, 1949.

[10] Editorial, "Publication of Stalin's Works in China," Canton *Nan-fang Jih-pao*, December 21, 1959.

that the real tactical policies, and the theoretical justifications of these policies, were sent to China in the form of numerous Comintern directives with Stalin's approval.[11]

### *"Leadership of the Proletariat"*

Because of the collapse of the KMT-CCP alliance in 1927, Chinese Communist writers make a special effort to prove that Mao at an earlier date had rejected the bourgeoisie as leader of the Chinese revolution. They then go beyond this and claim originality for Mao on the matter of leadership.

[11] Direct and regular contact with the Far Eastern Secretariat of the Comintern was established by the Chinese Communists in the spring of 1921 following G. Voitinsky's arrival in China in the previous spring. According to B. Z. Shumiatsky, chief editor of the Russian and English journal published by the Special Department of the Far Eastern Secretariat of the Comintern, the Special Department was established in Irkutsk in 1920 and a Chinese Section was set up one year later. The duties of the Chinese Section were outlined by Chang T'ai-lei, later a hero of the Canton Commune (December, 1927), as follows:

"1. A *Chinese Section* of the Far Eastern Secretariat in Irkutsk is established to attend to the problems connected with relations between the CCP and the Comintern, to supply information to the CCP and the R.S.F.S.R., as well as to pass on the directives of the Executive Committee of the Comintern to the CCP. . . .

3. The *Section* follows the pattern of Comintern organization by which the Communist parties of separate countries serve as Sections of the Comintern. Likewise, the relations between the Central Committee of the CCP and the Far Eastern Secretariat of the Comintern must be based on the similar principle of organizational contact. That is, the membership of the *Chinese Section* . . . will consist of the local representative of the Central Committee of the CCP in the Far Eastern Secretariat, and the *Section* itself will be subordinated to the Secretariat."

See Ch'en Kung-po, *The Communist Movement in China* (1924), ed. (with an excellent introduction) C. Martin Wilbur ("Columbia University East Asian Institute Series," No. 7 [New York, 1960]), pp. 25–26. Also, Tung Pi-wu's acknowledgment that in the 1920's "the CCP was a branch of the [Communist] International," in *Chung-kuo Ch'ing-nien*, July 5, 1961.

Comintern influence was exerted with increasing effectiveness. The Resolution of the First CCP Congress (July, 1921) is a short document which rejects compromise with the KMT, but the Decisions of the Second Congress (July, 1922) attack "imperialism," discard the no-compromise policy in order to permit Communists to join the KMT, and provide the theoretical rationale that the proletariat must help the bourgeoisie at this stage against "imperialism and feudalism."

Ch'en Po-ta claims that Mao "consistently adhered to . . . the Lenin-Stalin theory concerning the *leadership* of the proletariat and developed this theory in a concrete manner."[12] But how Mao had done this, Ch'en never informs us. Chang Ju-hsin implies that Mao developed this theory in *Analysis* by pointing out that "the national bourgeoisie's aim of establishing a state under its own rule is impracticable."[13] Chang continues: "The *leader* of the Chinese bourgeois-democratic revolution against imperialism and feudalism will not be the national bourgeoisie, but the proletariat," as this is a "bourgeois-democratic revolution of a new type."[14] To settle the matter decisively, he quotes from *Analysis*: "The leading force in our revoluion is the industrial proletariat."

This is merely Lenin's view of proletarian leadership in a revolution against feudalism — one of his minor revisions of Marx and Engels. According to Marx and Engels, revolution in modern times will progress in two distinct stages: first, a "bourgeois, democratic" revolution places the bourgeoisie in power after an attack upon feudalism and monarchy, and, second, a "socialist" revolution slowly ripens and overthrows the bourgeoisie, establishing a dictatorship of the proletariat. Thus Engels says in 1848:

> Fight on bravely then, gentlemen of capital. We need your help: We need even your rule upon occasions. For it is you who must clear from our path the relics of the Middle Ages and of absolute monarchy. You must abolish monarchy, you must centralize, you must change the more or less destitute classes into real proletarians — recruits for us. It is your factories and trade connections that must lay the foundations for the liberation of the proletariat. Your reward shall be a brief

[12] Ch'en Po-ta, "Mao Tse-tung's Theory of the Chinese Revolution Is the Integration of Marxism-Leninism with the Chinese Revolution, *Hsüeh-hsi*, July 1, 1951.

[13] Chang Ju-hsin, *On Two Works of Comrade Mao Tse-tung during the First Revolutionary Civil War Period* (Peking: Jen-min Ch'u-pan She, 1953), p. 6. (This pamphlet is the published version of a lecture given by Chang at the Marx-Lenin Academy, Peking, in June, 1953.)

[14] *Ibid.*, pp. 7–8.

> period of rule. You shall dictate laws, and bask in the sun of your own majesty. But remember, "The hangman's foot is upon the threshhold." [15]

In his *Two Tactics of Social Democracy in the Democratic Revolution* of June–July, 1905, however, Lenin insists that the proletariat must not be a subsidiary to the bourgeoisie, and that it must become the leader of the bourgeois-democratic revolution.[16] "Marxism teaches the proletariat not to keep aloof from the bourgeois revolution, not to be indifferent to it, not to allow the leadership of the revolution to be assumed by the bourgeoisie." [17] "The proletariat being, by virtue of its very position, the most advanced and the only consistently revolutionary class, is for that very reason called upon to play the leading part in the general democratic revolutionary movement in Russia." [18]

The 1905 peasant uprising in Russia opened Lenin's eyes to the revolutionary potential of the peasants. In the *Agrarian Program of Social Democracy* of November–December, 1907, Lenin goes so far as to define the bourgeois-democratic revolution in Russia as a "peasant revolution," but he denies that the bourgeoisie can lead the rural movement: "The proletariat must in its own interest assume the leadership of the peasant revolution." [19]

Turning his attention to colonial revolutions — "national liberation movements in the East" — Lenin at first does not stress proletarian leadership of these "bourgeois, democratic" revolutions and seems to have believed that his *Two Tactics* theses need

[15] Engels, "Die Bewegungen von 1847," in Marx and Engels, *Gesamtausgabe*, Section I, Vol. VI (Berlin: Marx-Engels Verlag, 1932), pp. 397–98.

[16] Lenin, *Two Tactics of Social Democracy in the Democratic Revolution* (June–July, 1905) (New York: International Publishers, 1935), p. 41.

[17] *Ibid.*

[18] *Ibid.*, p. 59. According to Trotsky, in 1905 Lenin did not accept the view that the bourgeois-democratic revolution would "pass over" into the socialist revolution, and it was only in the spring of 1917 that he advanced this idea, re-equipped with Trotsky's theory of "permanent revolution."

[19] Lenin, *Selected Works*, III (New York: International Publishers, n.d.), 258 (hereafter cited as *Selected Works*).

not be applied to China's bourgeois revolution of 1911. In his *Democracy and Narodism in China* of July, 1912, Lenin contrasts the bourgeoisie of the West who are "rotten to the core" with Sun Yat-sen, "a revolutionary democrat, who symbolizes the nobility and heroism inherent in a class that is on the rise." He says:

> The Western bourgeoisie is in a state of decay; it is already confronted by its grave-digger — the proletariat. In Asia, in contrast, there is *still* a bourgeoisie capable of championing sincere, militant, consistent democracy, a worthy comrade of France's great enlighteners and great leaders of the close of the 18th century.[20]

Continuing in an orthodox Marxist vein, Lenin points to the "virgin naivete" of Sun's idea that "capitalism can be 'prevented' in China"[21] and assigns the small Chinese proletariat only the task of criticizing Sun's utopias while it "defends and develops the revolutionary-democratic core of his political and agrarian program."[22]

By November, 1912, however, Lenin is prepared to return to his *Two Tactics* thesis of proletarian (that is, Communist party) leadership of the bourgeois-democratic revolution. In his *Regenerated China*, he says:

> China's freedom was won by an alliance of peasant democracy and liberal bourgeoisie. Whether the peasants, without the leadership of a proletarian party, will be able to retain their democratic positions *against* the liberals, who are only waiting for a suitable moment to shift to the Right — this the near future will show.[23]

[20] Lenin, "Democracy and Narodism in China" (July, 1912), in *The National Liberation Movement in the East: Lenin* (Moscow: Foreign Languages Publishing House, 1957), pp. 43–44 (Lenin's emphasis).

[21] *Ibid.*, p. 45

[22] *Ibid.*, p. 47.

[23] Lenin, "Regenerated China" (November, 1912), *ibid.*, p. 52 (Lenin's emphasis). M. N. Roy, the chief Indian delegate to the Second Congress of the

When, therefore, Stalin in May, 1925, calls on students in the University of the Toilers of the East to "ensure the hegemony of the proletariat" in the national-revolutionary bloc [24] and Mao in March, 1926, allegedly designates the industrial proletariat as the "leading force" in the bourgeois-democratic revolution, they are not expounding a new idea.

To return to Chang's and Ch'en's claims, they are open to another objection: at no point in the original 1926 version of *Analysis* does Mao designate the proletariat as the "leading" force. Why not? Because Mao and the other Chinese Communist leaders at that time were carrying out Comintern directives, which designated the KMT as a bloc of four classes and as the "leader" of China's democratic revolution. The sentence which Chang is emphatic in quoting—"The leading force in our revolution is the industrial proletariat"—was inserted into the October, 1951, version of *Analysis*.[25]

Mao's *Analysis* is indeed a Marxist-Leninist essay but it certainly was not, as claimed, "the earliest and most clear-cut Marxist-

---

Comintern, held in July and August, 1920, opposed Lenin's view that a "temporary alliance" with all the bourgeoisie in colonial areas should be established. Roy insisted on a "distinction" between revolutionary and reformist capitalists, viewing the latter as dangerous. As a compromise, Lenin on July 26 told the Congress that " we should speak of the national-revolutionary and not of the 'bourgeois-democratic' movements" in the East. Thus in the 1920's the Chinese Communists designated the KMT as leader of the "national revolution," but many Communist leaders feared the "temporary alliance."

[24] Stalin, "The Political Tasks of the University of the Peoples of the East" (May, 1925), in *Works*, VII (Moscow: Foreign Languages Publishing House, 1954), 151. P'eng Shu-chih was one of several Chinese Communist theorists who discussed proletarian leadership before Mao allegedly did. In his *Who Are the Leaders of the Chinese National Revolution?* of late 1924, P'eng states that the proletariat is stronger than the industrial bourgeoisie, as it extended to both Chinese-owned and foreign-owned industries. The "natural leader" of the revolution, therefore, was not the bourgeoisie but the proletariat. See P'eng Shu-chih: "Basic Problems of the Chinese Revolution," in *Chung-kuo Ko-ming Wen-t'i Lun Wei-chi* (A Collection of Essays on Problems of the Chinese Revolution) (Shanghai: Hsin Ch'ing-nien She, 1927), p. 29.

[25] Mao, *Selected Works*, I (1951), 9.

Leninist document in China."[26] As for Mao's alleged "development" of the "leadership of the proletariat" in 1926, it is not an advance on Lenin's position in 1905 and 1912, and even his agreement with Lenin on this point was inserted into Mao's *Selected Works* many years later.

### *Importance of the Peasants*

Mao's estimate of the importance of the peasants in revolution is, on first consideration, a departure from Communist doctrine, from the Russian Communist prejudice that only the industrial workers can be the creative class and spearhead in making a revolution. Stalin's statement in 1932 is a typical expression of this prejudice:

> Isolated peasant revolts, even when they are not of the unorganized kind . . . cannot be successful. Peasant revolts can be successful only if they are combined with revolts of the workers and if the peasant revolts are led by the workers. Only a combined revolt led by the working class has any chance of achieving its aim.[27]

But Stalin is by this not denying the importance of peasant revolts; he is insisting that these revolts maintain contact with the leaders—the industrial urban workers—and not become "isolated." This position is in line with Lenin's view that although peasant forces in the countryside are vital for the Communist revolution, the city should lead the countryside. Both Stalin and Lenin do not deny the importance of the peasants.

Thus, on further consideration, Mao's stress on the importance of the peasants in revolution is not a departure from Soviet doctrine. The really unique aspects of Mao's road to power will be

[26] Ho Kan-chih, *A History of the Modern Chinese Revolution* (Peking: Foreign Languages Press, 1959), p. 108.

[27] "J. Stalin's Interview with Emil Ludwig," *International Literature* (Moscow), Nos. 2–3 (combined), 1932, p. 106.

discussed later in this chapter with the rural base area and guerrilla warfare.

Chinese Communist writers nonetheless claim that Mao somehow went beyond Lenin's and Stalin's position, expanding it. Chang Ju-hsin states that "Comrade Mao Tse-tung developed Lenin's and Stalin's directives on the special and important role of the peasant question in colonial and semi-colonial revolutionary movements, making a complete estimate of the peasants' revolutionary attitude. He said that the poor and middle peasants, who comprise more than 80 per cent of China's population, are the most important and reliable ally of the proletariat in the democratic revolution."[28] Chang's emphasis on the role of the poor peasants is the key to his claims for Mao's originality.

*Analysis* (March, 1926) and *Report of an Investigation into the Peasant Movement in Hunan* (March, 1927) (hereafter cited as *Report*), Chang continues, contain Mao's contributions.

In *Analysis*, Mao says, "The overwhelming majority of the semi-tenant peasants, together with the poor peasants, constitute a very large section of the masses in the countryside. The 'peasant problem' is essentially their problem."[29] Mao centers his attention on the poor peasants even more forcefully in *Report*, the most striking thing he ever wrote:

> The main force in the countryside which has always put up the bitterest fight is the poor peasants. From the period of underground organization to that of open organization, the poor peasants have fought militantly all along. They accept most willingly the leadership of the Communist party. They are the deadliest enemies of the local bullies and bad gentry and attack their strongholds without the slightest hesitation. . . . They are the backbone of the Peasant Association, the vanguard in overthrowing the feudal forces, and the

[28] Chang Ju-hsin, *On Two Works of Comrade Mao Tse-tung*, pp. 11–12.
[29] Mao, *Selected Works*, I (1961), 6.

> foremost heroes who have accomplished the great revolutionary undertaking left unaccomplished for many years. Without the poor peasants (the "riff-raff" as the gentry call them) it would never have been possible to bring about in the countryside the present state of revolution, to overthrow the local bullies and the bad gentry, or to complete the democratic revolution. Being the most revolutionary, the poor peasants have won the leadership in the Peasant Association. . . . This leadership of the poor peasants is absolutely necessary. Without the poor peasants there can be no revolution. To reject them is to reject the revolution. To attack them is to attack the revolution. The general direction they have taken in the revolution has never been wrong.[30]

According to Chang, therefore, Mao demonstrated originality by maintaining that (1) revolutions in backward countries (such as China) are primarily peasant revolutions and (2) the poor peasants are the most important force and reliable ally in these revolutions.

1. *Revolutions in backward countries are primarily peasant revolutions.* In view of Lenin's statements as well as Stalin's and those of several Chinese Communists, Mao appears not to have made a contribution to theory on this point. For it was Lenin who sharply departed from Marx's reluctance to use the peasants as an important revolutionary fighting force.

Following the peasant uprisings of 1905 in Russia,[31] certain

[30] *Ibid.*, pp. 21–22.

[31] Early in his career, Lenin maintained the orthodox Marxist position, which argued against making concessions to the peasants' proprietary instincts and rejected the policy of defending small peasant holdings. By the end of 1905, however, he became aware that confiscation of the landed estates without subsequent redistribution held little attraction for the peasants, and in 1906 made a decisive reversal of his position. His new policy was: adopt the idea of distributing the land to the peasants and even designate the future bourgeois-democratic government a "peasant (farmer) republic." See Karl A. Wittfogel, "The Legend of Maoism," *China Quarterly* (London), No. 1, January–March, 1960, p. 77. Bertram D. Wolfe points to the role played by the revolutionary priest, Gapon, in convincing Lenin in 1905 that "all" of the land must be given to the peasants. *Three Who Made a Revolution* (Boston: Beacon Press, 1955), pp. 304–5.

parts of Lenin's writings began to sound — to orthodox Marxists — like the plans of a revolutionary calling for peasant insurrectionism. In his *Agrarian Program of Social Democracy* of 1907, Lenin emphatically states that "The agrarian question [in Russia] is the basis of the bourgeois-democratic revolution. . . . We must have a clear idea of the character and significance of precisely the peasant agrarian revolution as one of the varieties of bourgeois revolution." Further: "The peasant revolution, as Kautsky justly pointed out, leads also to state bankruptcy, i.e., it damages the interests not only of the Russian, but of the whole international bourgeoisie." Further:

> A section of the Marxists, the Right wing, persistently made shift with an abstract, stereotyped conception of the bourgeois revolution, and failed to perceive the peculiar features of the present bourgeois revolution, which is precisely a peasant revolution. . . . The Bolsheviks, on the other hand . . . singled out the concept of peasant revolution as one of the varieties of bourgeois revolution. . . . Thus we see that Plekhanov completely collapsed on the question of fundamentals of the general Social-Democratic tactics in a bourgeois revolution that can be victorious only as a peasant revolution.[32]

Later, turning to the task of formulating Communist tactics for backward countries as the "East," Lenin in effect sees only the peasants as the revolutionary army. It is as a proponent of peasant revolutionary movements that Lenin speaks to the Second Congress of the Comintern in July, 1920:

[32] Lenin, *Selected Works*, III, 159, 286. However, Lenin displayed no deep sympathy for the peasants and desired to use them only as allies. Thus in his *The Attitude of Social Democracy toward the Peasant Movement* of 1905 he had stated: "We support the peasant movement in so far as it is revolutionary and democratic. We are making ready (making ready at once, immediately) to fight it in so far as it becomes reactionary and anti-proletarian. . . . At first we support to the end by all means, including confiscation, the peasantry generally against the landlords and then (or rather, not 'then,' but at the same time) we support the proletariat against the peasantry in general" (pp. 144–46).

> The most important feature of backward countries is that the precapitalist relations still prevail there and that, therefore, there can be no question of a purely proletarian movement in them. There is almost no industrial proletariat in those countries. . . . The idea of soviet organization is a simple one, and it can be applied not only to proletarian conditions but also to feudal and semifeudal peasant relations. . . . we must base the theses of the Communist International on the assumption that the peasant soviets . . . are applicable not only to capitalist countries but also to the countries of precapitalist conditions, and that it is the absolute duty of the Communist parties . . . to propagate the idea of peasant soviets, the soviets of the toiling people everywhere . . . and to try, wherever conditions permit, to create peasant soviets or soviets of the toilers.[33]

Actually, despite Lenin's directives on the importance of peasant soviets and peasant revolution for backward countries, most of the very early leaders of the CCP directed their activities toward organizing the urban working class, which was few in number.[34] Mao says that prior to the May 30 Incident (1925), "I had not fully realized the degree of class struggle among the peasantry" and that in 1922–23, "I returned to Hunan and vigorously pushed the work among the labor unions."[35]

But at least one prominent Chinese Communist leader, P'eng Pai, who in the late 1920's became a politburo member, had real-

[33] "Report of the Commission on the National and Colonial Questions to the Second Congress of the Communist International (July 26, 1920)," in *The National Liberation Movement in the East: Lenin*, pp. 267–68.

[34] In line with Lenin's Comintern thesis of 1920, the Manifesto of the CCP adopted in July, 1922, by the Second Congress states: "Three hundred million Chinese peasants are the most important factors of our revolutionary movement. . . . We believe that the Chinese revolution will quickly succeed when the majority of the peasants ally themselves with the workers." Ch'en Kung-po, *The Communist Movement in China*, p. 120. Nevertheless, the CCP's major effort in the early 1920's was concentrated on organizing factory workers, railroad workers, seamen, and dockworkers in the cities.

[35] Snow, *op. cit.*, pp. 159–60.

ized the degree of class struggle among the peasants and carried out Lenin's instruction to organize peasant soviets.

In 1921, P'eng Pai went to the Kwangtung countryside to carry out "organization and propaganda" work among the peasants. He organized the first village peasants' association in China in Kwangtung Province which, by September, 1922, had enrolled more than 500 members. On January 1, 1923, the Haifeng County Peasants' Association was formally established with a membership of about 20,000 families — 100,000 persons — or one-quarter of the population of the county. By mid-1923, he established the Kwangtung Provincial Peasants' Association and raised the slogan, "Down with the landowners! Long live the peasants!" Demands for reduction of land rent became demands for its total abolition. Peasant struggles against landlords and local officials spread throughout Kwangtung Province and into Hupeh and Hunan. Peasant associations were firmly established in Honan by September, 1925. In Hunan, by late November, 1926, there were fifty-four counties with a total registered membership in the peasants associations of 1,071,137. By January, 1927 — when Mao began his Hunan investigation — this number exceeded 2,000,000.[36]

P'eng Pai set up the first peasant soviet in China — the Hailufeng Soviet Republic of Kwantung — in November, 1927. Thus it was P'eng who organized the early peasant movement and worked out an organizational model.[37]

Peasant revolution was rapidly developing in the rural areas when the KMT began its own revolutionary activities among the peasants in 1924. In August, 1926, the KMT Peasant Department published its declaration of Current Tactics for the Peasant Movement in Hunan, which extensively discussed policies for expand-

[36] Hua Kang, *The Great Chinese Revolution of 1925–1927* (Shanghai, 1931), chap. iv, sec. 4.

[37] P'eng Pai, "Report on the Peasant Movement in Haifeng," in *Chung-kuo Nung-min*, January 1, March 1, April 1, and May 1, 1926. See also T. C. Chang, *The Peasant Movement in Kwangtung* (Shanghai, 1928).

ing and strengthening Hunan's peasant associations, especially among the "poor peasants." [38] Mao did not go out to inspect these Hunan associations for the Central Committee of the CCP until January, 1927, when he was also training activists for the peasant movement for the KMT.

It was precisely one year earlier that the young Mao went out to learn from the organizational model established by P'eng Pai in the rural areas of Haifeng and Lufeng, Kwangtung. According to an on-the-spot account of his trip, Mao and his trainee charges learned much at Haifeng:

> At the time [early 1926], the peasant movement had been developed in extensive areas in the country, and the peasant movement in the East River area of Kwangtung led by Comrade P'eng Pai was the most outstanding of all. Chairman Mao organized the whole body of students for a visit to Haifeng county to see the movement's progress. We landed at Swabue, and throughout the night we waded along the coast, flanked on the other side by rice fields. All along our route, the organized peasants (those who had attained political awakening and economic improvement) greeted us during our night's march with lion dances and lantern shows.
>
> It was in Haifeng, therefore, that we first came into contact with a class of peasants who had gone through a fierce class struggle and achieved considerable success. The movement had greatly educated us, and we felt ourselves drawn into the ranks of the peasants themselves, feeling as well that it would be glorious to be able to shed our blood in their cause. That visit laid the foundation of subsequent decisions to dispatch the students to various parts of the country to engage in the peasant movement.[39]

[38] "Current Tactics for the Peasant Movement in Hunan," *Chung-kuo Nung-min*, August 1, 1926.

[39] Tu Sung-shou, "Some Matters Connected with Chairman Mao during His Stay in Canton in 1926," printed originally in Sian *Ch'ün-chung Jih-pao* and reprinted in Hong Kong *Wen-hui Pao*, June 24, 1951. In early 1926, the period

Mao, therefore, was not the first Chinese Communist peasant organizer.

Moreover, he was not the first Chinese Communist to emphasize the importance of the peasants. In addition to P'eng Pai, several Communist writers working with the KMT's Peasant Department placed almost exclusive emphasis on the peasants. In August, 1925, they were designated the "major force for destroying feudalism" by the Communist Kan Nai-kuang. Kan says, "The peasant class is the basic class of the national revolution. In other words, the peasantry is the main force in the national revolution." He explicitly *reverses* the view held by Marxist-Leninists on the role of the peasants as allies of the proletariat: "We consider that the working class is the most reliable ally of the peasants."[40]

Stalin, too, had underscored the importance of a peasant revolution for China before Mao stressed the point. Thus the Theses of the Seventh Plenum of the Comintern Executive Committee which Stalin and Bukharin drafted with the assistance of T'an P'ing-shan, the Chinese Communist delegate, in November, 1926, states:

> Not to deal boldly with the agrarian question, not to support in their entirety the political and economic aims of the peasant masses would be a real danger for the revolution. It would be wrong not to place the program of the peasant movement first in the program of national liberation for fear of alienating the uncertain and perfidious cooperation of a part of the capitalist class.[41]

---

to which the author refers, Mao was in Canton in charge of the Peasant Movement Training Institute of the KMT.

[40] Kan Nai-kuang, "What Is the Main Force of the National Revolution?" *Chung-kuo Nung-min*, August, 1925.

[41] "Theses on the Situation in China," adopted by the Seventh Plenum, Executive Committee, Communist International, November-December, 1926, *Inprecor* (Paris), February 20, 1927. The theses directed the Communists to confiscate only the land of "reactionary" militarists — a loose formulation which had the effect of restricting the force and scope of the peasant revolution.

In his *Prospects of the Revolution in China* of November, 1926, Stalin considered as correct the view of T'an P'ing-shan, who maintained that the immediate satisfaction of the most urgent peasant demands is an "essential condition for the victory of the Chinese revolution." [42]

Actually, Stalin in late 1926 did not deal very "boldly" with the agrarian question and did not really believe that peasant soviets and peasant revolution could survive "isolation" from the urban workers' movement in China.

But peasant revolution as an important part of the national revolution was in the air. Inasmuch as land held by KMT officers was not to be confiscated, KMT delegate Shao Li-tzu reported to the November, 1926, Comintern plenum that "Comrade Chiang Kai-shek declared in his speech before the members of the KMT that the Chinese revolution would be unthinkable if it were unable to solve correctly the agrarian, i.e., the peasant question." [43]

2. *The poor peasants are the most important force and reliable ally.* So much for Mao's pretensions to originality on the matter of peasant revolution in backward countries, particularly in China. Is there any stronger foundation for the claims of uniqueness regarding the peasants?

It seems that there is not, for Lenin, not Mao, first underscored the importance of the *poor* peasants in a revolutionary movement. In his *Agrarian Program of Social Democracy*, Lenin speaks of the "poor peasantry" which he describes as crushed by the feudal landlords. He also distinguishes a small group of "middle peasants," who possess land sufficient to conduct farming in a tolerable way, a small group of "well-to-do peasants," and "feudal

[42] Stalin, "Prospects of the Revolution in China" (November 30, 1926), *Works*, VIII, 385. But, unlike T'an, Stalin said that the only way to organize the peasants was through the KMT government.

[43] Shao Li-tzu, "Speech to the Seventh Plenum, Session of November 30, 1926," *Inprecor*, December 30, 1926. In his *Report*, Mao speaks repeatedly of "bad" gentry, "evil" landlords, and local "bullies." This was KMT terminology of the time, as "good" gentry and "good" landlords were permitted to retain their land.

latifundia."[44] In a work written two years earlier, he speaks of a "rural proletariat" and says that "we lay the main emphasis on . . . the special organization of the rural proletariat into a class party . . . we are keen on *revolutionary peasant committees*. . . . Class antagonism between the rural proletariat and the peasant bourgeoisie is inevitable, and we reveal it in advance, explain it *and prepare for the struggle on the basis of it*."[45]

Thus Lenin seems to use the term "rural proletariat" as Engels had done in his *The Peasant Question in France and Germany* of 1894, that is, to designate poor farm workers as distinct from big and small landowners. For Lenin, it is the rural proletariat who will make the revolution in the countryside.

### *Mao's "Report" of March, 1927*

Viewed in its time and circumstances, Mao's *Report* of his investigation of peasant uprising in Hunan was evidently not considered a heresy by Communists. Because rural revolution was rapidly increasing in 1925 and because Stalin had designated it the "essential condition for the victory of the Chinese revolution" in November, 1926, the *Report* of March, 1927—its publication date—seemed appropriate to the time. It apparently was a fairly accurate estimate of the revolutionary potential and total forces of the peasants in Hunan. To provide an accurate picture of the peasants as he saw their activities, Mao gave the peasants credit for 70 per cent of the revolutionary work in Hunan and attributed only 30 per cent to the Hunan urban dwellers and military units.

That this was viewed as a useful estimate of the peasants' revolutionary enthusiasm rather than a piece of heretical writing is suggested by the fact that it was reprinted by the Russian-dominated CCP in its official journal[46] as well as by Moscow.[47] Karl A.

[44] Lenin, *Selected Works*, III, 167.

[45] *Ibid.*, pp. 144–45 (Lenin's emphasis).

[46] *Hsiang-tao Chou-pao* (Guide Weekly) (Shanghai), No. 191, March 12, 1927.

[47] *Revoliutsionnii Vostok* (Revolutionary East), published by the Scientific Association for the Study of National and Colonial Problems, Moscow, 1927, No. 2.

Wittfogel points out that in May, 1927, Bukharin, at a plenary session of the Comintern's executive committee, spoke of the document as "an excellent and interesting description" in which "one of our agitators describes his trip in Hunan Province." [48]

Similarly, P'eng Pai's reports of experiences in organizing the first peasants' association in China in the early 1920's and the first peasant soviet in 1927 were reprinted in the Soviet publication *International Literature* (1932). Moscow did this, despite the fact that P'eng speaks almost exclusively of the peasants' revolutionary activity without any significant urban support. In describing Haifeng County as divided into two big camps—"landowners and the peasants"—P'eng speaks of the workers not as leaders but as subsidiary allies of the peasants: "The workers were on the side of the peasants." [49] That is the extent of his discussion of the workers.

In October, 1951, however, when the Chinese Communists were laboring to build Mao Tse-tung's prestige as an eminent *theorist*, the emphasis on reportorial accuracy was replaced. The new emphasis was on doctrinal maturity, on theoretical excellence. What in March, 1927, and in the years immediately following, was viewed as a good on-the-spot account of the Hunan peasant revolts, in October, 1951, was viewed as a "brilliant" Marxist-Leninist theoretical analysis of the Chinese revolution in general. As such, it was subjected to the test of doctrinal rather than *practical* accuracy, and, as a result, the sentence slighting the "urban dwellers'" role in the Hunan revolts was deleted.[50]

[48] Wittfogel, "The Legend of Maoism," *loc. cit.*, p. 21.

[49] P'eng Pai, "Red Haifeng," *International Literature*, p. 95.

[50] In his brilliant and pioneering book, Benjamin I. Schwartz describes this sentence as the most remarkable in the entire *Report.* (*Chinese Communism and the Rise of Mao* [Cambridge, Mass.: Harvard University Press, 1951], p. 75). We agree, but suggest that it is remarkable if the work is viewed as an essay in doctrine rather than a practical report on peasant revolt. The original sentence states: "To give credit where it is due, if we allot ten points to the accomplishments of the democratic revolution, then the achievements of the urban dwellers and the military rate only three, while the remaining seven should go to the peasants in their rural revolution." See Mao, *Selected Works* (1947), p. 215.

Also deleted in 1951 were the italicized portions of the following sentences which indicated that the poor peasants rather than the CCP were the organizers of revolutionary work:

> *Only one group* in the countryside has fought hard and relentlessly from the very start: the poor peasants. Out of the secret stage into the open stage, it was they who fought, *who organized, and who did the revolutionary work*. They *alone* were the deadly enemies of the local ruffiians and bad gentry, whose bastions they attacked unreservedly. *They alone were capable of doing the destructive work*.[51]

In its original form, this passage also neglects the role of the "middle peasants," and by 1951 such neglect may well have seemed too extreme and too narrow, for Mao was by then reputed to have coined the slogan "Unite all the forces that can possibly be united" for the revolution. Accordingly, the passage was made less restrictive.

A doctrinal content was supplied by insertion. Thus, theorist Li Ta claims that "in the *Report*, Comrade Mao Tse-tung established the theoretical foundation of the worker-peasant alliance."[52] But in the original version of the *Report*, Mao does not mention the alliance or allude to anything like it. Another theorist, Chu Chien-nung, claims that in the *Report* Mao solved the question of leadership of the peasant revolution. To prove this doctrinal point, Chu cites the following sentence from the *Report*: "the poor peasants accept most willingly the leadership of the Communist party."[53] But this crucial sentence appears only in the 1951 version of the *Report* as an insertion; it was not in the 1927 original. For the Comintern had designated the KMT as leader of the

[51] Compare Mao, *Selected Works*, I (1951), 21–22 with Mao, *Selected Works* (1947), p. 220.

[52] Li Ta, "Read Comrade Mao Tse-tung's Four Works Written between 1926 and 1929," in *Read the "Selected Works of Mao Tse-tung, Volume I"* (Peking: Hsin-chien She Tsa-chih She, 1952), p. 37.

[53] Chu Chien-nung, "Read *Report of an Investigation into the Peasant Movement in Hunan*," *ibid.*, pp. 53–54.

national revolution, not the CCP. At the time, Mao was working for the KMT as well as for the CCP, and part of his *Report* was therefore published in the weekly organ of the Central Executive Committee of the KMT, *Chinese Correspondence*.[54]

### *The Bourgeois Ally*

Regarding the question of allies, Li Ta claims that in *Analysis*, Mao indicated that the Chinese bourgeoisie is different from the bourgeoisie in capitalist countries and "came to the conclusion" that the "*left-wing of the national bourgeoisie* could be friendly toward the revolution." Li asserts that by including the "national bourgeoisie" in the worker-led united front of peasants and petty bourgeoisie, "Comrade Mao Tse-tung has further developed the Marxist-Leninist theory of classes." "Clearly, *Analysis* established the theory of a revolutionary united front led by the workers."[55]

Li mentions no early Communist literature on the subject of the national bourgeoisie probably because his claims would crumble were he to do so. For Lenin and Stalin were explicit in discussing the "revolutionary" section of the bourgeoisie.

In *The Stages, Trends, and Prospects of the Revolution* of 1906, Lenin makes a distinction between two sections of the Russian bourgeoisie:

> The labor movement flares up into a direct *revolution*, while the liberal bourgeoisie has already united in a Constitutional-Democratic party and thinks of stopping the revolution by compromising with tsarism. But the *radical* elements of the bourgeoisie and petty bourgeoisie are inclined to enter into an alliance with the proletariat for the *continuation of the revolution*. . . .[56]

Thus Lenin goes beyond the concept of "liberal bourgeoisie" discussed by Marx and Engels, positing a radical section.

[54] *Chinese Correspondence*, No. 8, May 15, 1927.
[55] Li Ta, *loc. cit.*, p. 35.
[56] Lenin, *Selected Works*, III, 134 (Lenin's emphasis).

Discussing revolution in backward countries, particularly in China, Stalin in 1925 speaks of the split of the "national bourgeoisie . . . into a revolutionary and an anti-revolutionary wing." "Hence the task of the Communist elements in the colonial countries is to link up with the revolutionary elements of the bourgeoisie. . . ."[57] Like Lenin, Stalin makes the distinction very explicit.

When, therefore, roughly one year later Mao says in *Analysis* that "some sections" of the middle class (i.e., the national bourgeoisie) will "turn left and join the ranks of the revolution" and the other section will become anti-revolutionary,[58] he is merely repeating Stalin's formulation.

But in order to credit Mao with originality, Li Ta cites Ch'en Po-ta's statement that Mao in the 1920's "did not have an opportunity to make a systematic study of Stalin's many works on China" (see page 32 above). The whole basis of Ch'en's arguments is untenable. Few Chinese Communist leaders, if any, had the opportunity to make a "systematic" study of Stalin's "many" works on China. The point is that they received his directives on policy regularly and in considerable detail through Comintern channels. These directives included the matter of a united front with the "revolutionary" section of the bourgeoisie — a distinction which appears frequently in the writings of early Chinese Communist leaders.

In at least one decisive case, the Comintern directive was given forcefully and orally in Moscow. At the Fourth Congress of the Comintern, which met from November 5, to December 5, 1922, Karl Radek attacked the Chinese delegates for being too "leftist" in their view of the bourgeoisie. "You must understand, comrades, that neither the question of socialism nor of the Soviet

[57] Stalin, "Results of the Work of the 14th Conference of the R.C.P. (B) — The Immediate Tasks of the Communist Elements in the Colonial and Dependent Countries" (May 9, 1925), *Works*, VII, 108–9.

[58] Mao, *Selected Works*, I (1961), 4.

republic is now the order of the day. . . . the immediate task is: (a) to organize the young working class; (b) to adjust its relations with the revolutionary bourgeois elements in order to organize the struggle against European and Asiatic ]Japanese] imperialism." [59] Once again the positing of a "revolutionary" section of the bourgeoisie.

To sum up the discussion thus far, Chinese Communist spokesmen acknowledge that Mao's early analysis of the Chinese revolution owes a general debt to Lenin and Stalin, but they minimize that debt, and they conceal the importance of Comintern directives in Mao's early thinking. All their specific claims for this early work appear to be spurious. Mao's alleged "development" of the concept of "leadership of the proletariat" in 1926 is not an advance on Lenin's position in 1912, and even his agreement with Lenin on this point was inserted into Mao's works many years later. Mao's alleged discovery that revolutions in backward countries are primarily peasant revolutions was anticipated by Lenin, Stalin, and other Chinese Communist leaders such as P'eng Pai. Similarly, Lenin, not Mao, first emphasized the importance of the *poor* peasants in a revolution, and, with respect to the responsiveness of the poor peasants to Communist party leadership, again the Chinese Communists have faked a date to credit Mao with making this point years before he actually did. Further, Mao's alleged discovery that a part of the bourgeoisie was friendly to the revolution was simply a repetition of Lenin and Stalin.

Mao's earliest writings, then, contain nothing to substantiate the claim of a creative development of Communist revolutionary doctrine. But the Chinese case for Mao does not stop there. It is a familiar Communist thesis that the leader who directs a Communist party in revolution contributes, by his formulations of

[59] *The Fourth Congress of the Communist International* (Abridged Report of Petrograd and Moscow Meetings Held November 7–December 3, 1922) (London: published for the Communist International by the Communist Party of Great Britain, 1922), p. 221.

actual strategy and tactics, to the "theory" of revolution itself. If the scope of "theory" is thus broadened, Mao can indeed be credited with two distinctive contributions — the strategy of waging revolution from self-sustaining rural bases and the tactics of guerrilla warfare.

### *The Rural Base Area*

According to Ch'en Po-ta, Mao "worked out a series of complete conclusions . . . that it was possible for the revolution to achieve victory first in the countryside and that it was possible to establish long-term revolutionary bases there." [60]

Mao and his supporters apparently believed that they had little choice but to achieve "victory first in the countryside." In *The Chinese Revolution and the CCP* of December, 1939, Mao and his co-authors say that since "powerful imperialism and its reactionary allies in China have occupied China's key cities for a long time," the relatively weak Communists "must build the backward villages into advanced, consolidated base areas." [61]

Mao's idea of a rural base area is a contribution to the Marxist-Leninist *strategy* of revolution. It is unique in Communist literature.

The prerequisites for establishing "long-term revolutionary bases" in the countryside were enumerated by Mao in November, 1928. In *The Struggle in Chingkang Mountains*, Mao says that in order to survive, an "isolated base" [62] requires, "(1) a sound mass basis, (2) a first-rate party organization, (3) a Red Army of adequate strength, (4) a terrain favorable to military operations, and (5) economic strength sufficient for self-support." [63] We can agree with Ch'en Po-ta's statement that "to establish

[60] Ch'en Po-ta, "Mao Tse-tung's Theory of the Chinese Revolution . . . ." *loc. cit.*

[61] Mao, *Selected Works*, I (1961), 629.

[62] "Isolated base" or "cut-off base" is a more literal translation of the Chinese than the English-language rendition, "independent regime" (ko-chü ti-chü).

[63] Mao, *Selected Works*, I (1961), 59.

revolutionary bases by armed force was the starting point of the road along which Comrade Mao Tse-tung led the revolution to nation-wide victory." [64]

We can also agree with Benjamin I. Schwartz's view that in addition to these prerequisites is the peculiar, unique preference of Mao's for bases in "border areas," bases from which it would be possible "to influence both provinces." [65] It can reasonably be argued, as Professor Schwartz does, that Lenin had opened the door and Mao stepped through it. That is, Mao's strategy for waging the revolutionary struggle in China constituted a *practical* advance over Lenin's general idea of establishing peasant soviets in backward countries.

## *Guerrilla Warfare*

Ch'en Po-ta singles out guerrilla warfare, as well as rural bases, as an important component of Mao's strategy of revolution. Ch'en says: "The main strategy of the revolutionary war as expounded by Comrade Mao Tse-tung was to develop guerrilla warfare to the fullest possible extent and on a large scale and then, under certain conditions, after the growth of our strength, to transform it into regular warfare." [66] Ch'en then quotes from *The Chinese Revolution and the CCP*: "The protracted revolutionary struggle in such revolutionary bases is chiefly a peasant guerrilla war led by the Chinese Communist Party."

Chinese claims for the originality of Mao's concept of guerrilla warfare tactics are marked by considerable detail.

> In this series of lectures [*On Protracted War*, May 26 to June 3, 1938], Comrade Mao Tse-tung . . . worked out his strategic concept of 'conducting independent and

[64] Ch'en Po-ta, "Mao Tse-tung's Theory of the Chinese Revolution . . . ," *loc. cit.*

[65] Schwartz, *Chinese Communism and the Rise of Mao*, p. 190.

[66] Ch'en Po-ta, "Mao Tse-tung's Theory of the Chinese Revolution . . . , *loc. cit.*

> isolated guerrilla warfare in mountainous terrain' and 'prosecuting primarily guerrilla warfare coupled with a war of movement in favorable circumstances' for the Eighth Route Army and the New Fourth Army.[67]
>
> With regard to the problem of engaging the enemy, it was Comrade Mao Tse-tung who always determined military strategy and military art. Precisely coincident with the promulgation of guerrilla warfare, he created his famous 16-word formulation: "Enemy advances, we retire. Enemy tarries, we harass. Enemy tires, we fight. Enemy retires, we pursue." . . . To summarize the 25 years of experience in guerrilla warfare, Comrade Mao Tse-tung wrote many famous military treatises: *Strategic Problems of China's Revolutionary War*, *Strategic Problems of the Anti-Japanese Guerrilla War*, etc. In these works, he explains the sources, nature, and theories of war involved in strategic military thinking, the laws of war, and even problems of military art.[68]

International importance is also claimed for Mao's guerrilla warfare theories. Thus Kuan Meng-chüeh in 1952 states that Mao's *Strategic Problems of China's Revolutionary War* of December, 1936, "is one of the most brilliant Marxist works of the world Communist movement on military science."[69] Kuan's statement carries considerable authority, as he seems to have taken it verbatim from Hu Ch'iao-mu's *Thirty Years of the CCP*, the party's official history in 1952.

Despite their references to Lenin and Stalin, Soviet writers had paid Mao great tribute in discussing his treatises on guerrilla warfare. Thus, in discussing *Strategic Problems of China's Revo-*

[67] Kuo Hua-jo, "On the Occasion of the 15th Anniversary of the Publication of *On Protracted War*," Peking *Jen-min Jih-pao*, June 3, 1953.

[68] Mo Wen-hua, in Peking *Jen-min Jih-pao*, February 23, 1953. Mo concludes by stating that "the military science of Comrade Mao Tse-tung is the military science of Marxism-Leninism sinicized."

[69] Kuang Meng-chüeh, "Read *Strategic Problems of China's Revolutionary War*," in *Study the "Selected Works of Mao Tse-tung, Volume I"* (Peking: Hsin Chien-she Ch'u-pan She, 1952), p. 144.

*lutionary War*, M. Mitin states: "It is an extremely valuable and useful military text. . . . Mao shows himself to be not only a major military figure and leader of great dimensions, but also a military theoretician who skillfully and creatively applied Lenin's and Stalin's ideas in the concrete conditions of the revolutionary war in China."[70] I. Plyshevskiy and A. Sobolev state that "Mao Tse-tung's working out of strategic and tactical problems is an important contribution to the art of warfare."[71] This Plyshevskiy-Sobolev statement, which was made in a review of the second volume of the Russian edition of Mao's *Selected Works* is one of the more genuine and unequivocal tributes to Mao made by Soviet writers, who have frequently qualified their praise and, in recent years, suspended it altogether.

The idea of a popular revolutionary guerrilla war as it was fully and brilliantly developed by Mao is another contribution to the Marxist-Leninist strategy of revolution. Mao-Tse-tung is clearly the "classical" guerrilla leader in the world Communist movement, as his writings on partisan warfare as a means to national power broke new ground in Communist literature.

How much of this strategy is exclusively Mao's? The entire system of ideas is by no means his own. It is a curious fact that as he begins to relate the history of the Chinese Red Army to Edgar Snow in 1936, Mao recedes from a discussion of personal history which had hitherto been the main subject of his account. It is no longer "I" but "we," no longer Mao Tse-tung, but the Red Army.[72] This sudden reticence on his own role in formulating military policy may have reflected a certain modesty. It is equally possible, however, that Mao was not the sole or even the main formulator of Red Army policy in the period from 1928

[70] M. Mitin, "First Volume of the *Selected Works of Mao Tse-tung*," *Bol'shevik*, No. 17, September, 1952, p. 67.

[71] I. Plyshevskiy and A. Sobolev, in *Pravda*, June 13, 1953.

[72] Snow, *op. cit.*, p. 175.

to 1938 and that when he talked with Snow, he was willing to credit his comrades with military vision.

Throughout a large part of the above-mentioned period, Chu Te seems to have had the major role in devising military tactics. When the famous Fourth Red Army was created in 1928 at Chingkangshan in the Hunan-Kiangsi border area, Chu Te was named military commander and Mao served as "political commissar." Mao says that apart from the "political" basis of the Communist effort at Chingkangshan, Red Army tactics explained much of the "military" successes.[73] As for his own role in 1928–29, Mao is silent, probably because Chu, as commander, was the chief military strategist. He then says that from October, 1932, until the beginning of the Long March in October, 1934, he devoted his time "almost exclusively to work with the Soviet Government, leaving the military command to Chu Te and others."[74] During the Long March, however, he participated in some military conferences. For example, Mao joined Chu, Lin Piao, P'eng Te-huai, and Chou En-lai in making the military decision to cross the Tatu River in Szechuan at the Liu Ting Bridge.[75] Nevertheless, the genius of partisan warfare was Chu Te. In 1936 Snow gave the following appraisal of Chu:

> . . . it must be admitted that for tactical ingenutiy, spectacular mobility, and richness of versatility in maneuver, he repeatedly proved his superiority to every general sent against him, and established beyond any doubt the formidable fighting power of revolutionized Chinese troops in partisan warfare. . . .
>
> For pure military strategy and tactical handling of a great army in retreat nothing has been seen in China to compare with Chu Te's splendid generalship of the Long March.[76]

[73] *Ibid.*, p. 177.
[74] *Ibid.*, p. 185.
[75] *Ibid.*, p. 205.
[76] *Ibid.*, pp. 388–89.

A less glowing albeit more professional estimate of Chu was given by another on-the-spot observer. Major Evans F. Carlson described Chu Te cryptically but decisively as "pre-eminent in his field." [77]

It is, therefore, difficult to determine the extent of Mao's debt to Chu. The evidence suggests that he, together with P'eng Te-huai, has been Mao's teacher in guerrilla warfare tactics. In any case, Chu steps aside:

> We must not absorb foreign countries' [Soviet] theories . . . mechanically and regard them as unchanging dogmas. The Great Revolution, the Agrarian Revolution, and the War of Resistance have given birth to a correct military science. . . . it is a military science that has both theory and practice. . . . the many books on warfare written by Comrade Mao Tse-tung are representative works of this *new* military science. . . . the strategy of the people's war is the outstanding result of Comrade Mao Tse-tungs method of waging war.[78]

This is Chu's tribute to Mao in April, 1945. Writing in *Pravda* in August, 1952, Chu praises in particular his former student's military-political treatise *On Protracted War* (May, 1938), in which Mao laid it down that the fight against the Japanese would be "protracted" and that final victory would have to be won in three

[77] Major Evans F. Carlson, "The Chinese Army: Its Organization and Military Efficiency," *Institute of Pacific Relations*, VII (October 6, 1939), 20.

[78] Chu Te, *Military Report to the 7th Congress, CCP*, given on April 25, 1945, published by Foreign Languages Press, Peking, 1952, pp. 63–64 (emphasis supplied). According to the Japanese Foreign Office Information Department's 7th report — *The History of the CCP: 1937* (Tokyo, 1937) — Chu Te wrote *Promoting Anti-Japanese Warfare* (July 15, 1937) and P'eng Te-huai wrote *On Guerrilla Warfare* (summer, 1937). Early Chinese Communist sources indicate that Chu also wrote *On Guerrilla Warfare* (1938), *On Anti-Japanese Guerrilla Warfare* (1938), *Experiences and Lessons Gained in the Past Six Months of the War of Resistance by the 8th Route Army* (1938), and *The Problem of Striving for a Quick-Decision Victory in the Protracted War of Resistance* (1938). Current Chinese Communist publications make no mention of these works, suggesting that Chu Te's light has been concealed so that Mao's can shine brighter.

stages — withdrawal, stalemate, and offensive.[79] A more ambitious study, however, is the earlier work by Mao — *Strategic Problems of China's Revolutionary Wars* (December, 1936). In *Strategic Problems*, Mao attempts to make accurate generalizations on the "laws" of the Chinese revolution, of the cause of victory and defeat in war, of the "laws" of war as well as "the process of understanding the laws of wars." The official CCP history does not exaggerate in appraising this fine work as "one of the most brilliant Marxist works on military science in the world Communist movement." [80]

## *The "Paper Tiger" Concept*

For Mao, the revolutionary process had always been one of turning weakness into strength. He has met the continuing problem in the military field by attacking only dispersed and isolated enemy units with overwhelming — "ten to one" — force, avoiding battle with the main enemy force while it is still superior in numbers and weapons. In the political field, he has sought out allies — even the "middle-of-the-road national bourgeoisie" — everywhere and entered negotiations in order to gain time. In the psychological field, he has tried (and succeeded remarkably well) to instill into the party and army firm revolutionary confidence and determination by advancing slogans, or concepts, of optimism. Mao's "paper tiger" concept is just such a concept of optimism.

Prospects for the continued existence of the CCP and Red Army as an effective revolutionary force were dimmed when, in July, 1946, Chiang Kai-shek with total military forces of approximately 4 million men and field forces of 1.6 million launched

[79] Chu Te, "Twenty-Five Years of the Chinese PLA," *Pravda*, August 1, 1952.

[80] Hu Ch'iao-mu, *op. cit.*, p. 42. Keeping in mind Mao's early dependence on Chu Te and, to a lesser extent, on P'eng Te-huai, we can agree with Hu's overall appraisal of the Chinese leader: "Comrade Mao Tse-tung has made outstanding contributions to Marxist-Leninist military theory in his works on the strategic problems of the Chinese revolutionary wars" (*ibid.*, p. 96).

major offensives against the Communist-led "People's Liberation Army" (PLA). The PLA's strength at the time was roughly less than one-third that of the KMT troops which they faced. PLA forces were cut off from one another in more than ten base areas, and PLA weapons and equipment were poor. It was in this situation (where the enemy had military superiority) that defeatist attitudes were bound to rise and grow.

Aware that morale would begin to ebb, Mao, in an interview in August, 1946, with American correspondent Anna Louise Strong, who was being used by Yenan to gain international sympathy for the CCP, enunciated his concept of optimism. It was a concept with which he was to indoctrinate the party and the army. He stated:

> All reactionaries are paper tigers. In appearance, they are frightening, but in reality they don't amount to much. From the long-term point of view, it is the people who really have great strength, and not the reactionaries.[81]

This was not the metaphor of an impetuous man blind to the reality of KMT military superiority. Because he was speaking of the "long term," these were in fact the words of a cautious man.

On first consideration, Mao's caution is not obtrusive. He says that the atom bomb, too, is a "paper tiger." [82] On second consideration, however, Mao's *actions* show him to have been very cautious indeed. For at the time when he enunciated the concept to Miss Strong, he and his lieutenants were preparing to evacuate Yenan, which had come under air attack from General Hu Tsung-nan's forces. He was retreating, using the cautious guerrilla tactics of "dispersing forces" because it was clearly a matter of survival.

Mao was cautious in yet another sense of the word — in the political-psychological sense. His "paper tiger" concept deliber-

[81] Mao, *Selected Works,* IV (1961), 1193.
[82] *Ibid.*

ately minimized certain facts — such as KMT military capability in the air and on the ground — or avoided all mention of them. As a cautious leader, he stated the case for Communist strength to the rank and file *from the most favorable aspect,* namely, the "long-term point of view." He carefully avoided discussing the short-term prospects, reserving deliberation on such matters for the secrecy of the conference tent.

In short, Mao showed caution by trying to save his forces from drowning in a sea of pessimism. A frank revelation of the desperate military situation would have been demoralizing. He therefore replaced all concepts of pessimism with one simple concept of optimism. As Marshal Lin Piao put it many years after the event, Mao's "paper tiger" concept "*ideologically* armed our entire party and army, inspired and strengthened the *confidence* of the people throughout the country in victory over the KMT reactionaries, and *swept away the fear* that some people had of US imperialism and the KMT reactionaries and their pessimism regarding the future of the revolution." [83]

It was, therefore, not a *military* estimate of enemy strength which Mao set forth in 1946; it was a political-psychological estimate of the debilitating effect the aura of KMT power would have on Communist forces. Thus the very expression of the "paper tiger" concept, reiterated so often, belies its value as anything but a psychological artifice, and it has been used as such in critical times.

The concept was used, for example, in the 1958 Taiwan Strait crisis. In mid-August of that year, shortly before the Communists began heavy shelling of Quemoy, the journal *Hung Ch'i* carried a belligerent article describing the United States as nothing but a "paper tiger," something not to be feared. Mao's August, 1946, enunciation of the concept was recounted, but there was still no

[83] Lin Piao, "The Victory of the Chinese People's Revolutionary War Is the Victory of the Thought of Mao Tse-tung," *Hung Ch'i,* October 1, 1960 (emphasis supplied).

mention of the dialectical qualification that the enemy was at the same time a "real tiger." The article was intended partly to provide Communist forces with confidence in the face of joint United States–Chinese Nationalist units in the Taiwan Strait and partly to strike a pose of determination not to be "blackmailed" by nuclear threats into backing down. When, by early October, the Communists failed to cut off Quemoy and were forced to back away from a commitment to annex the small islands, the United States "paper tiger" actually proved to be a real tiger. Faced with the awkward task of explaining the Communist backdown, the Chinese Communist leaders apparently decided to revise the "paper tiger" concept for the rank and file by insisting that one must be cautious.

The revision, which introduced for the first time an explicit statement on the need for caution (heretofore only implicit or expressed privately by Mao on November 18, 1957), was published in a special collection of Mao's remarks entitled *Imperialists and All Reactionaries Are Paper Tigers.* The special collection, consisting of extracts from Mao's writings and speeches, was published by the Peking *Jen-min Jih-pao* editorial board in the October 31, 1958, issue of the newspaper. The new—i.e., openly stated—component of the "paper tiger" concept first appeared unobtrusively in a quotation which the editorial board cited from Mao's Central Committee directive, *Concerning Several Important Problems in the Present Party Policy* (1948):

> We have reason to despise [the enemy]. . . . But with regard to each part, each specific struggle (military, political, economic, or ideological), we must never take the enemy lightly. On the contrary, we should take the enemy seriously. . . . While we correctly point out that, strategically, with regard to the whole, we should take the enemy lightly, we must never take the enemy lightly in any part, in any specific struggle.[84]

[84] "Imperialists and All Reactionaries Are Paper Tigers," Special Collection, Peking *Jen-min Jih-pao*, October 31, 1958.

At no point in the special collection of quotations was the openly expressed component—taking the enemy "seriously"—applied to the Chinese backdown in the Taiwan Strait. The new component was applied gradually, and Premier Chou En-lai was assigned the onerous task.

Speaking to a hastily convened meeting of the CCP Central Committee's propaganda department on November 10, 1958, Chou discussed "the present situation of the struggle in the Taiwan Strait area and the anti-imperialist task of the Chinese people." Following his analysis of Mao's view that "imperialists and all reactionaries are paper tigers," Chou "then clearly explained certain viewpoints concerning the situation of the struggle in the Taiwan Strait area and on the related international situation,"[85] but his report was not published in the press. That Chou probably linked the Taiwan Strait backdown with the concept of taking the enemy "seriously" is suggested by a Peking *Jen-min Jih-pao* editorial printed two days after his report. The editorial stated that "in the actual struggle and practical problem of the fight against imperialism, the revolutionary people should nonetheless take the enemy seriously. . . ."[86] That the United States–Chinese Nationalist enemy was taken seriously is indicated by Communist reduction of heavy shelling of the Quemoy complex and adoption of the face-saving tactic of alternate-day shelling on a small scale. The Chinese Communist leaders have maintained the option of shelling at a low and sporadic rate ever since in their effort (1) to deny the United States the Communist-Nationalist cease-fire it seeks and (2) to underscore their position that shelling is a "domestic affair" between Mao and Chiang and, therefore, no third party should intervene.

The November 12 *Jen-min Jih-pao* editorial not only carries the rationalization for Peking's failure to take Quemoy, but also contains highly polemical remarks, which apparently were di-

[85] Peking *Jen-min Jih-pao*, November 10, 1958.
[86] *Ibid.*, November 12, 1958.

rected at Soviet Premier Khrushchev. It attacks "some people" for insisting that (1) "the strength of the West should not be underestimated" and (2) "the imperialists should not be irritated . . . as this will not be in the interests of world peace." Both points had been used by Khrushchev to support his line of "peaceful coexistence between states of different social systems" during and following the twentieth Soviet party congress in 1956. Both points were largely incompatible with Communist-created tension in the Taiwan Strait. The peaceful coexistence line of Khrushchev was rejected by the Chinese Communists, who seem to have interpreted it as an attempt to stabilize East-West relations at a time when Peking had not gained its "rightful" status among the world's major powers. The Chinese leaders also viewed a possible United States–USSR–United Kingdom rapprochement as a Soviet maneuver to move toward an agreement limiting the "nuclear club" to three powers. Since the Chinese Communists could not gain either their military objective (the offshore islands and eventually Taiwan) or their political objective (international recognition of the mainland regime as the only Chinese government), they had decided by mid-1958 to return to a long-term, tough cold war policy vis à vis the West. Their attack by implication against Khrushchev (he was not named as their target) was particularly venomous in November, 1958, because Peking was compelled to admit in effect that the United States "paper tiger" had to be taken "seriously"—a view which Moscow had been pressing them to accept *publicly*. Privately, of course, Mao and his lieutenants were aware of their military limitations and of the decisively superior United States–Chinese Nationalist military capability.

Sustaining the rationalization for the failure to isolate and annex the offshore islands and responding to Soviet charges of "adventurism," Mao himself amended his 1946 "paper tiger"concept and for the first time since his secret speech in November, 1957, personally spoke of the "real tigers" as well. Speaking to a meeting of the party's politburo held at Wuchang, Mao on December 1, 1958, stated:

> Just as there is not a single thing in the world without a dual nature (this is the Law of the Unity of Opposites), so imperialism and all reactionaries have a dual nature — they are *real tigers* and paper tigers at the same time. . . . imperialism and all reactionaries, looked at in essence, from a long-term point of view, from a strategic point of view, must be seen for what they are — paper tigers. *On the other hand, they are also living tigers, iron tigers, real tigers, which can eat people.* On this we should build our tactical thinking).[87]

This important statement is highly defensive in tone, as indicated by Mao's laborious stress on the point that his original concept was designed only for the "essential, long-term, and strategic" point of view rather than for any tactical military situation. Mao is clearly compelled to fall back upon dishonest dialectics and to use flippantly the Law of the Unity of Opposites, cheapening it in order to provide balance to the lopsided "paper tiger" concept (lopsided, that is, as it had been *publicly* expressed heretofore). Like Lenin and Stalin, Mao played fast and free with a "law" of dialectical materialism, employing it in the crudest manner to make an important political and military point.

This revised "paper tiger" concept was seized upon by Mao's eulogists, who tried to absolve him from Soviet (and probably Chinese)[88] charges of left adventurism. A considerable insurgence

[87] Mao, *Selected Works*, IV (1961), p. 1190 (emphasis supplied). Mao's correction of his concept was inserted as a footnote in Volume IV of his *Selected Works* first published in 1960.

[88] Following Mao's probe of United States determination to support the Chinese Nationalist offshore island positions in the fall of 1958, the Chinese leader apparently was the target of criticism from within the CCP because of his seeming impetuosity. The author of a pamphlet on defying "ghosts" ("imperialists") stated in the spring of 1959 when "revisionists" (Khrushchev and other Soviet leaders) organized a big anti-Peking chorus, "revisionists inside the country rose in response to this international revisionism and launched their frenzied attack against the *leadership* of the party" (emphasis supplied). See Ho Chi-fang, "Preface to

against the pre-1958 concept was generated. In July, 1959, General Tu P'ing criticized "some of our comrades . . . who tactically see the enemy as a paper tiger" rather than as a real tiger.[89] An editorial in the party's theoretical journal, *Hung Ch'i*, in October, 1960, warned the party rank and file "we should not adopt a rash attitude in our struggle against the enemy," as Mao had advised "taking full account of the enemy tactically."[90] The editorial went on in a strongly defensive tone to insist that Mao "always stressed" that in fighting a battle (that is, in any real military situation), "the balance of forces between us and our enemy needs to be calculated accurately." The defensiveness of the editorial suggests that it was intended as another counter

---

*Stories about Not Being Afraid of Ghosts*," *Peking Review*, No. 10, March 10, 1961. Mao's impetuous economic policy was also under attack.

[89] Tu P'ing, "Study Chairman Mao's Standpoint, Viewpoint, and Method of Research in and Leadership of Warfare," *Hsin-hua Pan-yüeh K'an* (New China Semi-Monthly) (Peking), No. 13, July 10, 1959. Tu goes on to make the important point that Mao's views on actual combat have been formulated for a militarily weak country. He says: "Chairman Mao has formulated many leadership principles pertaining to war. A close study of these principles will reveal that they *all* derive from one basic fact, namely, 'the enemy is strong and we are weak' " (emphasis supplied). The "strong enemy" provides Tu with a premise for hammering home the important conclusion that major engagements must be avoided, as they are too risky: "Because the enemy is strong and we are weak, we cannot be obstinate and take risks with the enemy, nor can we swallow the enemy in one gulp." He makes it clear that the "paper" aspect of the imperialist tiger refers only to political-psychological matters, that is, to "confidence in inevitable victory" and "unbending will to fight on." Actual military combat, however, is a different matter: "But as to how to beat the tiger, that is a different thing, regarding which Chairman Mao has always told us to carry out a thorough investigation, demonstrate refinement in judgment, and, under the most difficult conditions, organize logistics and actual combat. There must be several plans for each battle, and each battle must be prepared for fully. . . . In short, we must fight the enemy as though he were a real tiger." Regarding estimates of all specific combat situations, Tu's argument reflects the low-risk emphasis of Mao's writings on guerrilla warfare. Tu's discussion is a defense of Mao's Taiwan Strait backdown of 1958. We do not accept the implication that all PLA tactics can be deduced from a close reading of Mao's works on military matters, inasmuch as Chinese military operations in the Korean War in several important respects deviated from several of his principles.

[90] "Slighting the Enemy Strategically and Taking Full Account of Him Tactically," *Hung Ch'i*, October 10, 1960.

against Khrushchev, who in mid-1960 by implication had criticized Mao as a "war maniac." This interpretation is supported by the editorial's chief complaint—that "there are some people who . . . consider that to slight the enemy strategically and regard all reactionaries as paper tigers represents an 'adventurist' point of view"—and by its attack on "modern revisionism," a term used by the Chinese to describe Khrushchev's views.

A *Hung Ch'i* article of November 1, 1960, is similarly defensive in the face of apparent Soviet criticism, as its authors insist Mao "always" studies and analyzes actual military situations "objectively," always opposes "left adventurism," and always disapproves of any Chinese Communist commander who becomes "a rash and reckless hothead."[91] The authors argue in effect that the "paper tiger" concept is not a one-sided, "leftist" strategy for carrying out revolution. On the contrary, it is in their view a balanced, "dialectical" approach to revolution. This rather qualified justification for retaining the concept is followed by some notorious nonsense, namely, the authors' claim that "slighting the enemy strategically and taking full account of him tactically" is "a new development of enormous significance in the theory of Marxist-Leninist strategy and tactics." It is nothing of the sort; it is just a platitude.

As interpreted by the Chinese *publicly* after mid-1958, the concept enjoins Communists to have faith in their eventual triumph, but to respect the enemy in particular situations. But this was the way of many revolutionary leaders. For example, the non-Communist nationalist guerrilla in Morocco, Abd-el-Krim, measured his cloth seven times over before acting when faced with a superior enemy military force. As a fighter in the cause of Soviet national interests, Stalin himself was a past master in showing contempt for the enemy strategically while exercising caution tac-

[91] Teng Li-ch'un and Wu Chiang, "Dialectics Is the Algebra of Revolution—Read the *Selected Works of Mao Tse-tung, Volume IV*," *Hung Ch'i*, November 1, 1960.

tically. Only a lunatic would fail to act cautiously if what he considered a "paper tiger" appeared for the moment to have the capacities of a real one.

Psychologically, if not logically, it is difficult to take full account of any enemy in a particular situation without also taking full account of him in the long view. Conversely, if an enemy is slighted in the long-view (as Mao prefers), the inclination is to slight him in a particular situation as well. Thus it may well be that the "paper tiger" concept prior to the fall of 1958 tended to create a simplistic view among the Chinese Communist rank and file of the United States as a military "pushover." This rank-and-file simplification apparently had to be altered publicly by the Chinese leaders when the United States tiger showed its teeth and determination to support the Chinese Nationalist effort to resupply the Quemoy garrison troops.

Mao and his lieutenants continue to use the "paper tiger" concept as a political-psychological weapon against Khrushchev's policies and against those of the West. In March, 1961, the Chinese Communists insisted that all Communists must view the West's economic and military power as "merely a transient phenomenon, historically speaking" and criticized Khrushchev (not by name) for his fear of "ghosts," i.e., of the United States.[92] Mao, they asserted, would prefer that "all Marxists . . . should be tough-willed men who fear nothing at all." But this is self-interpretation. It is Chinese self-interpretation of Mao as a Marxist who fears nothing at all. Khrushchev obviously does not accept this as a precise and true picture of Mao's courage. He rejects this Chinese self-interpretation and strongly implies that Mao is brave for others, brave for the Russians. That is, Mao would have the Russians fight and be "tough-willed men" for him and the Peking regime. Speaking to delegates of the twenty-second Soviet party congress in October, 1961, Khrushchev said:

[92] Ho Chi-fang, "Preface to *Stories about Not Being Afraid of Ghosts.*"

> You will have seen in films about Africa and Asia how kings, princes, rajahs and other notables go tiger hunting on elephants. They do this because they know that this form of tiger hunting is not dangerous.[93]

Khrushchev is saying that Mao is aware that the Western tiger fears the military strength of the Soviet elephant. It is not the Chinese notable who shows courage but rather the Soviet elephant on which he rides. The notable calculates that if the tiger attacks while being hunted, he is bound to clash with the elephant. Khrushchev would prefer that the Chinese notable either prove his courage by hunting the Western tiger on foot or stop spurring the elephant to hunt for him.

Mao continues to use the "paper tiger" concept (revised to include publicly the element of caution) for the following primary reasons.

First, it helps Mao bluff his way through a period in which Peking does not have, and the United States has, nuclear weapons. The Chinese leader is trying to convince the United States that Communist China is not militarily weak or psychologically cowed. They say: a nuclear attack on China would still leave 200 million Chinese to continue the war and win. In a highly emotional and vituperative response to United Nations Ambassador Adlai Stevenson's effective criticism of Peking's militant views, the Peking *Jen-min Jih-pao* commentator, "Observer," stated in December, 1961, that Mao's singular view of nuclear war is "the biggest slight of United States imperialism's policy of nuclear blackmail."[94] Admitting that a nuclear war would be "a serious calamity for mankind" and that the United States possesses "guns in far greater number than China does," "Observer" hints that consciously fostered tough-mindedness is absolutely necessary for the morale of the CCP and Peking's armed forces. "If we take fright, we shall

[93] *Pravda*, October 29, 1961.

[94] Observer, "Denounce Stevenson," Peking *Jen-min Jih-pao*, December 10, 1961.

be disarmed spiritually, the enemy will become more rabid, and the danger of nuclear war will become more serious." It is for this reason that the Chinese in 1958 had been disseminating the view that they are really not afraid of a nuclear war.

Second, the concept is intended for use as a psychological substructure on which to build a revolutionary — that is, anti–United States — attitude among emergent and newly emerged peoples. Thus the Chinese insist that "to expose the United States as a paper tiger, to have no fear of its nuclear threat, and to stir up the fighting will of the people" is an extremely important step to take in the struggle against the West.[95]

Regardless of how this attitude might or might not serve the interests of other peoples, Mao calculates that it definitely provides Peking with an important tool for rolling back United States influence in the underdeveloped areas of the world, which in turn helps to extend Communist China's influence. It is in these areas that the strength of the United States is most easily sapped. From the long view, it is in *Peking's interest* to create and intensify — to focus — anti–United States attitudes, but it is not in Peking's interest to say so.[96] The Chinese, therefore, are careful to avoid stressing their own national interests. Mao has acted in this matter appropriately with a view to what is useful, and he clearly thinks less of what is useful for other nations than what is useful for

[95] Sun Tu, "Answers to Readers' Questions on War and Peace," *Chung-kuo Ch'ing-nien*, February 16, 1960.

[96] That the Chinese Communists give top priority to having the United States isolated throughout the world is apparent from their statements and their persistent effort to insert into bilateral and multilateral communiqués the ideas of the United States as "the world's number-one enemy." They advance anti–United States appeals in a way that reflects a morbid obsession: "Like a rat running across the street while *everyone* shouts, 'Throw something at it,' the US imperialists run into bumps and bruises *everywhere*, and *everywhere* arouse a new upsurge of the people's revolutionary struggles, contrary to their intentions" (emphasis supplied). This is an application of Mao's own imagery to international politics. In this and other discussions, Peking's own interest in pushing revolutions is only suggested but rarely explicitly stated. See "Long Live Leninism," *Hung Ch'i*, April 19, 1960.

the Peking regime. He has succeeded in persuading many people that what he says about their interests must be taken seriously, inasmuch as he resorts to explicit statements and unambiguous language. He has also persuaded many that, after all, he is Lenin's heir because he gives priority to world revolutionary interests rather than Chinese revolutionary interests. And he has succeeded partly because he and other Chinese Communist leaders have stated Peking's own goals and interests ambiguously when discussing revolutions in Asia, Africa, and Latin America.

Third, the "paper tiger" concept is retained as another of Mao's creative developments of Communist doctrine on revolution. As stated above, it is hardly that but rather a psychological device for establishing faith in eventual victory in the minds of dispirited (or potentially dispirited) comrades and, as such, it is similar to Lenin's well-known remark that the imperialists are not invincible because they have "feet of clay."

## *A Text for Backward Countries*

The Chinese Communists believe that Mao's contribution to the strategy of revolution should be applied to other backward countries. But Mao's writings of 1928, in which he formulated the idea of establishing rural revolutionary bases, carried the implication that this was a strategy specifically applicable to the peculiar political and geographical environment of China. After 1949, however, the Chinese Communists began taking the line that Mao's formula for revolution — now designated "the road of Mao Tse-tung" — furnished a model strategy for all backward countries. Thus, when one of Mao's original writings — *Why can China's Red Political Power Exist?* (October, 1928) — was republished in the first volume of his *Selected Works* in 1951, a footnote was appended to it emphasizing the applicability of the Chinese revolutionary experience to other countries of "the East." The key passage in the footnote reads:

> Thus, just as the Chinese people have done, all or at least some of the colonial peoples of the East can hold big or small base areas and maintain revolutionary regimes for an extended period, carry on protracted revolutionary war to encircle the cities from the countryside, and proceed gradually to take over the cities and win nationwide victory in their respective countries.[97]

It is this prescription that is the uniquely Maoist formula for revolution. Ever since 1949, this prescription for revolutionary victory has been a thorn in Moscow's side—and it is even more irritating now that the Peking regime is actively competing for influence in the underdeveloped countries. Peking can claim, if only by implication, that every leader of a rural-based nationalist revolutionary movement in backward areas is following the "road of Mao Tse-tung," whether he ever heard of Mao or not.[98] Here Moscow is at a disadvantage, as it cannot cite Lenin and Stalin as architects of this special kind of revolutionary strategy. The Russians, however, can rely on their greater capability to supply rural revolutions with arms and other means of support to exert an influence.

To sum up, Chinese spokesmen acknowledge that Mao's early *Analysis* of the Chinese revolution owes a general debt to Lenin and Stalin, but they minimize that debt, and they conceal the importance of Comintern directives in Mao's early thinking. All their specific claims for this early work appear to be spurious. Mao's alleged development of the concept of "leadership of the proletariat" in 1926 is not an advance on Lenin's position in 1912, and even his agreement with Lenin on this point was inserted into Mao's works many years later. Mao's alleged discovery that revolutions in backward countries are primarily peasant revolutions was anticipated by Lenin, Stalin, and other Chinese Communist lead-

[97] Mao, *Selected Works*, I (1961), 57.

[98] At one time, the Chinese Communists stated, and now clearly imply, that the "revolution" in Vietnam has moved along "Mao's road" of rural-based guerrilla warfare.

ers such as P'eng Pai. Similarly, Lenin, not Mao, first emphasized the importance of the *poor* peasants in a revolution, and, with respect to the responsiveness of the poor peasants to Communist party leadership, again the Chinese have faked a date to credit Mao with making this point years before the fact. Further, Mao's alleged discovery that a part of the bourgeoisie was friendly to the revolution was simply a repetition of Lenin and Stalin.

Subsequently, Mao made two contributions to the *practical* problem of working out a viable strategy for revolution. The first of these, forced on him by circumstance, was the concept he developed of an isolated and self-sustaining rural base; the second, taken in part from Chu Te and P'eng Te-huai, was his elaborate doctrine on guerrilla warfare. Soviet writers themselves at one time had paid Mao tribute in the matter of guerrilla war tactics, but those halcyon days of the Sino-Soviet relationship are over. Another of Mao's concepts — the "paper tiger," enjoining Communists to have faith in their eventual triumph, but to respect the enemy in particular situations — is not a contribution at all. Although Chinese theorists say it is a "new development of enormous significance" for theory, it is simply a platitude.

Despite the spurious nature of most of these claims, there remains a unique hard core in Mao's strategy for revolution. To many Communists in backward countries, Mao's "contribution" to the strategy of revolution is his formulation of a number of very practical guidelines for organizing and directing a peasant revolt. No other Communist leader has written so much and so well on the tactics of rural warfare. No other Communist leader has been so influential in making rural-based revolution a supreme law unto itself. And no other Communist leader can claim with as much conviction that, while Lenin planned and executed the archetype of urban revolution, he, Mao, formulated and carried out the archetype of rural revolution.

# 3

# Mao and the State Form

When, on November 7, 1917, Lenin stood on the rostrum of the Soviet Congress to speak of "our victory," he asked, "What is the significance of this revolution?" and answered directly, "Its significance is . . . that we shall have a Soviet Government, without the participation of a bourgeoisie of any kind." [1] The workers and peasants would form the class basis of the new government and, under the guidance of the Bol'shevik leaders, they rapidly would acquire the necessary skills for helping in the administration without relying on the talents of the former ruling class. Lenin discovered, however, that he had to fall back on the administrative and technical (and even commercial) talents of some members of the Russian bourgeoisie. But they were never given formal rights in the Soviet Republic's "dictatorship of the proletariat."

Having learned the lesson, Mao took a more pragmatic approach from the start, telling his colleagues on July 1, 1949, that in the Chinese "people's" republic the national bourgeoisie — the small, native capitalists — definitely would have a formal place and formal rights.[2] As one Chinese writer put it, the national

[1] Quoted in David Shub, *Lenin* (special abridged edition; New York: New American Library of World Literature, 1959), p. 136.

[2] Mao, *Selected Works*, IV (1961), 1480. Mao stated: "Who are the people?

bourgeoisie and its political parties would have "more representatives" in the government than during the period of the rural bases (pre-1949) because this class can play "a definite role during the transitional period since it possesses a fairly rich knowledge of modern science and culture and a fairly large number of intellectuals and specialists."[3] In addition, Mao clearly recognized that this class was needed as part of the general effort to expand the industrial and commercial sectors of China's economy. It was as though he were starting a NEP policy in 1949.

The class composition of Mao's new state raised a problem in doctrine. If a bourgeoisie "of any kind" was not included in the formal structure of the prototype—the Soviet Republic—was it not a departure from doctrine to permit national bourgeoisie membership in the ruling group of the "people's" republic?

It *was* a departure from doctrine but not a clear break with precedent. Mao was not the first to lead the native capitalists into the group slated to control the state *after* the Communist seizure of power. Eastern European regimes had preceded Mao in this policy following World War II; Stalin, however, decided to reverse it in 1948 during the CPSU dispute with the Yugoslav Communists. Mao seems to have been the first Communist leader to have *written extensively* about the matter, and his works in the early 1940's may well have provided the Eastern European leaders with the idea of including the native capitalists in the formal state structure. In order to expand Marx's concept of the dictatorship of the proletariat, Mao in 1939 and 1940 used the phrase "joint dictatorship" of several revolutionary classes to denote the broader nature of the ruling group in the future Communist state in China.

---

At the present stage in China, they are the working class, the peasantry, the urban petty bourgeoisie, and the national bourgeoisie. . . . The latter at the present stage is of great importance."

[3] Ho Kan-chih, *A History of the Modern Chinese Revolution* (Peking: Foreign Languages Press, 1959), p. 531.

Precisely in what sense was the formulation of a "joint dictatorship" unique, inasmuch as Lenin in 1905 had envisaged a ruling dictatorship of more than one class?

In attempting to answer this question, it is necessary to distinguish (as Marx does) two stages of revolution—the bourgeois stage and the "socialist" stage, when Communists finally seize total power.

According to Marx, the dictatorship of the proletariat comes *after* the bourgeois revolution and *before* the social revolution is completed—a kind of intermediate stage. That is, the proletariat establishes a transitional state in the form of the dictatorship of the proletariat.[4] "Between capitalist and Communist society," Marx says in his *Critique of the Gotha Program* of 1875, "lies the period of the revolutionary transformation of the one into the other. There corresponds to this also a political transition period in which the state can be nothing but the *revolutionary dictatorship of the proletariat*."[5] In 1905, and in polemics with Trotsky in 1906, Lenin discussed the *bourgeois* (or first) stage of the revolution. He proposed a "revolutionary democratic dictatorship of the workers and peasants" as a form which the bourgeois revolution would take in Russia (whatever it might have meant in practice). At that stage, the peasants were the "bourgeois" element. This was of course poles apart from Marx's theory of the capitalist plan of development as a necessary precondition for the *socialist* revolution. But it was not a departure from Marx's view of the dictatorship of the proletariat because he was still

[4] Marx first used the designation, "dictatorship of the proletariat," in his *The Class Struggles in France* of 1850. Two years later, Marx described his achievements in a letter to Weydemeyer (March 5, 1852): "What I did that was new was to prove: (1) that the *existence of classes* is only bound up with *particular, historic phases in the development of production*; (2) that the class struggle necessarily leads to the *dictatorship of the proletariat*; (3) that this dictatorship itself only constitutes the transition to the *abolition of all classes* and to a *classless society*" (Marx's emphasis).

[5] Marx-Engels, *Selected Works* (Moscow: Foreign Languages Publishing House, 1955), II, 32–33 (Marx's emphasis). (Hereafter, Marx-Engels, *Selected Works*.)

speaking of the bourgeois revolution and its "provisional" revolutionary government. When the *socialist* revolution was consummated in November, 1917, the idea of "democratic dictatorship" was replaced by that of proletarian dictatorship.

Chinese theorists claim that Mao arrived at a unique formulation. In 1949, Tu Shou-su[6] and Li Mien[7] both say that Mao "further developed the Marxist-Leninist theory of state" by advancing the new concept of "people's democratic dictatorship" for China. Similarly, in 1960, Liu P'ing-lin says that "Comrade Mao Tse-tung has creatively developed the Marxist-Leninist doctrine on the dictatorship of the proletariat, creating the theory of the people's democratic dictatorship."[8] Liu goes on to say that what Mao discovered "for China" was "a new form of revolutionary dictatorship of the proletariat."

Mao's originality (which is somewhat exaggerated by his eulogists) emerges only from his relatively late writings. For in at least two rather early works, Mao merely follows Lenin's and Stalin's formulations.

Thus in his *Why Can China's Red Political Power Exist?* of October, 1928, Mao speaks of an armed "workers' and peasants'" regime,[9] and in *A Single Spark Can Start a Prairie Fire* of January, 1930, he speaks of "the correctness of the slogan about a workers' and peasants' democratic political power."[10] This was Lenin's formulation. In his *Two Tactics of Social Democracy in the Democratic Revolution* of 1905, he includes the peasants in the dictatorship: "The task now is to define *which* classes must

[6] Tu Shou-su, "Chairman Mao's *On the People's Democratic Dictatorship* — a Program for the Development of the Chinese Revolution and the Crystallization of the Thought of Mao Tse-tung," in *The Theory and Practice of the People's Democratic Dictatorship* (Canton: T'uan-chieh Ch'u-pan She, 1949), p. 11.

[7] Li Mien, "The People's State — a Study Note on *People's Democratic Dictatorship*," in *ibid.*, p. 32.

[8] Liu P'ing-lin, "Seriously Study Comrade Mao Tse-tung's Doctrine on the Dictatorship of the Proletariat," Tsinan *Ta-chung Jih-pao*, May 12, 1960.

[9] Mao, *Selected Works*, I (1961), 52.

[10] *Ibid.*, p. 102.

build the new superstructure. . . . This definition is given in the slogan: The democratic dictatorship of the proletariat and peasantry. This slogan defines . . . the character of the new superstructure (a 'democratic' as distinct from a 'socialist' dictatorship) . . ." as bourgeois-democratic development was still the order of the day in Russia.[11]

Stalin applied Lenin's formulation to China in 1926:

> I think that the future revolutionary government in China will in general resemble in character the government we used to talk about in our country in 1905, that is, something in the nature of a democratic dictatorship of the proletariat and peasantry, with the difference, however, that it will be first and foremost an anti-imperialist government. This shall be an interim state power for China to attain non-capitalist development.[12]

This Leninist idea of workers' *and* peasants' political power was not only used by Mao in October, 1928, and January, 1930, but also appears in the 1931 constitution of the Chinese Soviet Republic (in Kiangsi). That constitution referred to the political power of "the state of the democratic dictatorship of the workers and peasants."[13] But in the late 1930's, Mao began to develop

[11] Lenin, *Selected Works* (Moscow: Foreign Languages Publishing House, 1952), I, Part 2, 137 (Lenin's emphasis). Trotsky saw use of the new worker-peasant formula as merely a tactic, concealing real "working class"—i.e., Communist or Social-Democratic—aims: "It is . . . absurd to speak of a *specific* character of proletarian dictatorship (or dictatorship of the proletariat *and* the peasantry) within a bourgeois revolution, viz., a *purely democratic* dictatorship. The working class can never secure the democratic character of its dictatorship without overstepping the limits of its democratic program" (Trotsky's emphasis). See Leon Trotsky: "Prospects of a Labor Dictatorship (1906)," in *Our Revolution—Essays on Working-Class and International Revolution, 1904–1917*, (New York: Henry Holt & Co., 1918), pp. 65 ff.

[12] Stalin, "Prospects of the Revolution in China" (November, 1926), *Works*, VIII, 382.

[13] "Outline Constitution of the Chinese Soviet Republic (Adopted at the First National Congress of Chinese Soviets on November 7, 1931)," in *Su-wei-ai Chung-kuo* (Soviet China), printed in Chinese (Moscow: Foreign Languages Publishing House, 1933), pp. 38–39.

his own idea of Communist post-revolutionary dictatorship, carrying Lenin's view one step further by bringing yet another class—the "middle," or "national," bourgeoisie—into the circle of the select. The "big" bourgeoisie, compradors, landlords, "bullying gentry," and the reactionary section of the "vagrants" (*Lumpenproletariat*) were excluded.

Mao's view was set forth well before the concept of "people's democracy" was discussed in Soviet literature for what became, after 1945, the East European satellites. In chapter 2 of *The Chinese Revolution and the CCP* (1939), Mao and his co-authors, describing what they call a "new democracy" revolution in China, say:

> Politically, it means the *joint* dictatorship of *several* revolutionary classes . . . Economically, it means nationalization of all *big* capital and *big* enterprises . . . distribution of the land of landlords among the peasants, and at the same time the general preservation of private capitalist enterprises.[14]

They go on to say that the "new democracy" revolution results in the "dictatorship of the united front of all revolutionary classes,"[15] without explicitly including the national bourgeoisie. But chapter 2 carries throughout the implication that this class is indeed a member of the new "united front," or "joint," dictatorship, as "The national bourgeoisie . . . oppressed by imperialism . . . constitutes one of the revolutionary forces."[16]

Within one month, Mao took another step toward firmly lodging the native capitalists in the future state structure of China. His *On New Democracy* (1940)—the definitive Chinese Com-

[14] Mao, *Selected Works*, II (1961), 642 (emphasis supplied).

[15] *Ibid.* The original text, published prior to the establishment of the Communist regime in 1949, also calls for the "dictatorship of the united front of several revolutionary parties" in addition to revolutionary classes. Cf. Mao, *Selected Works* (1947), pp. 185–86.

[16] Mao, *Selected Works*, II (1961), 634.

munist work which served as a guide for the following decade—implied that the national bourgeoisie would be one of the classes in the new state. Mao first says that the Chinese revolution aims at establishing "a new democratic society" and "a state under the joint dictatorship of all revolutionary classes."[17] He then sets forth the prime criterion for determining the loyalty to minimum Communist policies: an anti-imperialist attitude. "No matter what classes . . . join the revolution . . . so long as they oppose imperialism, their revolution becomes part of the proletarian socialist world revolution and they themselves become its allies."[18] Thus the Chinese national bourgeoisie "even in the era of imperialism" retains to a certain degree "a revolutionary quality which enables it . . . *to ally with the proletariat* and petty bourgeoisie to oppose the enemies it sets itself against."[19] It apparently is, therefore, one of the revolutionary classes destined to play a role in the "joint dictatorship."

The first *explicit* reference in Mao's works to the national bourgeoisie as one of the classes of the new, Maoist dictatorship is made in *On the People's Democratic Dictatorship* (1949).[20] Mao says:

> All the experiences of the Chinese people . . . tell us to carry out a people's democratic dictatorship. . . . Who are the "people"? At the present stage in China they are the working class, the peasantry, the petty bourgeoisie, and the national bourgeoisie.[21]

[17] *Ibid.*, p. 661.

[18] *Ibid.*, p. 664.

[19] *Ibid.*, p. 666 (emphasis supplied).

[20] In an earlier work—*On Coalition Government* (April, 1945)—Mao included the national bourgeoisie—together with workers, peasants, handicraftsmen, and the urban petty bourgeoisie—as one of the classes which desired a "new-democratic state system." But he avoided, with deliberateness, mentioning his "joint dictatorship" of several classes, and, in an additional effort to conceal the fact that a Communist-led "coalition government" would be a bogus system, he explicitly denied that a proletarian dictatorship "following the example of the Russian Communists" will be established in China.

[21] Mao, *Selected Works*, IV (1961), 1480.

"This clear and correct definition," says Tu Shou-su, "leaves no confusion."[22] It is primarily to these lines that Chinese theorists point when they credit Mao with having further developed the Marxist-Leninist theory of the dictatorship of the proletariat.

According to the Chinese, at precisely what point did Mao "develop" this theory? Liu P'ing-lin makes the inclusion of the national bourgeoisie the decisive factor. "The people's democratic dictatorship accepted the participation of the national bourgeoisie; it was, therefore, different from the 'Workers' and Peasants' Revolutionary Democratic Dictatorship' proposed by Lenin during the 1905 Russian revolution."[23]

Liu's rejection of Lenin's formula, which Stalin in 1926 had declared would be the future form of state power in China, is a reflection of Mao's persisting reluctance to accept the Russian formulation. It was Mao's desire, fired by personal and chauvinist conceit as well as practical considerations, to establish a new, Chinese formula to describe state power for a Communist regime. Liu states: "Comrade Mao Tse-tung has created a *new form* of proletarian revolutionary dictatorship for *our* country and found the most correct road, the road of the people's democratic dictatorship."[24]

Mao's Marxism-Leninism on the matter of Communist dictatorship as well as other issues is at once dogmatic and adaptive. He was suffiicently autonomous—free of Stalin's control—to modify doctrine where political circumstances and his own prestige required its change. Yet he did not alter the fire at the center—the rationale for the party's monopoly of power—when it came to the question of questions: Who has the hegemony in the government and through it in the country? On this question, Mao's *On the People's Democratic Dictatorship* reads like Engels' *On Authority* (1873), Lenin's *State and Revolution* (1917), and

[22] Tu Shou-su, *op. cit.*, p. 11.
[23] Liu P'ing-lin, *op. cit.*
[24] *Ibid.*, (emphasis supplied).

Trotsky's *Dictatorship vs. Democracy* (1922). (It is unnecessary to cite Stalin's views on the subject, as these are perhaps the best known of all his views.) Engels says that if the victorious party in a revolution does not want to have fought in vain, it must maintain its dictatorship "by means of the terror" which its arms inspire in the vanquished; Lenin declares that "the systematic repression of the exploiting minority calls for the greatest ferocity and savagery"; and Trotsky speaks of the "severe compulsion" with which the "workers'" state controls its enemies. That Mao is not a moderate or a revisionist on the matter of Communist party hegemony—that is, neither a moralist in method of persuasion nor an eclectic in thought—is indicated by his answer to non-Communist critics or imagined critics in 1949:

> "You are dictatorial." My dear sirs, you are right, that is just what we are. . . . we deprive the reactionaries of the right to speak and let the people alone have that right.[25]

Mao's *On the People's Democratic Dictatorship* is not an inspired work and merely reiterates rather than creatively develops what the classical texts say on the subject of hegemony and control.

On the matter of who the "people" are, however, Mao's formulation goes beyond the classical concepts. For Marx, Engels, Lenin, and Stalin, the Communist dictatorship following the Communist (as distinct from the bourgeois) stage of revolution was not to include the middle, or national bourgeoisie. (Moreover, for Lenin and Stalin, the national bourgeoisie could not conceivably continue to exist as an accepted class during the post-revolutionary period of "socialist construction.") They never saw this class as part of the "people" in a Communist-controlled state. Mao's definition of "people" is, of course, reducible to the simple question: who is a friend and who is an enemy of the CCP?

On at least two occasions, Lenin explains Marx's use of the

[25] Mao, *Selected Works*, IV (1961), 1480.

term "people" as indicating only the workers and peasants, the latter constituting part of the petty bourgeoisie.

In 1905, Lenin stated: "It now remains to define more precisely what Marx really meant by 'democratic bourgeoisie' [*demokratische Bürgerschaft*], which together with the workers he called the people, in contradistinction to the big bourgeoisie. . . . There is no doubt that the chief components of the 'people,' whom Marx in 1848 contrasted with the resisting reactionaries and the treacherous bourgeoisie, are the proletariat and peasantry." [26]

Regarding the "liberal bourgeoisie," Lenin in 1917 excludes them from the ranks of the "people" after the revolution, as they will betray the peasants by taking the side of the landlords. Lenin points out that in a letter to Dr. Kugelmann (April 12, 1871), Marx spoke of a "people's revolution." [27] He then says that "the idea of a 'people's' revolution seems strange on Marx's lips, and the Russian Plekhanovites and Mensheviks . . . might possibly declare such an expression a 'slip of the tongue' . . . but in the Europe of 1871, the proletariat on the Continent did not constitute the majority of the people. A 'people's' revolution, actually sweeping the majority into its current, could be such only if it embraced both the proletariat and the peasantry. [During the revolution] both classes then constituted the 'people.'" [28] After the revolution, when the new, transitional state is established, it can be, says Marx, only a dictatorship of the proletariat.

Lenin's own use of the term "people" also excludes the national bourgeoisie in the state form. In 1905 he defines the "people" as the "proletariat and peasantry, if we take the main, big forces and distribute the rural and urban *petty* bourgeoisie (also part of the 'people') between the two." [29] "The Jacobins of contempo-

[26] Lenin, "Two Tactics of Social Democracy in the Democratic Revolution," *Selected Works*, I, Part 2, 144–46.

[27] Lenin, *State and Revolution* (New York: International Publishers, 1935), p. 33.

[28] *Ibid.*, pp. 34–35.

[29] Lenin, "Two Tactics . . .," p. 56 (emphasis supplied).

rary Social-Democracy — the Bol'sheviks — want the people, i.e., the proletariat and the peasantry, to settle accounts with the monarchy and the aristocracy in the 'plebian way'. . . ."[30] "There remains the 'people,' that is, the proletariat and peasantry. . . ."[31]

The peasants, designated by Lenin as "democratic" or "petty" bourgeoisie, were to be used only to consummate a revolutionary seizure of power, after which the proletariat would mark them for discard: "In other words: when the democratic bourgeoisie or petty bourgeoisie ascends another step, when not only the revolution but the complete victory of the revolution becomes an accomplished fact, we shall 'substitute' (perhaps amid the horrified cries of new, future, Martynovs) for the slogan of the democratic dictatorship, the slogan of a socialist dictatorship of the proletariat."[32]

That is what Lenin did after the Bol'shevik takeover in 1917, and the dictatorship of the proletariat was formalized by Stalin in 1936. But Mao did not follow this precedent after the CCP takeover in China in 1949. In theory, China had just then completed the bourgeois-democratic revolution but had not yet completed the "socialist" revolution, requiring some form of "democratic" rather than purely "proletarian" dictatorship. Even in 1953, when the "socialist" revolution was proclaimed, for reasons of prestige and broad non-Communist support, Mao insisted on preserving the unique slogan of "people's democratic dictatorship."

Mao's "people's democratic dictatorship" was not a transitory stage to the dictatorship of the proletariat, inasmuch as the CCP had taken *full* power in 1949. His "people's democratic dictatorship" was, therefore, a pseudonym for proletarian dictatorship or a specific form of proletarian dictatorship — proletarian dictatorship "without the Soviet form," as Soviet theorists put it. By contrast, the concept of a "Workers' Government" set forth by Zinoviev and Radek at the Fourth Comintern Congress held in

[30] *Ibid.*, p. 59.
[31] *Ibid.*, p. 104
[32] *Ibid.*, p. 140.

Moscow in late 1922 was explicitly described by the latter as "one of the possible transitory stages to the proletarian dictatorship" *but* as "not yet the proletarian dictatorship."[33] Zinoviev explained that many "Workers' Governments" can be "bourgeois governments according to their social composition"—that is, can be united front governments which include liberal bourgeois groups—and as such cannot be proletarian dictatorships. Even a Soviet form of government "does not always mean proletarian dictatorship," witness the Kerensky government. The only type (he mentions four, but says there can be even more) of Workers' Government which can be designated a proletarian dictatorship is a "Communist Workers' Government":[34] Radek and Zinoviev therefore held that for the Communists to join a Workers' Government was good tactics (particularly in Australia and England in 1922) but made it clear that the presence of the liberal bourgeoisie in them by definition meant they were not and could not be any form of proletarian dictatorship.

The call for Communist participation in these governments in 1922 was in effect a pragmatic recognition of Lenin's mistaken belief that the Russian workers' uprising of 1917 would be repeated in the industrially advanced Western democracies. Radek and Zinoviev saw the need for a transitional formulation which would permit Communists to work in parliamentary governments while the fiery demand for "smashing" the bourgeois state apparatus and replacing it with a dictatorship of the proletariat—i.e., full Communist control—could be temporarily concealed. These Comintern strategists thus realized that a greater degree of flexibility in Western Europe was needed than had previously been shown by Bol'shevik theorists discussing world revolution in general, and revolution in capitalist states in particular. When, therefore, Khrushchev at the twentieth congress of the CPSU in 1956

[33] *Fourth Congress of the Communist International* (Abridged Report of Petrograd and Moscow Meetings Held November 7–December 3, 1922), p. 51.
[34] *Ibid.*, pp. 87–90.

called for a parliamentary road to eventual Communist power without stressing proletarian dictatorship during this transitional stage, he was in effect reviving the Radek-Zinoviev strategy of 1922.

The difference between their strategy and Mao's is that in the latter's view the Communists can participate in a government with the bourgeoisie only if they retain *their own sources of political and military power.* In Mao's view, a coalition, or united front, government must not mean a temporary union of the strong (bourgeoisie) with the weak (Communists) but rather an unstable union in which the Communists must be *as strong as or even stronger than* their temporary partners. They must not depend on mere voting strength; they must not merely strive to win a majority in parliament. They must rely primarily on Communist strength in the field. As for Mao's "people's democratic dictatorship" of 1949 and thereafter, it is not at all a united front or coalition government as conceived for Communists in Western countries, who are to co-operate with the still predominant bourgeoisie. It is a totalitarian dictatorship in which *the Communists are the predominant force* and the "democratic" parties and national bourgeoisie are weak puppets carried along to create the impression of broad popular non-Communist "support." It is a specific — Chinese — form of proletarian dictatorship. According to doctrine, neither the "big" bourgeoisie nor the "national" bourgeoisie (small capitalists) should retain political status in this dictatorship. By granting the national bourgeoisie paper political rights and extending the period of their existence as a class into the period of "socialist" revolution, Mao departed from doctrine, and in this sense was an innovator.

Since 1949 the Chinese have shown considerable sensitivity to apparent Soviet efforts to erode or conceal the uniqueness of Mao's slogan, "people's democratic dictatorship." The Russians tried persistently to equate the "people's democratic dictatorship" with Lenin's two-class slogan. At times, however, they would nod slightly in Mao's direction, conceding that his slogan was broader than Lenin's concept. In April, 1952, the Peking *Jen-min Jih-pao* noted with apparent delight the criticism by Soviet scholars of the book *Historical Materialism* (edited by Konstantinov), which had "incorrectly" described China's state form. *Jen-min Jih-pao* reports the criticism:

> In the last paragraph of Section 2, Chapter 9, "On the Soviet Socialist State," the writer states that the People's Republic of China has established a revolutionary democratic dictatorship of the proletariat and peasantry. This definition fails to indicate fully and correctly the characteristics and special features of the state power of the People's Republic of China (genuine *people's* and democratic state power). . . .
>
> The writer does not give attention to the alliance of the working class and the national bourgeoisie formed in New China, although this aspect should not be neglected in describing the characteristics of the development of the People's Republic of China.[35]

Despite this concession—i.e., that the worker–national bourgeoisie alliance was a "special feature" of Mao's version of the state in China—the Soviet practice was (in 1952) and is (now) to conceal the uniqueness of Mao's slogan. In discussing China's "people's democratic dictatorship," Soviet writers continued to make it a standard procedure to conceal its originality by using language which implicitly equated it with Lenin's two-class idea.

The Chinese effort to resist Soviet imposition of the Lenin idea is manifest in the device used by Chang Ju-hsin in treating this idea in his eulogy of Stalin in April, 1953. (Chang's essay is a tribute to Mao as well.) Chang's procedure is simple: he conspicuously deletes Stalin's phrase, "that is, something in the nature of a democratic dictatorship of the proletariat and peasantry":

[35] "The Problems of the Character of the Chinese Revolution Appearing in Discussions of the New Soviet Book, *Historical Materialism*," Peking *Jen-min Jih-pao*, April 28, 1952 (emphasis supplied). For an account of the Soviet discussion, see *Voprosy filosofi* (Problems of Philosophy) (Moscow), 1951, No. 4.

> In his treatise, *On the Prospects of the Revolution in China*, published in 1926, Stalin wrote: "I think that the future revolutionary government in China will in general resemble in character the government we used to talk about in our country in 1905 — — — — — — with the difference, however, that it will be first and foremost an anti-imperialist government. This shall be an interim state power for China to attain non-capitalist development" [Chang's dashes indicating deletion].[36]

Chang goes on to say that China's state power belongs to the general "type of state power" described by Stalin, but then quotes from Mao's *On the People's Democratic Dictatorship* the passage which specifically includes the national bourgeoisie.

We may now ask, Why did Moscow attempt to blur the distinction between Lenin's democratic dictatorship of the proletariat and peasantry and Mao's "people's democratic dictatorship"? There are several reasons, the most obvious being the Chinese claim that Mao had "further developed" the Marxist-Leninist theory of state.

Whether it was accurate to claim that a Communist-led state is anything but a dictatorship of the proletariat (i.e., of the Communist party) — whether the claim was true to life — is a matter which probably did not much concern the Soviets. They were not interested in the accuracy of the claim: they were concerned with the *prestige-value* of the claim. For it provided Mao with a means for appealing to Communists in Asia, the Middle East, and Latin America to set up not a Soviet-type "dictatorship of the proletariat" after revolutionary victory but a Maoist "people's democratic dictatorship." Were the claim to be accepted in the international Communist movement, Mao would become the mid-twentieth-century maker of doctrine for backward countries just as Lenin had been decades earlier.

[36] Chang Ju-hsin, "Stalin's Great Theoretical Contributions to the Chinese Revolution," Peking *Jen-min Jih-pao*, April 3, 1953.

The Soviets probably were also irritated by the independent way in which Mao had first formulated his new "people's democratic dictatorship" as clearly distinct from the Soviet model and by the international significance he assigned it. In 1940, describing his joint dictatorship of several revolutionary classes as a "new democracy republic," Mao openly makes the following distinctions:

> On the one hand, this new democracy republic is different from the old European-American form of capitalist republic under bourgeois dictatorship, for such an old democratic republic is already out of date; on the other hand, it is also different from the socialist republics of the type of the USSR, republics of the dictatorship of the proletariat; such socialist republics are already flourishing in the Soviet Union and moreover will be established in all the capitalist countries and undoubtedly will become the dominant form of state structure and political power in all industrially advanced countries. Yet, during a given historical period, they are not yet suitable for the revolutions in colonial and semicolonial countries.
>
> Therefore the form of state to be adopted by the revolutions in colonial and semicolonial countries during a given historical period can *only* be a third one, namely, the new democracy republic. This is the form for a given historical period and therefore a transitional form, but an *unalterable and necessary form.*[37]

That is, according to Mao, a dictatorship of the proletariat is applicable to the Soviet Union and industrially advanced countries, but is by no means pertinent to the backward, colonial, or semicolonial nations. In these nations, it will be replaced by his own "joint dictatorship of several classes" and acquire a significance distinct from — although within the framework of — inherited Marxist-Leninist doctrine.

[37] Mao, *Selected Works,* II (1961), p. 668 (emphasis supplied).

By advancing this idea, Mao has taken a step beyond Marx's statement in the *Critique of the Gotha Program*, i.e., that the state in the transition period "can be nothing else but the revolutionary dictatorship of the proletariat" and Lenin's two-class dictatorship. Mao insists that for backward countries, the state can be nothing but the revolutionary "people's democratic dictatorship" or a "people's dictatorship."

Chinese Communist theorists are aware that Mao's "people's democratic dictatorship" is a revision of Marx and have in effect said so. Thus in October, 1953, theorist Chi Yün says:

> The problem of the transition period had been raised in Marx's *Critique of the Gotha Program*, 1875, when he wrote: "Between capitalist and socialist society is the period of the revolutionary transformation of the one into the other. There corresponds to this also a political transition period in which the state can be nothing but the *revolutionary dictatorship of the proletariat.*"
>
> But at that time there was yet no practical experience in the building of socialism which could be used. Marx therefore was able to bring forth this problem only as a principle.[38]

Chi then says that Lenin found the concrete road for "Russia's transition" which was further developed by Stalin, but that the form adopted by China "differs from that of the Soviet Union and other people's democratic states because originally we were not a capitalist nation, but rather a semicolonial, semifeudal nation." China's form, he concludes, was "discovered" by Mao, who advanced the political theory of the "people's democratic dictatorship."

Stalin did not regard Mao's revision of Marx's dictatorship of the proletariat as an academic point; on the contrary, it was for him a practical matter. Acceptance of the slogan "people's dicta-

[38] Chi Yün, "The Economy of the Transition Period from Capitalism to Socialism," *Hsüeh-hsi*, October 2, 1953 (Marx's emphasis).

torship" by Communist parties in backward countries would afford—as we have said—a new channel for the spread of Chinese influence among these parties at Soviet expense.[39] Furthermore, Stalin had "predicted" in 1926 that the state form in China would resemble Lenin's two-class dictatorship, and Stalin was not a man who would permit his foresight on any matter to be taken lightly. But this is what Mao did in advancing his concept of a four-class dictatorship.

There is evidence that the Chinese were successful in inducing some acceptance of the Mao slogan among Asian Communists. Burmese Communist Myat Htoo stated in April, 1953, that the Communist party in Burma—that is, a unified party which he envisaged—must "set up a dictatorship of four classes: the workers, the peasants, the petty bourgeoisie, and the national bourgeoisie."[40] Also in 1953, the Indonesian Communists used Mao's

[39] The first significant extension of CCP influence among Asian Communist parties began shortly after the establishment of the Chinese Communist regime (October 1, 1949) when, on November 23, Liu Shao-ch'i told the Trade Union Conference of Asian and Australian Countries: "The road taken by the Chinese people in defeating imperialism . . . is the road that should be taken by the peoples of many colonial and semi-colonial countries in their fight for national independence and people's democracy. . . . This is the road of Mao Tse-tung" (Shanghai *Wen-hui Pao*, November 25, 1949). But within two years, Moscow turned the strategic line away from armed uprising and apparently prevailed on the reluctant Chinese for a time to discard their effort to impose Mao's military-revolutionary model on other Asian Communist movements. The concept, "Mao Tse-tung's road"—a feature of Chinese propaganda since Liu's 1949 speech—disappeared from Chinese publications in November, 1951.

This abrupt turn, resulting in silence, took place simultaneously with the presentation of a report to the Scientific Conference held in the Oriental Studies Institute of the Academy of Sciences of the USSR by the principal speaker, Ye. Zhukov, in November, 1951. In his report, Zhukov stated that "it would be risky to regard the Chinese revolution as some kind of 'stereotype' for people's-democratic revolutions in other countries of Asia" ("On the Character and Peculiarities of People's Democracy in Countries of the East," *Izvestiya Akademii Nauk SSSR, Seriya Istorii i Filosofii*, IX, No. 1 [1952], 80–87).

[40] Myat Htoo, "A Report from Burma's Liberated Areas—the United Front of the People Advances: A Single Marxist Party to Lead the National Fight against Imperialism and Feudalism," *Crossroads* (New Delhi), IV, No. 50 (April 19, 1953), 8–9.

slogan of "people's dictatorship" in their Draft Program and Election Manifesto. The Draft Program, approved in October, 1953, stated that, "considering the backwardness of our economy, the Indonesian Communist party holds that the future government should not be one of the 'dictatorship of the proletariat,' but rather a government of people's dictatorship."[41] The Indonesian Communist party's Election Manifesto of 1954 declared: "The party must carry through a people's dictatorship. . . . A people's dictatorship means the rule of workers, peasants, intellectuals, and petty and national bourgeoisie (entrepreneurs). . . . Without a people's dictatorship, there can be no complete independence and democracy for Indonesia. . . . "[42] The dictatorship of several revolutionary classes was a concept also incorporated into the program of the Malayan Communist party."[43]

Use of the Chinese slogan by these Asian Communist parties suggests that they rejected a Soviet effort to impose on all Asian Communist movements Lenin's formula of a two-class dictatorship in line with Stalin's 1926 "prediction."

The Russians had sought to establish their line in 1951. At the Scientific Conference in Moscow in November, 1951, Ye. Zhukov, a prominent Soviet orientalist, had laid it down that "people's democracy in countries of the Orient is a specific form of the revolutionary democratic dictatorship of the proletariat and peasantry . . ."[44] and earlier — in October — A. Sobolev had already written in *Bol'shevik* that the first stage of people's democracy is a revolution "in the course of which people's democracy emerges as the organ of revolutionary power, which is in content something like a dictatorship of the working class and peas-

[41] Reprinted in *Shih-chieh Chih-shih* (World Knowledge) (Peking), December 3, 1953.

[42] Reprinted in *Ibid.*, May 20, 1954.

[43] Chen Tsan-wei, "Malaya and the Five-Year War of Resistance," *ibid.*, October 18, 1953.

[44] "On the Character and Peculiarities of People's Democracy in Countries of the East," *Izvestiya Akademii Nauk SSSR*, IX, 80.

antry."[45] Both Russians were at pains to demonstrate that Communist regimes in Asia—Communist China in particular was their apparent point of reference—are patterned after Lenin's two-class concept, not Mao's.

What was the original source of the theory of "people's democracy" which was developed by Soviet theorists in 1947? Benjamin I. Schwartz has suggested that it came from China, from the hand of Mao, who had developed his theory of "new democracy" in the period from 1939 to 1945.[46] There are many striking similarities between the two theories: both contain concepts of a new type of transition to socialism based on a coalition of classes, land

[45] A. Sobolev, "People's Democracy as a Form of Political Organization of Society," *Bol'shevik*, No. 19, October, 1951. Sobolev applies the Leninist formula to China in the way Stalin had applied it: the revolutionary power established in China "is, in its content, something like a democratic dictatorship of the working class and peasantry." However, at least on one occasion a Soviet writer did not use Lenin's formula, but Mao's. Significantly, this occurred after Stalin's death. Colonel A. Martynov, reviewing the first three volumes of Mao's works in the organ of the USSR Ministry of Defense, *Krasnaya Zvezda*, December 1, 1953, says: "Creatively developing the ideas of Leninism, Mao Tse-tung, in his works, *The Chinese Revolution and the CCP* and *On New Democracy*, showed that the victory of the bourgeois-democratic revolution in China under the leadership of the proletariat would lead inevitably to the establishment of a people's democratic system with a dictatorship 'of the alliance of all anti-imperialist and anti-feudal forces led by the proletariat.'" The credit given Mao by Martynov is a striking departure from Soviet writers' earlier and subsequent treatment of his view of the future Communist dictatorship.

[46] Benjamin I. Schwartz has posed this question in his excellent article, "China and the Soviet Theory of People's Democracy," *Problems of Communism* (Washington), September–October, 1954, p. 10: "Of particular import . . . was Varga's use of the phrases 'democracy of a new type' and 'new democracy.' It invites the speculation that at this time, Soviet theoreticians were paying some attention to Mao Tse-tung's 'theoretical contribution' to Marxism-Leninism. . . . There is a strong resemblance between [features of] Varga's 'democracy of a new type' and Mao's 'new democracy.'" Discussing the *Soviet* theory of 1947, Samuel L. Sharp conjectured that "Mao Tse-tung seems to be the author of the term 'new democracy'" ("New Democracy: A Soviet Interpretation," *American Perspective*, Vol. I, No. 6 [November, 1947]).

H. Gordon Skilling has stated that among Soviet theorists in 1947 "the expression 'new democracy' was for some time in common usage. This was gradually superseded, without explanation, during 1948 by the term 'people's democracy,' which is invariably used at the present time" ("People's Democracy in Soviet Theory," *Soviet Studies*, Vol. III, Nos. 1 and 2 [July and December, 1951].

redistribution as a "bourgeois democratic" measure playing a large role in the transition period, "feudal vestiges" and the foreign enemy as forces which cause the union of the patriotic bourgeoisie with other revolutionary classes, and temporary rejection of the dictatorship of the proletariat as the state form.[47]

At the same time, traces of Mao's idea of the dictatorship of a bloc or "front" of several classes — rather than of one class — appear in G. M. Dimitrov's speech at the Seventh Comintern Congress in 1935. According to Dimitrov, a "people's front" government, which was to be broader than a united front government, should be established in the countries of Europe. It would include the workers, peasants, urban petty bourgeoisie, and certain "advanced sections" of the bourgeois intellectuals (intelligentsia).[48] The Resolution of the Seventh Congress ordered the sections of the International, if possible, "to create a *proletarian united front government or an anti-fascist people's front government*, which is not yet a government of proletarian dictatorship."[49] The workers would *not yet* be ready to rise under Communist leadership "for the achievement of Soviet power."[50] The people's front gov-

[47] Schwartz, in *Problems of Communism*, p. 10. Mao avoids mentioning "leadership" or hegemony over the front or "bloc" in his *On Coalition Government* of 1945. Only beginning in 1949 was Mao willing to state openly that the four classes in the new state "will be under the leadership of the working class *and the CCP*" and "we have the people's democratic dictatorship led by the working class (*through the CCP*) . . ." (emphasis supplied; Mao, *Selected Works*, IV (1961), 1480. The revision of the theory of "people's democracy" by Soviet writers in 1948, as a result of the Moscow-Belgrade break and signs of polycentrism in Eastern Europe, together with the final CCP takeover in China in 1949, obviated any further pretense by Mao that a genuine coalition of parties or classes would be established. When, therefore, *The Chinese Revolution and the CCP* and *On New Democracy* were reprinted in the post-1949 editions of Mao's works, the phrase "under the leadership of the proletariat" was inserted into those passages which discussed the joint dictatorship of several classes.

[48] "Report of Dimitrov on the Tasks of the Working Class," *VII Congress of the Communist International* (Abridged Stenographic Report of the Proceedings, Moscow, 1939), p. 149.

[49] *Ibid.*, p. 579 (emphasis in original).

[50] *Ibid.*, pp. 174–75.

ernments were, of course, tailored for Stalin's antifascist strategy in Europe—a strategy which required appeals to many non-Communists and which, therefore, had to conceal Communist revolutionary goals.

Dimitrov's statements of 1935 come close to Mao's 1939 and 1940 remarks on a "joint dictatorship" of several revolutionary classes which was to include the national capitalists. But neither Dimitrov nor the Resolution called for inclusion of the national capitalists in the "people's front government." They drew the line at the "bourgeois intellectuals," who are capable—according to the *Communist Manifesto*—of "going over to the proletariat" because they have raised themselves to the level of comprehending "theoretically the historical movement as a whole." The only similarity between the Radek-Zinoviev (1922) and the Dimitrov (1935) formulations and Mao's appears to be the explicit, temporary rejection of the dictatorship of the *proletariat*. For Mao, however, this rejection was extended into the period of the establishment of *full* Communist power.

Following World War II, small capitalists were permitted to exist in several of the Communist-led united front governments in Eastern Europe. However, the formal establishment of the Cominform in September, 1947, and doctrinal pronouncements by Soviet theorists—intensified in February, 1948—marked the beginning of the return to orthodox (i.e., Stalinist) practices and theory. The national capitalists were no longer permitted to exist as a separate class. The Dimitrov of 1948 took up the new policy of fashioning East European regimes into near-facsimiles of the Soviet regime, becoming as rigid in December, 1948, as he had been flexible—for Stalin's purposes—in the summer of 1935.

If Dimitrov in 1935 anticipated one aspect of Mao's theory of a people's government—temporary rejection of the dictatorship of the *proletariat*—he was, in 1948, eager to dispel the notion that Communist regimes could be anything but such a dictatorship. His report to the Fifth Congress of the Bulgarian Communist party (December, 1948) reflected Stalin's imposition of orthodoxy:

> Embodying the rule of the toilers under the leadership of the working class, the people's democracy . . . can and must successfully perform its functions of proletarian dictatorship for the liquidation of capitalist elements and the organization of a socialist economy.[51]

For his part, Mao clung to his idea of a joint dictatorship or a "people's democratic dictatorship" even when, in 1953, the first five-year plan for China was introduced and the "transition to socialism" was declared in progress.

To enter this transition period, that is, to begin the "building of socialism," without proclaiming a dictatorship of the proletariat was unprecedented in Communist theory. After 1948, all the East European "people's democracies" were declared to be "performing the functions of" proletarian dictatorship, although they were—theoretically—states without the "Soviet form" and were, therefore, not as advanced as the Soviet Union. They took the first steps to exclude the national capitalists from their structure as the "building of socialism" began.[52]

In contrast, the Chinese continued their independent course, as

[51] "Report of Dimitrov at the Fifth Congress of the Bulgarian Communist Party (December 19, 1948)," *Pravda*, December 21, 1948.

[52] Prior to the complete revision of the Soviet theory of people's democracy in 1949, Trainin stated that "the main driving forces of the new democracy are the people: the workers and peasants, who are joined by the progressive part of the bourgeoisie, its intelligentsia, and various democratic strata of the petty bourgeoisie" (I. P. Trainin, "Democracy of a Special Type," *Sovetskoie Gosudarstvo i Pravo* [Soviet Government and Law], No. I [Moscow, 1947]). Trainin's description is a Maoist one of the classes which participate in the state power structure. Also present is Mao's phrase, "new democracy."

Following the revision of the theory, the new line was expressed, among Soviet writers, by P. Yudin and Pospelov, the latter writing in *Pravda* on January 22, 1949, that "the regime of people's democracy performs the function of a dictatorship of the proletariat *in suppressing and abolishing capitalist elements*, thus solving the problem of the transition from capitalism to socialism" (emphasis supplied).

the CCP led by Mao demonstrated that Stalin's theorists might drum the Eastern European leaders—excluding Tito—into line but could not bend the independent leader of China. In July, 1951, the Chinese indicated their determination to retain the appearance of uniqueness; Hu Ch'iao-mu, author of the then standard history of the CCP, stated emphatically in his work:

> In the present historical period, the People's Republic of China still permits the national bourgeoisie to exist. Herein lies the difference between people's democracy in China and people's democracy in the countries of southeast Europe.[53]

When, in the late summer of 1953, the Chinese shocked the post-Stalin Soviet leadership by announcing that China's "transition to socialism" had begun, the people's democratic dictatorship was held to be the proper form for attaining "socialism." By a dialectical twist, one Chinese theorist denied that a continuation of the "alliance and coalition with the national bourgeoisie could be held to be a weakening of the class struggle."[54] Again by a dialectical twist, yet another theorist denied that there was a real ("essential") difference between the state power of proletarian dictatorship and the people's democratic dictatorship;[55] the dif-

[53] Hu Ch'iao-mu, *Thirty Years of the CCP* (Peking: Foreign Languages Press, 1954), p. 76. The preamble to the Constitution of the People's Republic of China (adopted September 20, 1954) states that the regime is a "people's democratic dictatorship." Article 5 includes "capitalist ownership" as a basic form of ownership of the means of production and Article 10 says: "The state protects the right of capitalists to own means of production and other capital according to law (*Constitution of the People's Republic of China* [Peking: 1954], Foreign Languages Press, pp. 3, 10, and 12).

[54] Wu Chiang, "The Transition Period and the Class Struggle," *Hsüeh-hsi*, June 2, 1954.

[55] Ti Chao-pai, "State Capitalism in Our Transition Period," *Hsüeh-hsi*, February 2, 1954. Other writers stated in late 1953 and 1954 that "in essence" the two dictatorships were similar. The logic of this argument escaped many. Theorist Yu Kuang-yüan ventured an explanation: "People might ask: Since the people's democratic dictatorship in China now is essentially a form of the dictatorship of the proletariat, how are we to explain the fact that the national capitalists have

ference was only a matter of "form." Soviet theorists agreed that this was so.

By 1956, a dialectical compromise had been worked out between Moscow and Peking. The new Chinese-Soviet view that the people's democratic dictatorship was only a different "form" of proletarian dictatorship apparently was intended to bring Mao's formulation a step closer to the mainstream of Leninism and, therefore, acceptable to the Soviet leaders. For Lenin had conceded that "the transition from capitalism to Communism will certainly bring a great variety and abundance of *political forms*, but the essence will inevitably be only one: the dictatorship of the proletariat." [56] Yet the Chinese maintain that a "people's democratic dictatorship" is sufficiently different in form from proleterian dictatorship to warrant retention of Mao's slogan. In its first definitive public statement on Khrushchev's and Mikoyan's attack on Stalin at the twentieth congress of the CPSU, the CCP politburo on April 5, 1956, discussed the history of proletarian dictatorship in the world Communist movement; gently — as though in passing — the statement reasserted Mao's view that in China this dictatorship was still a "people's democratic dictatorship." This was the "form" it had taken in China. Thus the dialectical distinction permitted the Chinese to have their cake and eat it too: different in "form" (and name) but similar in "essence." [57]

Speaking of this well-known philosophical distinction in the works of Aristotle, Bertrand Russell stated in his *A History of Western Philosophy* (1945) that the concept of "essence" is "muddleheaded . . . incapable of precision." Soviet and Chinese the-

---

the right to vote? . . . Under present conditions in China, the majority of capitalists find it possible to accept socialism; therefore, we must retain them as allies . . . and permit them to carry out important work in the government at all levels" (Yu Kuang-yüan, "The Class Nature of China's People's Democratic Dictatorship," *Hsüeh-hsi*, November 2, 1956).

[56] Lenin, *State and Revolution*, p. 31 (emphasis supplied).

[57] "On the Historical Experience of the Dictatorship of the Proletariat," Peking *Jen-min Jih-pao*, April 5, 1956.

orists subsequent to Stalin's death in 1953 did not desire precision; what they desired was ambiguity — ambiguity with which to conceal and reduce the doctrinal fencing — and they attained it.

The driving force behind this compromise probably was Khrushchev. In Peking in late September and early October, 1954, Khrushchev seems to have carried with him a new view of China, reflecting a change in Soviet thinking on China which (in the fall of 1954) was more radical than the cautious deference shown the Chinese leaders in the period immediately following Stalin's death. Starting in the fall of 1954, Khrushchev probably hoped to establish a viable working relationship with Mao and other Chinese leaders, partly in order to increase his own influence in the Soviet hierarchy. The Chinese leaders welcomed his initiative and supported him in turn.

What Khrushchev initiated in his new China policy was, in effect, the de-Stalinization of relations with Peking. Speaking in Peking on September 30, 1954 — the eve of the regime's National Day — the Soviet leader set forth the concept of the Soviet Union and China as comprising jointly the "bastion" of the Communist bloc. This meant *two* leaders, as Molotov made it clear. Molotov, speaking in Moscow on February 8, 1955, converted the concept of the joint "bastion" into a new formulation, namely, *dual* — Soviet and Chinese — leadership of the Communist bloc. Khrushchev may also have calculated that by increasing Peking's prestige (by calling China a co-leader) he was implicitly striking a blow for Soviet strategic security, dissociating the Soviet Union from automatic responsibility for any Chinese military initiatives. As an independent "leader" of the Communist bloc, he may have calculated, China's initiatives would be taken by the West as a Chinese affair and Moscow would not necessarily be blamed for them.

Regarding concrete actions, Khrushchev was primarily responsible for the January, 1955, sale of Soviet shares in the Sino-Soviet joint stock companies and the May, 1955, evacuation of Soviet troops from the naval base at Port Arthur.

In short, beginning in late 1954, Khrushchev moved vigorously to reduce sources of Sino-Soviet friction, including those of doctrine.

The Soviet leader's public recognition of China's "people's democratic dictatorship" was expresed in late 1956 at a time when developments in East Europe compelled Khrushchev to seek explicit Chinese support for his policy. Earlier, in reports to the twentieth congress of the CPSU in February, 1956, Khrushchev and Shepilov had taken a step in Mao's direction by describing as creative the "peaceful transformation" of private industry and agriculture in China. But neither speaker had mentioned the people's democratic dictatorship. Khrushchev referred to the Chinese state as a "people's democracy" and Shepilov spoke of "people's rule" in China, implying that the state form was similar to that of the satellite people's democracies.[58] Following the Polish "October" and the Hungarian revolt, however, Khrushchev for the first time (on November 26, 1956, at the Chinese embassy in Moscow) publicly acknowledged that his Chinese ally had established a state in the form of a "people's democratic dictatorship." For their part, the Chinese leaders were conceding that Mao's democratic dictatorship was *in fact* a dictatorship of the proletariat. Peking conceded this partly as an act of compromise and partly because China already had begun to "build socialism," requiring in theory a dictatorship of the proletariat. As the newfound Sino-Soviet cordiality began to crumble, however, the Russians gradually reversed their policy of occasionally acknowledging Mao's formula on dictatorship.

It is Mao's style to sustain pretenses. Mao's complaints against

[58] One Soviet theorist discussing China paid tribute, as did Khrushchev and Shepilov, to "peaceful transformations," but like the Soviet leaders, he did not mention the people's democratic dictatorship. See A. V. Sergivev's article on Marxism applied to China, *Voprosy filosofii*, No. 1, February, 1956.

Khrushchev were expressed not in terms of China's national interest and certainly not in terms of Mao's pretensions to be world Communism's most eminent living theorist and leader (to which they were primarily relevant), but in terms of doctrinal differences (to which they were only secondarily relevant). By April, 1960, the Chinese opened a sharp attack against Khrushchev, pillorying the Soviet leader by implication for betraying various broad goals of the world Communist movement for "narrow" (read Soviet) interests, without mentioning that Khrushchev's subordination of *Chinese* interests was really the basic motivation for the attack. The Russians hit back, and the Sino-Soviet polemic which was subsequently deepened affected the compromise on the "people's democratic dictatorship." The Soviet leaders moved to obliterate Mao's formula as a model state form for former colonial countries and replace it with a Soviet-formulated concept.

The original version of the Soviet textbook, *Fundamentals of Marxism-Leninism*, published in October, 1959, had quoted Mao's view that the Chinese revolution had as its object the establishment of a "democratic dictatorship of *all* anti-imperialist and anti-feudal forces." When the textbook was reprinted in July, 1960, during bitter Sino-Soviet polemics, this passage was deleted and the only remaining reference to a "democratic dictatorship" was to Lenin's *two-class* dictatorship.[59]

By July, 1960, the Russians were well on their way to working out their own concept of a new state form for former colonies. Enunciated formally in December, 1960 (in the Moscow Statement of 81 Communist parties), their concept — a "national democratic state"—included the national bourgeoisie (as Mao's "people's democratic dictatorship" did) but *failed* to insist on and deliberately avoided the stipulation of Communist party leadership (as Mao's did not). The Chinese were opposed to the Soviet concept of a "national democratic state" for two reasons:

[59] *Fundamentals of Marxism-Leninism*, English-language version (Moscow: Foreign Languages Publishing House, 1960), p. 656.

1. The idea departs — to the right — from Mao's own statements on the national bourgeoisie. It does not include a call for Communist leadership of the new state, allowing instead the exercise of leadership by representatives of the national bourgeoisie (for example, Sukarno, Nasir, Nkrumah, and Toure). These non-Communist leaders are said to have an understanding of "socialism" rather different from that of the Communists ("non-scientific," as the Russians put it), but they are nevertheless on the right track. In this state, full Communist power — as in a "people's democracy" such as Communist China — is not yet possible but neither is full bourgeois control. An explicit statement denying immediate Communist control was made in March, 1962, by the Soviet-oriented Secretary General of the Syrian Communist party:

> The national democratic state by no means implies rule by the Communists, as noisy reactionary propaganda would have it. It represents neither a socialist nor a people's democratic state. But neither is it a bourgeois democratic state in the classical sense of the term, on the lines of European states.[60]

The Chinese Communists reject this state form. In contrast to the Soviet view, they place considerable emphasis on the unreliability of the nationalist leaders who are not also Communists.

2. The idea replaces Mao's "people's democratic dictatorship" as the state form for *all* former colonies. Using it, the Soviet leaders in effect have confined Mao's ideas on backward states to China and North Vietnam for, as the Syrian party boss says, the national democratic state "is a state of a new type, corresponding to the stage that the recently liberated countries are now going through."[61] Soviet theorists now discuss the state form for newly independent backward countries primarily with reference to the "national democratic state," which most Communists recognize

[60] Khalid Bakdash, "The CPSU Program and the Present Stage of the National Liberation Movement," *Pravda*, March 23, 1962.

[61] *Ibid.*

as a concept originated by the Soviet, rather than the Chinese, leaders. Mao's March, 1926, prediction that in the future "it is completely impossible for the national bourgeoisie to create a state in which it would rule"[62]—a reference which Mao later extended to the bourgeoisie of all backward countries—is drastically undercut by the Soviet idea. Mao is confronted with the choice of accepting national bourgeois leadership by discarding his prediction or sticking to his 1926 statement. Partly from conviction but largely from conceit, Mao and his theorists have held tenaciously to his old statement, angered by Soviet infringement on his self-appointed role of theorist on backward countries for the world Communist movement.

Despite the impression that he is nothing but a dogmatist, Mao has made a revision in doctrine on the state form for Communist power. His use of the national bourgeoisie during an anti-imperialist revolution in the East as an ally is, as we have seen, a pure Leninist idea. (The current Soviet leadership has on occasion gone far to the right of this position, claiming that the national bourgeoisie is capable of acting as the leader of an anti-imperialist revolution.) But Mao's dictum that the national bourgeoisie as a class will continue to exist *after* the revolution and for a long time thereafter is a revision of Marxism-Leninism. In the Marxist-Leninist sense, Mao is thus a revisionist. In practice, however, he is not. The Communist dictatorship in China is applied to non-capitalists as well as capitalists with a vigor and terror that is offensive even to some members of the bloc.

There is no real difference between proletarian dictatorship in the Soviet Union and Mao's people's democratic dictatorship. Power is held as exclusively by the CCP as it is by the CPSU. In fact, Mao is probably more thorough about imposing his dictatorship than Khrushchev is. This is true not because the third program of the Russian Communists (adopted in October, 1961) has

[62] Mao, *Selected Works*, I (1961), 4.

complied with the Marxist doctrine on discarding the dictatorship of the proletariat, for it is clear from the same document that the dictatorship of the party will remain. It is true because the party under Khrushchev does not rule with the same *degree* of terror and total mobilization of the individual as it did under Stalin's rule, while the dictatorship of the CCP under Mao is as pervasive and total as it had been in Stalin's heydey. Khrushchev continues to attempt reform of Stalin's dictatorship and to reduce internal pressures on the individual without discarding one-party—that is, dictatorial—rule. Reduction of pressure and "within-system" reforms (as Bertram D. Wolfe puts it)[63] is a risky course, far riskier than Mao's temporary relaxation of pressure *while maintaining total organization of the individual's day-to-day activities.* We agree with Leonard Shapiro's judgment that "straightforward terror of the kind practiced by Stalin is a much safer form of despotism (for the despot) than the attempt at reform inaugurated by his successor."[64] There has been a change from a bad but stable tyranny in the Soviet Union. In China, however, Mao's tyranny is unrelieved (despite the retreat from the brutal pace of the 1958 policies) and probably will remain stable until his death.

[63] Bertram D. Wolfe, "The Durability of Soviet Despotism," *Commentary*, August, 1957.

[64] Leonard Shapiro, "From the Other Shore," *Encounter*, August, 1962.

# 4

# The "Transition to Socialism"

More than a decade before he became chairman of the first national Communist-led government in China's history, Mao Tse-tung gained experience as the leader of the regional government established by the Communists in the northwest. His experiences with rural egalitarianism and with a primitive economy which included small-scale private enterprise are reflected in his writings between 1936 and 1949, particularly in his concept of the mixed economy of "new democracy." Mao carried over the idea of preserving a small corner of private capitalism into the period of "building socialism"—that is, into the period when, according to doctrine, it should have been *completely* eliminated.

The "socialism" that Stalin established in the Soviet Union and the "socialism" that Mao hopes to build in China is not, of course, the socialism of democratic socialists. The economist Rudolf Hilferding tells us why:

> From a social democratic viewpoint, the Bol'shevik economy can hardly be called "socialist," for to us socialism is indissolubly linked to democracy. According to our concept, socialization of the means of production implies freeing the economy from the rule of one class and vesting it in society as a whole—a society which is democratically self-governed. We never imagined that the political form of that "managed economy" which

> was to replace capitalist production for a free market could be unrestricted absolutism.[1]

To Communists who follow in the Lenin-Stalin tradition, however, it is a phase distinct from full Communism—the final goal of the orthodox. The distinction in phases was made explicit by Lenin.

In chapter v of *State and Revolution* (August, 1917), Lenin makes a distinction between "socialist" society and Communist society in discussing the "transition from capitalism to Communism." Citing Marx's *Critique of the Gotha Program* (1875), Lenin says that the "political transition period" of which Marx spoke "must undoubtedly be a special stage or epoch" of transition, and this stage, he says, has been designated by Marx as the "first" phase of Communist society. It is, he continues, "generally called socialism."

### *"Peaceful Transformation" of Capitalist Enterprises*

The view that the elimination of the bourgeoisie as a class and the expropriation of their holdings must be carried out during the first transitional ("socialist") stage became for Communists a dogma. Marx, Engels, and Lenin, however, saw the need for more than one method of expropriating the bourgeoisie and thereby eliminating it as a class. Faced with economic problems in the Soviet state, Lenin was willing to make use of certain capitalists until the Soviet regime was able to establish a degree of economic stability. Lenin later claimed that he was compelled to resort to direct, violent methods of expropriating all capitalist property, as the capitalists had resisted his effort "gradually and peacefully" to transfer their holdings to the Soviet government.

There really never had been for Stalin a "soft" policy toward the capitalists, and his writings concerning them are not marked

[1] Quoted by Sidney Hook in his brief but helpful account of Marx's legacy: *Marx and the Marxists* (New York: D. Van Nostrand Co., 1955), p. 240.

by gentle phrases. The bourgeoisie must be "smashed," capitalists, merchants, kulaks, and profiteers must be "eliminated," and the exploiting class must be "liquidated" during the "transition to socialism." Describing the New Economic Policy (NEP) in 1925, Stalin says that it would be an "inevitable phase of the socialist revolution in all countries." Adhering to Lenin's view, Stalin goes on to concede that capitalists will be tolerated, but that is all he concedes:

> NEP is a special policy of the proletarian state, counting on the toleration of capitalist elements, the commanding heights being in the hands of the proletarian state, counting on the growth of the role of the socialist elements to the detriment of the capitalist elements, count- on the victory of socialist elements over capitalist elements, counting on the abolition of classes and the laying of the foundation of a socialist economy.[2]

Stalin later indicated that the "victory" of the socialist over capitalist elements in Soviet society had nothing to do with a peaceful transition. In the *History of the Communist Party of the Soviet Union (B)* of 1938, he and his writers strongly condemn as Bukharinite opposition (and, by implication, revision) the theory of "peaceful growing of the bourgeoisie into socialism . . . and the fostering and encircling of the bourgeoisie, not destroying it." [3] Thus the "transition to socialism" in the USSR was carried out following the liquidation of the capitalists and the total destruction of them as a class.

The Chinese Communists claim that Mao has discovered a peaceful *method* for handling capitalists, that the "transition to

[2] Stalin, "Report to the 14th Congress of the C.P.S.U. (B) (December, 1925)," *Works*, VII, 374. Attacking Zinoviev's moderate view of the NEP, Stalin in *Problems of Leninism* (January, 1926) emphasized the aspect of struggle: "NEP is the party policy which admits the struggle between the socialist and capitalist elements."

[3] *History of the Communist Party of the Soviet Union (B), Short Course* (1938), edited by a commission of the Central Committee of the CPSU (New York: International Publishers, 1939), p. 275.

socialism" in China is advancing with the continued existence of the "national" capitalists, and that such a transition is unprecedented. The claim in large part is valid.

The Chinese are, of course, referring to the only capitalists who were permitted to continue in their businesses after 1949, namely, the entrepreneurs engaged in the production and sale of consumer goods. All other capitalists were characterized as "bureaucratic-capitalists" and were expropriated and "smashed" in 1949. They no longer exist as a stratum. The remaining small entrepreneurs are designated the "middle" or "national" bourgeoisie and *their* enterprises gradually have been transformed.

Because the capitalists ("national bourgeoisie") in China are (*a*) weak, (*b*) obedient to the CCP and its program, and (*c*) willing to be transformed, the "transition to socialism" can be a "peaceful" process. Chinese writers contrast this with the history of the transition in the USSR, where the capitalists were "smashed" because they were (*a*) strong, (*b*) antagonistic to the CPSU, and (*c*) unwilling to change their ways.

The contrast between the Soviet and Chinese situations was described in 1956 by theorist Wu Ch'uan-che among others:

> Unlike the violent expropriation of the means of production of the bourgeoisie which was the form of struggle adopted in the USSR in the transition period, in China we have adopted peaceful transformation of the capitalists' enterprises during transition. . . .
>
> Regarding the elimination of classes, it can be carried out only by class struggle, as there is no other road. But the form of struggle adopted — armed or peaceful, bloody or bloodless struggle — must be changed according to the objective conditions.[4]

This "peaceful transformation" of the capitalists' enterprises into state-run enterprises has been made possible, Wu says in

[4] Wu Ch'uan-che, "Peaceful Transformation of Capitalist Industrial and Commercial Enterprises Is a Special Form of Class Struggle," *Che-hsüeh Yen-chiu*, No. 1, March 1, 1956.

an earlier article (1955), because Mao had mastered the law of "bloodless change." Wu says: "Because of his profound knowledge of this law, Chairman Mao has adhered to the correct line for the last 30 years of revolutionary struggle, opposing both tailism and adventurism, and thus had led the revolution to a victorious conclusion. He has created the basic conditions for a transition to socialism by peaceful means." [5]

We have suggested above that there is a warrant in Lenin's works for a transition by peaceful means. During the period of the NEP, Lenin spoke of the Soviet government's desire for a gradual transition. In his report delivered at the Seventh Moscow Party Conference on October 29, 1921, Lenin stated that the Soviet government in 1917 and 1918 "attempted to introduce its economic policy . . . which was originally calculated to bring about a number of gradual changes, to bring about a more cautious transition to the new system." [6] In discussing the policy of spring 1921, Lenin again referred to gradual, indirect methods: "The political situation in the spring of 1921 revealed to us that retreat to the position of state capitalism, the substitution of 'siege' tactics for 'direct assault' tactics was inevitable on a number of economic questions." [7] But when NEP was brought to an end, so was the existence of the "new bourgeoisie," i.e., the nepmen as a class.

The idea of "peaceful transformation" of capitalists' enterprises in China, therefore, may well have been a concept which Mao took over from Marx, Engels, and Lenin. In his *Peasant Question in France and Germany* of 1894, Engels had stated that

> once our party has seized state power, it should immediately expropriate the big landowners and the factory owners. Whether this expropriation requires the use of buying out, is a matter primarily to be determined not

[5] Wu Ch'uan-che, "The Basic Class Contradiction during China's Transition to Socialism," *Che-hsüeh Yen-chiu*, No. 1, June, 1955.

[6] Lenin, *Selected Work*, IX, 285.

[7] *Ibid.*, p. 286.

> by us, but by the conditions prevailing when we attain political power, and is even more determined by the actions of the big landowners themselves. We absolutely do not state that ransom is impermissible under all conditions. Marx told me (and how many times!) that in his opinion we would get off cheapest if we could buy out the whole lot of them.[8]

Thus Engels had sanctioned a relatively moderate form of expropriation, buying-out rather than violent requisition. Like Marx, he seems to have been less revolutionary in his later years.

Lenin goes beyond Engels' position and speaks of using the skills of capitalists in the service of the new state. Thus in his *Unavoidable Catastrophe and Boundless Promises* of 1917, Lenin says:

> As to the individual capitalists, or even the majority of capitalists, not only does the proletariat not intend to "strip" them (as Shulgin has been "scaring" himself and his ilk), not only does it not intend to deprive them of "everything," but, on the contrary, it intends to place them at useful, honorable tasks, subject to the control of the workers themselves.[9]

One year later, in his *"Left-Wing" Childishness and Petty Bourgeois Mentality* (1918), he speaks of "buying off" the capitalists and of a peaceful "transition to socialism":

> Marx was profoundly right when he taught the workers the importance of preserving the organization of large-scale production precisely for the purpose of facilitating the transition to socialism and that (as an exception, and England was then an exception) the idea was conceivable of paying the capitalists well, of buying them

[8] Marx-Engels, *Selected Works*, II, 438. The concept of "buying out" is not entirely inconsistent with all of the *Communist Manifesto*, the supreme work of their earlier years, as in one passage the authors call upon the proletariat after the revolution to wrest capital from the bourgeoisie "by degrees" rather than all at once.

[9] Lenin, *Selected Works*, VI, 148.

> off, if the circumstances were such as to compel the capitalists to submit peacefully and to come over to socialism in a cultured and organized fashion, provided they were bought off. . . . Well, and what about Soviet Russia? . . . Is it not clear that *certain* conditions prevail which correspond to those which might have existed in England half a century ago had a peaceful transition to socialism begun then? [10]

State capitalism was common to both NEP Russia and the transitional economy of Communist China. Lenin appears to have combined Engels' idea of "buying off" with the concept of state capitalism. In his *The Tax in Kind* (1921), Lenin says:

> We can and ought to *combine* the method of ruthless suppression of the uncultured capitalists who refuse to have anything to do with "state capitalism" or to consider any form of compromise, and who continue by means of profiteering, by bribing the poor peasantry, etc., to hinder the application of the measures taken by the Soviets, *with the method of* compromise, or "state capitalism," or buying off the cultured capitalists who agree to practice and who are useful to the proletariat as clever and experienced organizers of very large enterprises, which supply commodities to tens of millions of people.[11]

The NEP, defined succinctly by Lenin as "*capitalism* plus socialism," was shortlived. Within several years it was ended, and remaining capitalists were expropriated outright. In China however, the Communists are buying off the "national capitalists" by compensating them with fixed interest and combining this with the gradual takeover ("socialist transformation") of their enterprises.

Some of the Chinese methods of "peaceful" takeover of capi-

[10] *Ibid.*, pp. 368–70 (Lenin's emphasis).

[11] Lenin, *Selected Works in Two Volumes* (Moscow: Foreign Languages Publishing House, 1952), II, Part 2, p. 536 (Lenin's emphasis).

talist enterprises may have been taken over from early NEP experiences and from the considerable experience of the Eastern European satellite regimes from mid-1945 to 1948, but some methods are probably unique — for example, the nationwide campaign of "struggle" against the capitalists which intimidated them ("gave them a lesson in political power," as the Chinese Communists have put it) but did not entirely liquidate the private capitalist sector of the economy. Moreover, the precise details on how to "buy out" and on the matter of how to use the "national capitalists" in the production effort while permitting them no independent economic activity are probably uniquely Chinese Communist — Maoist — details.

Marx, Engels, and Lenin had set forth a theory of "buying out" the capitalists, of purchasing their means of production. Mao put the theory into practice, working out the policy of gradual "socialist transformation" of the capitalists' enterprises. This is his contribution to the doctrine of the expropriation of the bourgeoisie. East European leaders in the satellites were in a position to, and did, make contributions in the mid-1940's. But the decisive factor — independent political control of the Communist party — was denied them by Stalin, who stifled any effort to proclaim individual doctrinal originality and drove the satellites into sterile conformity in 1948, when they were compelled by Moscow to reject "peaceful transformation" of national capitalists. That Mao's theorists could proclaim originality for their leader was a clear indication of his independence from Stalin in sustaining control of the CCP apparatus.

Precisely what were the details of the policy worked out by Mao for gradual, "peaceful transformation"?

In the first years following the establishment of the regime in 1949, transformation of the private capitalist enterprises took the following form: a number of the most simple forms of state capitalism were applied, such as private enterprises working on government orders, the sale of their products to the state, trading on government commission, etc. At the same time, the administration of the enterprises was completely in the hands of the capitalists.

Beginning in 1952, that is, after the end of the reconstruction period, the CCP began to create mixed, public-private enterprises, administered jointly by representatives of the government and private capitalists, but with the government having the deciding role. Actually, there was nothing very "peaceful" about the process. The "5-anti's" movement of January to June, 1952, was used by Mao to take a big step forward in the direction of placing private business more completely under CCP control; this required, in Mao's view, mobilization of the party and the masses for a class war against the bourgeoisie.

Even the smallest merchants were forced to exhaust their savings and liquidate all concealed assets under conditions of persecution and terror. There were many suicides, and those who escaped with their lives saved nothing but a small share in their own businesses. The latter meant that such merchants continued to exist as capitalists, and for this reason the Communists insist that their buying-out is a "peaceful" process.

From 1952 and 1953 to 1955, the capitalists were bought out by means of a system of distributing profits according to the principle of "four horses per measure of oats." That is, the capitalists received 25 per cent of the profits of the enterprises. But in 1955, the process of transforming capitalist enterprises into state-capitalist enterprises was intensified. The CCP began to create specialized companies in entire branches of industry and commerce, to which the individual enterprises were subordinate. The administration of the small enterprises went entirely into the hands of the party. The new (1955) situation is described by a Chinese Communist writer as follows:

> After this change-over (to joint state-private operation by whole trades) was realized, the state made the following important provisions which are still current. A fixed rate of interest was paid by the state for the total

> investment of the capitalists in the joint state-private enterprises. Irrespective of locality and trade, the interest was fixed at a rate of 5 percent per annum. In the meantime, the state declared that this system would not be changed for seven years starting from 1956. This was the continuation of the policy of "buying off" the capitalists after the change-over by whole trades, only the form of payment was changed. The fixed rate of interest took the place of the distribution of profit according to definite proportions. In all the joint state-private enterprises, the total investment of the capitalists amounted to about 2,418 million yüan, of which 1,693 million yüan were in industry; 586 million yüan in commercial and catering trades; 102 million yüan in communications and transport; and 36 million yüan in personal services. Under the fixed interest system, the annual outlay from the state treasury was over 120 million yüan. There were 1,140,000 recipients in all.[12]

As a result of the complete transformation of small capitalist enterprises into state-capitalist enterprises in 1956, and the introduction of a new form of "buying out"—in the form of a guaranteed percentage of the capital invested in the mixed enterprises—all private ownership of the means of production was converted into joint enterprises.

Thus Mao showed considerable originality in *applying* Marx's, Engels', and Lenin's theory of "buying out" by transforming capitalist industry and commerce into mixed, public-private industry and commerce, transforming capitalists into shareholders, and transferring the administration of private enterprises into party and government hands.

Actually, the "socialist" transformation of agriculture in 1955 was a more noteworthy accomplishment of Mao's than the transformation of small capitalist enterprises. The 1955 collectivization of hundreds of millions of peasants without large-scale bloodshed

[12] Kuan Ta-tung, *The Socialist Transformation of Capitalist Industry and Commerce in China* (Peking: Foreign Languages Press, 1960), p. 53.

stands in stark contrast to Stalin's brutal and chaotic collectivization in the late 1920's. The methods employed by Mao in 1955 in collectivizing the Chinese peasants could well serve as the basis for a claim that in 1955 he had made an original contribution to Communist methods of rural cooperativization. Mao, at the beginning of his July 31, 1956, speech, "On Agricultural Cooperativization," came close to making such a claim, stating that rural cooperativization in China "has a very great world significance." An editorial in the Peking *Kuang-ming Jih-pao* of October 21, 1955, already had claimed that it "will indicate to billions of peasants all over the world" the real way to advance toward socialism."

### *From New Democracy to the "Transition to Socialism"*

Before the Chinese Communists attained national power in 1949, Mao had promised that the capitalist sector of the economy would be permitted to develop.

As early as 1934, Mao stated in *Our Economic Policy* that "so long as private enterprises do not transgress the legal limits set by our government, we shall not only refrain from prohibiting them, but shall promote and encourage them."[13] In *The Chinese Revolution and the CCP* (1939), Mao and his co-authors described an important aspect of New Democracy: "Economically, it means nationalization of all big capital and big enterprises of the imperialists, collaborators, and reactionaries, distribution of the land of the landlords among the peasants, and at the same time *the general preservation of private capitalist enterprises* without the elimination of the rich-peasant economy."[14] In his report to the Seventh Congress of the CCP of April, 1945, Mao stated that "the task of the New Democracy we advocate . . . is to assure the Chinese people of the possibility of . . . freely developing a private capitalist economy which, however, must not 'hold in its grasp

[13] Mao, *Selected Works*, I (1961), 128.
[14] *Ibid.*, p. 642 (emphasis supplied).

the livelihood of the people.'" His quotation on livelihood of the people is drawn from the ideas of Sun Yat-sen and represents one of many ways used by Mao to persuade non-Communists as well as Communists in China that he rather than Chiang Kai-shek and the KMT defended the "true" ideals of Sun.

Following the establishment of the Chinese Communist regime in 1949, Mao reaffirmed his New Democracy view that a private capitalist sector of the national economy should exist alongside a state-owned "socialist" sector. In his report to the party's Central Committee of June 5, 1950, Mao made it policy that national planning must take into account the interests of "all sections" of the economy and improve relations between state-run and private capitalist enterprises. Ten days later, politburo member Ch'en Yün said: "The state allows private capital to conduct commercial activities in order to develop the circulation of commodities. . . . The People's Government protects the interests of all capitalists who benefit the nation's welfare and the people's livelihood." These top level statements revealed a desire among the leaders to go slow at the beginning.

Thus in 1950 Mao and his lieutenants in the party continued to stress a moderate line toward the economic activities of small capitalists in China. The "transition to socialism" was not mentioned as an immediate goal. This was still the period of New Democracy which had been discussed by Mao ever since the 1930's. That is, it was still the period which was to precede the start of China's "transition to socialism." "New Democracy," not "socialism," was the term used and most fully discussed by Chinese Communist writers throughout the period from 1940 to 1953.

In mid-1953, however, following Stalin's death and as hostilities in Korea were subsiding, the Chinese leaders changed the line. In July, 1953, the Chinese began to claim that the "transition to socialism" was at hand in China.

On July 10, 1953, the transition had been made the immediate task in a decision of the All-China Federation of Trade Unions

(ACFTU) at a closed session of the union's executive committee. This was indicated by the following statement which appeared in an August issue of the official newspaper of the CCP: "The task of attaining national industrialization and the gradual transition to socialism is *now placed* before the people of the entire nation."[15] By October, the phrase "transition to socialism" began to appear with increasing frequency in Chinese published materials and on October 27 a full-blown "general line" for the transition period was discussed by Li Wei-han, director of the CCP Central Committee's United Front Work Department. Like Stalin, Mao laid down a general line for building "socialism."

Li Wei-han presented the official formulation of the general line for the transition in the form of a directive of Mao Tse-tung. He quoted Mao's directive in full:

> With regard to the general line of the state in the transition period, Chairman Mao has given the following directive: "From the founding of the People's Republic of China [PRC] to the basic conclusion of socialist reform is the period of transition. During this stage of transition, the general line and the general task of the state is the gradual realization, over a relatively long period of time, of the socialist transformation by the state of agriculture, handicrafts, and private industry and commerce. This general line is the lighthouse that illuminates our various tasks. Divorced from this general line, we shall commit rightist or leftist mistakes in our various tasks."[16]

Li did not reveal the occasion on which this directive was formulated and issued. In view, however, of the circumstance that the gradual "transition to socialism" was laid down as an immediate mission at the July 10 session of the ACFTU's executive commit-

[15] Peking *Jen-min Jih-pao*, August 27, 1953 (emphasis supplied).

[16] "Speech Given at the National Congress of the All-China Federation of Industrial and Commercial Circles," Peking *Jen-min Jih-pao*, November 10, 1953 (originally given on October 27).

tee, referred to above, it is likely that the formulation of the general line was under active consideration by Mao and other members of the CCP leadership in the summer of 1953.

We may now ask: why was the line on transition *gradually* introduced in the period from July to October and raised to a nationwide propaganda campaign only in October? A possible answer is that Mao went slow at first. By going slow at first, the Chinese leader and administrators in the party were able to "grope their way" toward the best methods of carrying out the politburo decision on transition and, when these methods were finally determined through trial and error, the nationwide campaign to implement the new policy was launched. Gradual introduction of the new line, while the phrase "New Democracy" was dropped by Chinese writers as smoothly as feasible, may also have been an attempt to make the transition appear as having been in process for sometime prior to 1953.

According to Mao's directive revealed by Li in October, 1953, private industry and commerce would now be subjected to "socialist transformation by the state." This statement, and the announcement that the "New Democracy" stage *really* had ended and the "socialist" stage had simultaneously begun in October of *1949* (founding of the regime), apparently came as a surprise to many people in China.

They soon learned that Mao's promise to retain a private sector in China's economy for a long time to come was somehow really a short-term proposition. Starting in late October, 1953, as the national campaign for the transition grew in intensity, the notion of the New Democracy economy as one in which the private sector would "flourish" unimpeded by central controls was brought under crass attack and gave way to the line that the private sector gradually was to be *crowded out* and eventually taken over by the state.

Indicative of this change in line, theorist Yao P'eng-chang, in criticizing the heretofore authoritative book in which Meng

Hsien-chang had recorded the concept of an expanding private sector, found it a matter of concern that "this book was able to circulate for three years without having been censured."[17] Meng was berated for "not criticizing private capitalism" which inevitably would be displaced from the economy. Capitalism would not be permitted to develop at will, Yao continued, and the leniency toward private business would be qualified. Yao condemned Meng's interpretation of New Democracy in the following manner:

> The author's information concerning the leading role of the state-run economy is incorrect. He says that "State-run enterprises in their so-called leading role merely *guide*, but do not *squeeze out*; merely are of *relative*, not *preponderant importance*; merely pose as *hosts*, not as *monopolists*; merely function *in coordinating*, not *in opposing*; and merely have the power *to help*, not *to restrain*" (*A Course in New Democracy Economy*, p. 37). These phrases reveal the author's ignorance of the corrupt, backward face of private capitalist economy. . . . From the viewpoint of the leading role of the state-run economy, for it merely *to help* is incorrect and to say that it merely shall *co-ordinate* is even more erroneous.[18]

The attack indicated that Mao's general line formulation was significantly more radical, more restrictive of private capitalism than his earlier concept of New Democracy in which "socialist" and capitalist economic sectors were to grow side by side. The earlier concept had been helpful — but by no means decisive — in winning over many non-Communists and smoothing Mao's way to power in 1949. Now that Mao and the other members of the leadership were prepared to move on, private enterprise became in October, 1953, more and more a declining, temporary supplement to the swelling state economic sector.

[17] Yao P'eng-chang, "Criticism of *A Course in New Democracy Economy*," Shanghai *Wen-hui Pao*, January 7, 1954.
[18] *Ibid.* (Yao's emphasis).

Mao's statements since 1934 that the small private sector would be protected and permitted to develop were suddenly revealed to be part of a certain kind of promise, namely, a dialectical promise (to use Karl A. Wittfogel's phrase). The early promise of a freely developing small-capitalist economy had been transformed: although the private sector would be "used," it was now to be "restricted and reformed." Mao's theorists promptly took up the task of trying to prove to the perplexed and disillusioned Chinese that Mao, after all, had said "socialism" was the key goal.

That this change was unexpected—that is, that New Democracy was to be replaced by the "transition to socialism"—is also attested to by Chu Kuang-chien, the seemingly bewildered professor of the Western Language Department of Peking University, when he wrote the following:

> Upon studying the general line, I heard that the period of transition to socialism actually had begun when the PRC was founded. I also heard that the general line was not suddenly espoused.
>
> It was mentioned by Chairman Mao in *On New Democracy* and *On the People's Democratic Dictatorship* and was stipulated with clarity in the Common Program. I read these documents again and found that the general line governing the transition from the New Democracy stage to socialism clearly had been outlined. I had read these essays many times in the past, but now I know that I had failed to understand them. I did not grasp the essence of New Democracy and failed to appreciate that it was a period of transition to socialism.[19]

Reading Professor Chu's confession carefully, one concludes that he was only seemingly bewildered and was in fact writing between the lines. Professor Chu apparently was informing careful readers among China's intellectuals that he "failed to appreciate" that the "essence" of New Democracy pointed to a period of "transition

[19] Chu Kuang-chien, "I Have a Role in the General Plan of the General Line," Peking *Kuang-ming Jih-pao*, January 15, 1954.

to socialism" precisely because the documents he cites are ambiguous on the matter. We are shown once again the perverse way in which Mao would have Chinese intellectuals view the concept of "essence" when it serves the regime's purpose. Professor Chu apparently was also telling his readers that in the 1953 directive, Mao *for the first time*, and in one stroke, had pushed back to October, 1949, the starting date for the transition and the completion date for New Democracy. Professor Chu concluded: "I have come to understand that studying is no easy matter. One might have read an essay a number of times and thought its import had been comprehended. Actually, however, one had not grasped it at all."

The authoritative understanding of the New Democracy society prior to the general line campaign of October, 1953, was that it consisted of two stages, the first of which prepared for "socialism," and the second, after a long time, made the direct transition. This concept was attacked by Yao P'eng-chang, who was anxious to show continuity by merging these two stages and blurring them. Yao's assertion that the "New Democracy society *is* the transitional society" on the road to "socialism"—a point of particular emphasis in general line propaganda—exemplified the new element in the CCP claim of Chinese political and economic progress and maturity. It was a claim to the prestige which accrues to a Communist-led state when it proclaims that "building socialism" is the new task at hand.

Mao apparently was reluctant to accept for long a position for China which placed it in a doctrinally inferior status. That is, according to Soviet theorists, the "democratic," or "New Democracy," stage in Eastern Europe had been completed in late 1947, after which time all Eastern European Communist regimes were acknowledged to be in the second stage, the more advanced stage of "transition to socialism." China, however, was still held to be in the first stage, and this clearly was intended to imply that the Chinese Communist regime was less advanced and revolutionary than the regimes of Eastern Europe. Mao apparently decided, therefore, to move at least abreast of these countries by proclaiming that the transition was in progress and had been ever since October, 1949.

Mao did not begin the transitional campaign until after (*a*) the national economy had been "rehabilitated" and the first five-year plan was being prepared (December, 1952), (*b*) Stalin had died (March, 1953), and (*c*) the Korean hostilities had ended (July, 1953). The *timing* of the campaign was probably influenced by all three factors.

### *Soviet Reluctance To Accept China as "Building Socialism"*

As of October, 1953, when the Chinese made clear that they had entered upon the "building of socialism," the Russians in effect denied this claim. According to the Soviet view, China was still in the first stage of a people's democratic revolution, the task of which was to carry out only "general democratic" reforms and to establish the prerequisites for the future proclamation of the "transition to socialism." Soviet propagandists and the Soviet leadership apparently were unprepared for the turn of events in China and seemed reluctant to accept the transition claim.

Clear signs of this reluctance appeared at the start. The Russian October Revolution slogans, which had been promulgated on October 25, 1953, had sent greetings to the Chinese people "who are struggling for industrialization, economic and cultural advance, and for the strengthening of the people's democratic state." The specification "socialist" did not appear. Nor did the *Pravda* editorial of November 9 take into account Mao's characterization of China's new stage. The editorial merely repeated the formulation as given in the October Revolution slogans, while explicitly referring to the building of "socialism" in the European Communist countries:

> The great Chinese people are successfully struggling for the industrialization of their country, for the further

> advance of their economy and culture, and for the all-round strengthening of their people's democratic state. . . . The European people's democracies are marching forward with confidence. Utilizing the rich Soviet experience, the toilers of Poland, Czechoslovakia, Rumania, Hungary, Bulgaria, and Albania are successfully struggling for the further advance of their national economy and for an increase in the material and cultural level of the life of the people, and for the *building of a socialist society.*[20]

And, *Pravda*'s year-end editorial on December 31 read:

> Shoulder to shoulder with the Soviet Union along this path of progress and happiness march the great Chinese people, who have rapidly rebuilt their economy and have raised the banner of struggle for further economic progress and for industrialization, and the European people's democracies, which are confidently building socialism.[21]

The circumlocution used in describing China's status was quite deliberate: China was "great" but not yet ready for the transition.

The first overt acknowledgment by a Soviet publicist of China's "transition to socialism" came around the middle of January, 1954. In the review by the CPSU's theoretical journal, *Kommunist*, of the fourth volume of Mao Tse-tung's *Selected Works* (third volume in the Chinese edition), G. Yefimov stated:

> The People's Government and the Communist party are planning to bring about, over a relatively prolonged period of time, the socialist industrialization of the country, socialist transformations in agriculture. trade, and other sectors of the national economy. The policy of the People's Government and the CCP is directed, thus, to the gradual transition from the minimum program, the creation of a new democracy state, to the maximum program, the building of a socialist society in China.[22]

[20] *Pravda*, November 9, 1953 (emphasis supplied).
[21] *Pravda*, December 31, 1953.
[22] G. Yefimov, "Fourth Volume of the *Selected Works of Mao Tse-tung*," *Kommunist*, No. 1, January, 1954 (approved for printing January 12).

The entire statement stands as unique in the January issues of Soviet journals and magazines. There was no Soviet-originated statement (in any other Soviet publications in January, 1954) that China was "building socialism." On the contrary, the traditional distinction between European satellites and China continued to be made in a number of the January publications, including *Pravda*, on January 17.

Toward the end of April, 1954, the Soviets began to give general recognition to the claim advanced by the Chinese the preceding October that they were engaged in the "building of socialism." Kaganovich, for example, declared to the Soviet of the Union of the USSR Supreme Soviet that "the ruling circles of the imperialist states, especially the United States, are following with hatred and anger the successes of Communist construction in the USSR and the successes of socialist construction in the great PRC and in all countries of people's democracy."[23] However, until the end of May, there was no discussion by a Soviet theoretician or publicist directed specifically to this new phenomenon, no extended article on the stages of the Chinese revolution in the light of this new development, no echoing of the Chinese claim that the second stage—the stage of "socialism"—had begun in October, 1949.

Soviet theorists did insist, however, that with the second stage in any Communist country must appear the change from "democratic dictatorship" of the proletariat and peasantry to "dictatorship of the proletariat." But this, as we have suggested in the preceding chapter, is precisely what Mao refused to do until the compromise in 1956. Mao had taken the unorthodox step, therefore, of entering the stage of "transition to socialism" without declaring, as a theoretical proposition, a proletarian dictatorship. Mao's line on transition was in this sense different from that prescribed by the Soviets for all people's democracies. It was unique.

[23] *Pravda*, April 27, 1954.

The long delay in Soviet recognition of China's "transition to socialism" suggests that Moscow opposed the unorthodox — that is, Maoist — line on transition under a "people's democratic dictatorship." During the entire period of Soviet resistance, the Russians may have attempted to maneuver the Chinese into a position requiring the declaration of proletarian dictatorship. Certainly, Soviet propaganda made it clear that this should be done, as the proletarian dictatorship was held to be *necessary* for the transition. Mao's failure to yield unequivocally and the compromise of 1956, which was reqiured to conceal the Sino-Soviet variance on proletarian dictatorship, can be taken as a measure of Mao's ability in 1953–54 to undertake a policy of which Moscow did not approve.

The Chinese claim that Mao has arrived at a new form and method for the transition. They do this by insisting that "peaceful transformation" of capitalists' enterprises differs from that of the Soviet Union and the European people's democracies. To nations engaged in drawing up plans for "mixed economies," the claim that "socialism" was entered upon in a unique way in China would keep the Chinese post-revolutionary example of economic behavior at the center of their attention.

Mao's application of the Marx-Engels-Lenin concept of "buying out" the capitalists (squeezing out is more accurate) and taking over their businesses is alleged to constitute a "model" for underdeveloped countries. In 1956, Wu Ch'uan-che declared:

> The experiences and achievements of China's socialist transformation of capitalist industry and commerce have created the following model: for countries which at one time were semi-feudal and semi-colonial, just as China had been . . . the model shows how the working class should handle its relations with the national capitalists and, after revolutionary victory, how to eliminate exploitation and complete the transition to socialism. It is for this reason that China's peaceful transformation of capitalist industry and commerce has a very important significance as a form of class struggle. We may say that China's experience in transition regarding

> elimination of exploitation and of classes certainly has enriched the Marxist-Leninist theory of the transition period.[24]

It is, therefore, not just Mao's strategy of rural-based guerrilla warfare as a road to power that is said by the Chinese to be a model for backward countries; added to this model is the model of "socialist transformation." Moreover, in 1960, the Chinese extended the relevance of their model beyond "semi-colonial" countries to include capitalist, or formerly capitalist, states.

For a brief period in 1960–61, the East Germans were prepared to learn something from the Chinese on the matter of handling small capitalists. On May 13, 1960, two members of the Berlin Bezirk organization of the National Democratic party discussed with Chinese embassy officials "a number of questions concerning the incorporation of the members of the middle class [national bourgeoisie] into the building of socialism in the German Democratic Republic and democratic Berlin."[25] The Chinese precedent was again alluded to in 1961, but in more guarded form, without the implication that the East Germans regarded the Chinese as their teachers in the matter.[26]

## *"Peaceful Transformation" of the Capitalists*

Now the claim for Mao that the Chinese make it not merely that the capitalists' enterprises will be transformed (that is, gradually placed under state control), but that the capitalists will be

[24] Wu Ch'uan-che, "The Basic Class Contradiction. . . ." *loc. cit.*

[25] East Berlin *National Zeitung*, May 14, 1960.

[26] *Wirtschaftswissenschaft* (East Berlin), May, 1961. An article in this journal states that the "German Democratic Republic" (GDR) differs from that of other East European regimes where the bourgeoisie was not prepared to support "socialism." "But in the GDR (another example is China), a large part of the nationally minded bourgeoisie have been prepared to cooperate in building socialism. Thus the possibility arose . . . of eliminating capitalist exploitation and, with this, the antagonism . . . through the form of state participation" (in private enterprises).

transformed as men, that is, they will be mentally changed or remolded. Thus theorist Wu Ch'uan-che says: "The ideology of the capitalist, who cares only for profits, is not absolutely impossible to transform. . . . We can . . . use the method of education to transform this ideology."[27] The term, "education," actually means intensive indoctrination and, in practice, it is a form of brainwashing—Mao's attempt to force men's minds.

The claim for Mao was stated in 1955 in such a way as to set off Chinese methods from other bloc countries. Theorist Shu Wei-kuang put it this way:

> In a state where the proletariat has seized political power, under definite social and historical conditions, establishment of the principle that *capitalists* can be basically transformed under socialist guidance is another brilliant contribution of Comrade Mao Tse-tung to the treasure house of Marxism-Leninism. This theory has never appeared in the classical works of Marxism-Leninism, and no country in the world has ever gone through this kind of experience.
>
> In the Soviet Union and the state of people's democracy in Eastern Europe, violent and forcible methods of expropriation were used to eliminate the bourgeoisie. But, under our concrete conditions in China, the identical goal of eliminating the bourgeoisie can be attained by taking the road of peaceful transformation.[28]

As noted above, there is some evidence that the concept of a peaceful transformation of capitalist industry and commerce was seminal in Marx, Engels, and Lenin. But whereas they gave a warrant for "buying out" the capitalists and Lenin saw that they could be put to work for the Soviet state, they never went as far as Mao. For what Mao wants, and believes he can get, is not just the capitalists' business, their co-operation, and the use of their

[27] Wu Ch'uan-che, "Peaceful Transformation . . ." *loc. cit.*

[28] Shu Wei-kuang, "The Gradual Leap in China's Transition Period," *Che-hsüeh Yen-chiu*, No. 1, June, 1955.

talents. Actually, he has these already. He wants their souls as well.

Mao apparently believes that men who had been small capitalists can be *mentally changed* and will be willing, under "education," to exchange their capitalist soul for that of a wage earner. In his report to the Eighth Congress of the CCP, Liu Shao-ch'i expressed this Maoist view with considerable confidence:

> In the course of bringing about the socialist transformation of capitalist industry and commerce, we have carried out the transformation of enterprises in conjunction with the remolding of individuals. That is, while the enterprises are being transformed, educational measures are adopted to remold the capitalists gradually, enabling them to be transformed from exploiters into working people earning their own living. . . .
>
> It can now be stated with conviction that with the exception of a very few diehards who still attempt to put up resistance, it is possible, in the economic sphere, for the overwhelming majority of the national bourgeoisie to accept social transformation and gradually change into real working people.[29]

To suggest even the possibility that "exploiters" can be changed and transformed "into working people" is to go against the whole grain of orthodox doctrine and practice. Liu's confidence is not based, of course, on the belief that the small capitalists will transform their ideology, their world view, voluntarily. This is, granted, possible, but experience undoubtedly shows Mao and Liu that only few individuals will accept a complete change of their moral, political, and economic outlook except when they are *compelled* to do so.

When Liu says that the capitalists must be "educated and re-

[29] Liu Shao-ch'i, "The Political Report of the Central Committee of the CCP to the 8th National Congress of the Party," given on September 15, 1956, in *8th National Congress of the CCP* (Peking: Foreign Language Press, 1956), Vol. I: Documents.

molded" into adopting a "socialist" world view, he is paraphrasing Mao. In 1949 and in 1950, Mao had stated that the capitalists would be educated when the time came. In his report to the party plenum of June, 1950, Mao says that "toward the people, [the people's democratic dictatorship] . . . does not use compulsion, but democratic methods, namely: it does not compel them to do this or that, but uses democratic methods in educating and persuading them."[30] However, both Liu and Mao are uttering euphemisms, for the line between persuasion (through education) and compulsion (through terror and threats) is a fine one indeed in China. "Education" of the capitalists has been carried out in conjunction with "struggle" campaigns of various degrees of intensity. As Li Wei-han, director of the CCP's United Front Work Department put it in 1960: "During the past 10 years, we have waged several violent struggles against the national bourgeoisie, while at the same time we have launched massive and regular educational work among them. . . . They have gradually turned from their passiveness into an active attitude, and they have accepted socialist transformation without too much reluctance."[31] The Chinese leaders in this sense seem to view the capitalist's brain as Pavlov viewed his dog's.

Li concedes that there are still some difficulties, as "human transformation is an *unprecedented* and great task in the history of mankind. . . . While transformation on the economic front is relatively easy, the real difficulty lies in the transformation of man, i.e., political and ideological transformation.[32] In late 1959 and 1960, the "rightists," who were skeptical of the feasibility of the commune program and the "great leap forward," were a problem. Regarding non-Communist "rightists" among intellectuals

[30] Mao Tse-tung, "Report to the Party Plenum (June 6, 1950)," *People's China*, July 1, 1950.

[31] Li Wei-han, "Study Chairman Mao's Works; Gradually Improve Your World View," Peking *Jen-min Jih-pao*, September 25, 1960.

[32] *Ibid.* (emphasis supplied).

and capitalists, Li speaks of transforming them gradually by means of "criticism, isolation, education, and help." He uses the term "isolation" again in connection with bourgeois intellectuals in general, and it emerges that he is not referring to physical isolation but rather to the feeling of having been left out: "Intellectuals among the working class have made unprecedented progress and in this situation some of the bourgeois intellectuals feel they are isolated. I see nothing wrong in this. It is rather desirable."[33] Li's remarks that it is "desirable" implies that creation of this feeling of isolation is deliberately fostered by the CCP cadres, whose responsibility is to "help" in this way to transform the capitalists' way of thinking.

The Chinese Communists are clearly aware of the psychological effects of each of their tactics in changing the thinking of the capitalists and bourgeois intellectuals, and Li Wei-han says that "fundamental transformation is a thoroughgoing process which entails pains and shocks." Transforming the world view of the capitalists, remolding their thinking through shocks, is a protracted process. In his *On the Correct Handling of Contradictions among the People* (1957), Mao lays it down that the capitalists "will still need ideological remolding for quite some time" even in the future when they rid themselves of the label "bourgeoisie."[34] Mao recommends a combination of work among wage earners in the enterprises and "study."

To help them in their "study," the Chinese Communists apparently apply certain aspects of their experiments in brainwashing captured Japanese soldiers in the 1930's, and criminals and political prisoners more recently, to more recalcitrant capitalists—"diehards." Many of these unfortunate souls are either too old or have too much self-respect to submit easily to the degrading process of having their minds forced through thought reform.

[33] *Ibid.*

[34] Mao Tse-tung, *On the Problem of the Correct Handling of Contradictions among the People* (New York: New Century Publishers, 1957), p. 18.

The methods used by the Chinese Communists in indoctrinating political prisoners apparently are decisively different in several respects from Soviet methods. These differences are:

1. Unlike the Russians, the Chinese attempt to ensure that the political prisoner will develop a long-lasting change in his attitude and overt behavior which will be sustained after his release. Nothing less than the establishment of a "new moral code" in the prisoner's mind is a major goal.

2. Unlike the Russians, the Chinese make extensive use of group interaction among prisoners in obtaining information, applying pressures, and carrying out indoctrination.

3. Whereas in the Soviet Union and the Eastern European regimes the ritual of public self-criticism, confession, self-degradation, punishment, and rehabilitation is a party procedure, the Chinese have extended this practice to the non-party population and have made it an important aspect of their thought-reform procedure.

4. In China, the period of detention is greatly prolonged. Whereas in the Soviet Union trial and sentencing take place fairly soon after the completion of the interrogation, in China the preparation of a first confession is only a prelude to a long period of indoctrination and re-education, which may go on for years and is not terminated until the authorities believe that the prisoner has finally adopted the "correct" attitude and behavior.[35]

It appears that Mao has taken over the Soviet practice of requiring a public confession, or "self-criticism," and further developed it with traditional Chinese emphasis of *sustained* learning by rote and endless repetition. One Chinese writer described protracted learning and "self-reform" as follows:

> Many businessmen call for a change in their status.
> Certainly a good sign, this is comprehensible to us. It

[35] L. E. Hinkle and H. G. Wolff, "Communist Interrogation and Indoctrination of "Enemies of the State,'" *Archives of Neurology and Psychiatry*, August, 1956.

> indicates that they realize exploitation is shameful and labor glorious. But to change an exploiter into a real laborer is a matter which requires colossal effort in self-reform. If any capitalist thinks that he can be made into a real laborer simply by acquiring the status of laborer and if he pays no attention to the bourgeois mentality hatched and developed through a long life of exploitation and, therefore, relaxes his effort, his self-reform will be impeded. . . . A change in status cannot be attained simply by waiving his income from interest. He must be subjected to a tough course of ideological remolding. For this reason, the problem of changing status can be solved only gradually and individually, according to the actual conditions of each person, the principle of voluntariness, and the possibilities of success.[36]

Capitalists presumably will continue to be capitalists even beyond 1964 (in 1962, this period was extended to 1965). The payment of fixed interest to industrialists "will continue until after the second five-year plan," according to Vice-Premier Po I-po's statement of December 10, 1956. Thus the Chinese Communists envisage a prolonged period of thought reform for the small capitalists, and Li Wei-han says, "We must be patient and meticulous in our work."[37]

Patient and meticulous work has begun to produce in China a type of capitalist never seen before in other countries. And a new type of capitalist in a *Communist* country is indeed a novelty. Khrushchev was at one time compelled to make, however ambiguously, an acknowledgment of the novelty. In a speech at the Chinese embassy in Moscow on November 29, 1956, Khrushchev praised the "original forms" of revolution in China and then centered his attention on the capitalists in the Chinese delegation. "I am no longer a young man and in the days gone by, I worked

[36] Li Kuang-yu, "How To Understand Correctly the Problem of Change-of-Status for Capitalists," *Shih-shih Shou-ts'e* (World Affairs Handbook), No. 24, December 25, 1956.

[37] Li Wei-han, "Study Chairman Mao's Works . . . . ," *loc. cit.*

in capitalist enterprises. I had occasion to take part in strikes, to be in workers' delegations, and to negotiate with capitalists. But at that time, we did not sit side by side, but were opposed to each other and our interests were irreconcilable." There is a definite note of orthodoxy in Khrushchev's last phrase. This was his equivocal way of flattering the Chinese. Moreover, he paid tribute to Mao's innovation without praising Mao himself. In late 1956 the Soviet leader, trying to re-establish Soviet hegemony in Eastern Europe which Gomulka and Nagy had called into question,[38] felt the need to agree with the cocky Chinese at least to the extent that in China a new approach to the capitalist man had been discovered. But they credited the Chinese party or the Chinese people with the unique approach, not Mao, who was in China the object of the kind of personality cult which the Russians were trying to discourage during de-Stalinization.

Soviet acknowledgment of uniqueness was guarded. Choosing his words carefully, Mikoyan had told the Chinese party congress in September, 1956, that "each country has its distinctive features and contributes something specifically its own in effecting the transition to socialism." He stated that the bourgeoisie in China had "found it more convenient not to clash with the people's state, but to work under its control," and that, compared with the setting of the Russian revolution, there had been in China "new historical conditions, a more favorable situation." This fact explained differences in Soviet and Chinese "experience," and left room for certain innovations. Contrasted with Chinese claims that Mao's innovation enriched the treasure house of Marxist-Leninist theory as well as practice, Mikoyan's words seem rather colorless and restrained.

While conceding that the Chinese view on "peaceful transformation" of small capitalists was something new, the Russians

[38] Zbigniew K. Brzezinski discusses this development in chapters 10 and 11 of his precisely detailed account: *The Soviet Bloc* (Cambridge, Mass.: Harvard University Press, 1960).

stressed that it was *specifically China's own*. That is, it had limited applicability elsewhere. In its editorial of November 23, 1956, *Pravda* applauded the Chinese, "who always make it clear that their methods, though perfectly correct in their country, are not necessarily of universal application." This remark, intended for the Yugoslavs, who at the time were urging the Eastern European regimes to accept Titoist internal policies, cut also in China's direction. The Russians undoubtedly were aware that the Chinese, too, were trying to export Mao's ideas on internal policies. The matter of whether Mao's innovations were of international applicability continued to be a source of concern for the Soviet leaders then as it is today.

As we have noted earlier in this chapter, the Chinese claim that Mao's handling of the small capitalists is applicable even to capitalist countries. A forceful statement of this view was made in 1960:

> Peaceful transformation of the capitalists' enterprises has now been attained in China. China's experience in this matter is of universal significance. The truth underlying this experience is not limited to colonial and semi-colonial countries. We are aware that with the East Wind prevailing over the West Wind, revolution will triumph in several capitalist countries and the big capitalists will be deprived of their rights. At that time, it is entirely possible for these countries to adopt the guideline of peaceful redemption toward the middle ["national"] and petty capitalists.[39]

Maoist proselytizing of this kind has angered the Soviet leaders, who are now attempting to take the wind from the Chinese leader's sails by insisting—rightly—that Marx and Lenin were the first to discuss the policy of "buying out" the bourgeoisie.[40] This

[39] T'ao Chu, "Speech to the Political Economy Class of the Kwangtung Provincial Party Committee (March 30, 1960)," Canton *Nan-fang Jih-pao*, May 13, 1960. This passage was deleted in the version of T'ao's speech published in the Peking *Jen-min Jih-pao* on August 5, 1960.

[40] In mid-1961, the author of an unsigned article in *Kommunist* asserted that

line has been incorporated into the new Program of the CPSU of 1961 — the document which replaced the Program of 1919 — where it is explicitly stated that "buying out" was a procedure which "Marx and Lenin foresaw."[41] Nevertheless, China retains the unprecedented "experience" to export.

### *Chou En-lai's Idea?*

The idea that a capitalist could be made to change his stripes, so to speak, appears to have evolved from Mao's works in the late 1930's and 1940's. Mao speaks repeatedly in this period of "preserving" the capitalist economy in China and of sustaining the alliance with the "patriotic capitalists." But it is difficult to determine just when and how the unorthodox thought occurred to him that the capitalist man could be transformed into the workingman.

Chou En-lai claims some of the credit. During a discussion with former premier of France, Edgar Faure, who was visiting China in 1957, Chou recalled his own stay in France between 1924 and 1927. He had worked there as a student and as a manual laborer, in Paris and Rouen. Said Chou:

> It was while I was amongst you that I was converted to Communism. I observed, I shared the life of my fellow-workers and I came to the conclusion that it was not possible to transform the wage earners into capitalists, but that it was possible to transform the capitalists into wage earners.[42]

M. Faure says that this was a jest on Chou's part, but Chou's statement stands as an assertion of a bit of personal creativity

---

in China "the state began gradually to buy out the property of the national bourgeoisie." He then implicitly denied Mao any originality: "Marxists have always considered this specific method of liquidating a class of capitalists as possible under the specific conditions of one or another country" ("Forty Years in the Vanguard of the Chinese People," *Kommunist*, No. 10, July, 1961).

[41] *Izvestiya*, November 2, 1961.

[42] Edgar Faure, *The Serpent and the Tortoise* (New York: St. Martin's Press, 1958), p. 18.

which is very unusual among Chinese leaders other than Mao and Liu Shao-ch'i. We may ask: how many ideas attributed to Mao's genius were really the product of other Chinese minds? The question is as legitimate in Mao's case as it was in Stalin's.

Chou's "jest" appears, nevertheless, as a slender reed beside the claims made for Mao regarding various aspects of transition—claims which proliferated in 1960. According to his eulogists, Mao had shown originality on *all* aspects of the transition, and no other Chinese leader is given credit on this matter.

We have seen how Mao made a minor revision in doctrine and how the continued existence of certain small capitalists as a class in China represents a Communist anomaly. Their contribution had carried some importance immediately after the Communist regime came to power, but by 1964 their continued, separate existence is economically meaningless. They are permitted to exist separately, we suspect, primarily as showpieces to be displayed as "proof" of a Maoist innovation. Actually, their existence as capitalists is really proof of how Mao allows himself to make minor revisions in dogma, while denying the privilege to Khrushchev.

To sum up, Marx and Engels had originated the dogma, which Lenin further developed, that the elimination of the bourgeoisie as a class and the expropriation of their holdings must be carried out during the "socialist" stage of revolution. Lenin was willing to make use of certain Russian capitalists until the Soviet regime had been strengthened, but, as it turned out, he expropriated capitalist property violently, and in Stalin's time the "transition to socialism" was carried out following the total destruction of the capitalists as a class.

In contrast, the Chinese claim that Mao has discovered a peaceful *method* for handling capitalists. The national capitalists—that is, those who remained after the bureaucratic capitalists had been "smashed" in 1949—are said to be a part of the transition in China, and it is asserted that such a transition with capitalists is unprecedented. This claim is partly valid, as Mao's method is a departure from previous practice.

Whereas Eastern European leaders after 1948, following Soviet practices imposed by Stalin, felt obliged to reject the "peaceful transformation" of capitalists, Mao was able *to work out the details and put into practice* the Marx-Engels-Lenin idea of "buying out" the capitalists during a period of gradual transformation. What Mao did in stages was to transform capitalist industry and commerce into mixed public-private industry and commerce, to transform capitalists into shareholders, and to transfer administration of private enterprises into party and government hands. The *practical* aspects — that is, the planning and day-to-day execution — of this imposed totalitarian control system were unprecedented in the history of Communist regimes. Eastern European leaders had not gone as far as Mao in planning and execution, nor do their propagandists claim they ever did.

The Chinese claim that Mao not only worked out a new method for the "transition to socialism" by peacefully transforming — that is, gradually taking over — capitalist enterprises, but that the capitalists themselves are being transformed mentally. This mental change is effected by intensive indoctrination which, differing somewhat from Soviet practices, seeks to effect permanent changes, makes extensive use of group pressures, is applied to non-party as well as party personnel, and is a very prolonged process. The entire *method* is uniquely Maoist. The small capitalists are generally not sent to prison or camps for this transformation; they keep working in their businesses and several, selected as showpieces, are used to demonstrate that Mao is a benevolent innovator who permits them to wash their minds in the ease of rather comfortable home life.

Even Khrushchev, no admirer of Chinese practices, paid a backhanded compliment in 1956 to the Chinese method of handling small capitalists. So did Mikoyan. Soviet spokesmen were careful, however, to restrict the applicability of these practices to China, and by 1960 Moscow was reluctant to concede that they were innovations and retired into silence at the end of the year.

Mao's ideas on the transition — in particular, on the method of "buying out" and "transforming" capitalists — are communicated to other Communists with a missionary zeal. These ideas are said to be of "universal significance" for all Communists even those in the West. This kind of proselytizing has angered the Soviet leaders, who attempted to take the wind from Mao's sails by insisting that Marx and Lenin were the first to discuss the "buying out" policy and by incorporating the policy into the new draft program adopted by the twenty-second Soviet party congress in October, 1961. The degree to which they will prove successful in undercutting Mao's methods will depend on the degree of control they can exert, or influence they possess, in the various Communist parties.

# 5

# "Contradictions" in a "Socialist Society"

In 1956 and 1957, Mao Tse-tung, a fanatic, sought to do away with fanaticism. The original impulse for his move came from the Soviet Union, where the fanaticism of Stalin was being assaulted by men who were less dogmatic than the dead despot in their approach to political life. They held that Stalin had created an enormous gap between himself (as God) and Soviet man and that had he not been cruel, suspicious, and insanely self-exalting, the gap would never have opened, for in a "socialist" society there can be no tension between the rulers and the ruled. Only the subjective mental aberrations of a madman, not the objective conditions of "socialist" society, can create such tension. Mao, who had learned over many bitter years that Stalin was quite fallible in political matters when he lived, nevertheless defended him when he died, and taught that it was not in Stalin's subjective nature but in the objective nature of all societies — including a Communist-led society — that tension ("contradiction") can arise between the leaders and the led.

In Mao's professed view, the task of the great leader was to accept the existence of these "contradictions" and to prevent them from erupting by treating political deviation with moderation rather than deadly animosity. Mao developed this point of view from early 1956 to spring 1957 in the obscure language of dogma which made it seem profound when actually it was but a lesson in the obvious.

In order to determine which of Mao's contributions are merely alleged and which are actual, we begin with a glimpse of the classic doctrine on "contradiction." "Contradiction," in the Communist vocabulary, is variously used to express the ideas of dissimilarity, mutual opposition, contrariety, conflict, and antagonism. It is, therefore, adaptable to almost any connotation by a clever writer or leader. These discussions on "contradiction" often seem to be a stupid and tiresome verbal game, but real issues are sometimes the topics, as in Mao's statements in 1956–57.

Adopting an idea of early Greek philosophers, Hegel held that oppositions, which he also called contradictions, are found everywhere in nature and thought, and that history proceeds through them. Marx accepted this in part but stressed the concept of "class," maintaining that class contradiction is the driving force of all social development. The appearance of a major contradiction between the bourgeoisie and the proletariat in capitalist society would be, Marx asserted, the harbinger of the ultimate demise of that society and of the victory of the proletariat. He made no comment, however, regarding contradictions in a "classless" society — the envisaged Communist society.

### *"Non-antagonistic" Contradictions*

It was Lenin who maintained that contradictions would still exist under "socialism." In discussing class struggle, Marx had used the terms "antagonism" and "contradiction" interchangeably.[1] Lenin, however, at times did not:

> Antagonism and contradiction are by no means the same. Under socialism the first will vanish, the second

[1] In his *Poverty of Philosophy* (1846–47), Marx says: "From the very moment in which civilization begins, production begins to be based on the antagonism of orders, of states, of classes, and finally on the antagonism between capital and labor. No antagonism, no progress." Marx also used the term "contradiction" to convey the same idea regarding the relationship between capital and labor.

> will remain. If in developed socialism there were no contradictions — contradictions between productive forces and relations of production, between production and demand, no contradictions in the development of technique, etc. — then the development of socialism would be impossible, then instead of movement we should have stagnation.[2]

Not antagonism but contradictions, which according to Marx were the motive force of all social development, were thus to continue under "developed socialism."

Chinese Communist theorists acknowledge Lenin's contribution to the matter of contradictions in a "socialist" society. And well they might, as Mao himself, in *On Contradiction* (first published in China in April, 1952), quotes Lenin's above-mentioned statement.[3]

But in order to clear the way for Mao as a creative thinker on contradictions, the theorists go on to minimize Lenin's contribution. Theorist Pien Chang says that "Lenin was restricted by historical factors and was therefore not able to make a detailed elaboration of the basic theory of contradiction,"[4] and theorist Sun Ting-kuo alleges that "Lenin in his day had come too late to make an all-round observation on the matter of internal contradictions in a socialist society."[5] Stalin's statements on contradictions under "socialism" are also mentioned, but only in a general way, and are similarly minimized.

Actually, Stalin discussed the matter in considerable detail in many of his works. In 1925, Stalin acknowledged the existence of contradictions within Soviet society and insisted that these

[2] Quoted in M. Shirokov, *Textbook of Marxist Philosophy* (Leningrad Institute of Philosophy), revised and edited translation by John Lewis (London: Gollancz, c. 1935), p. 175.

[3] Mao, *Selected Works*, I (1961), 324.

[4] Pien Chang, "A Preliminary Discussion of Comrade Mao Tse-tung's Development of Marxist-Leninist Philosophy," *Li-lun Hsüeh-hsi* (Studies in Theory) (Mukden), September 1, 1960.

[5] Sun Ting-kuo, "A Tremendous Development of the Law of Marxist Dialectics," *Che-hsüeh Yen-chiu*, No. 3, June 15, 1958.

"internal contradictions" can be solved through the "directing role" of the state.[6] Among the various contradictions mentioned by Stalin in 1925 was the contradiction between the proletariat and the peasantry, which, together with other "internal contradictions," is perpetuated by the continued existence of "external contradictions" between capitalist states and the Soviet state. Stalin enumerated more internal contradictions in his speech to the Stakhanovites in 1935.[7] In his *Letter to Ivanov* of 1938, he implied that the internal contradictions had been solved, but in *Economic Problems of Socialism in the USSR* (1952) Stalin once again conceded their existence under "socialism."

Lenin's statement that antagonism would disappear and Stalin's 1925 position that "internal contradictions" could be resolved on the basis of common interests provided the foundation for a general theory of "non-antagonistic" contradictions. Soviet writers had begun to develop the theory by 1935. Thus in the Soviet *Textbook of Marxist Philosophy*, a distinction is made between "antagonistic contradictions . . . and contradictions that do not have an antagonistic character. . . . Not all contradictions are antagonistic."[8] A similar distinction is made in 1935 in an article in the *Great Soviet Encyclopedia*.[9] In 1939, Mr. Rozenthal and P. Yudin wrote that "the contradiction between the working class and the working peasantry does not carry the character of antagonism."[10]

Starting in 1947, discussion of non-antagonistic contradictions increased among Soviet theorists. A. Zhdanov gave national and international prominence to the view that "criticism and self-criticism" would serve as a technique for preventing contradictions

[6] Stalin, "Results of the Work of the 14th Party Conference (1925)," *Works* (Russian-language version; Moscow: Gospolitizdat, 1946–51), VII, 90 ff.

[7] Stalin, *Leninism* (New York: International Publishers, 1942), p. 368.

[8] Shirokov, *op. cit.*, p. 174.

[9] "Historical Materialism," in *Bol'shaia sovetskaia entsiklopediia* (Great Soviet Encyclopedia) (1935), 727–50.

[10] M. Rozenthal and P. Yudin, *Kratki filosofsky slovar* (Short Philosophical Dictionary (Moscow: Oggizo, 1939), p. 11.

from becoming antagonistic.[11] P. Yudin in 1948 distinguished "different types of contradictions." "Contradictions and antagonisms are not one and the same thing. There are contradictions that are antagonistic and [those that are] not antagonistic."[12] Enlarging their 1939 statement on contradiction, Rozenthal and Yudin stated in 1951 that "Marxist dialectics distinguishes antagonistic and non-antagonistic contradictions. . . . The Soviet Union gave a clear example and model of the resolution of the non-antagonistic contradiction between the working class and the peasantry, which had enormous international significance."[13] The authors seemed to predict that other bloc countries would follow the Soviet precedent in handling non-antagonistic contradictions: "Countries of people's democracy are learning by the great example of the Soviet Union how, on the basis of the worker-peasant alliance, to overcome the contradictions which still exist between them and to turn small, fragmented agriculture into large-scale socialist agriculture. With the victory of socialism, the antagonistic contradiction inside the country disappears. . . . Lenin and Stalin teach that under socialism, antagonistic contradictions disappear, but that non-antagonistic contradictions remain."[14] And in August, 1951, the Soviet theorist B. Kedrov wrote in *Bol'shevik*, "The Marxist dialectic recognizes two fundamental types of contradictions: antagonistic and non-antagonistic."[15]

[11] A. A. Zhdanov, *On Literature, Music, and Philosophy* (London: Lawrence & Wishart, 1950), pp. 107–8.

[12] P. Yudin, "The Prime Source of Development of Soviet Society," in the symposium *O sovetskom sotsialisticheskom obshchestve* (On Soviet Socialist Society), ed. F. V. Konstantinov, M. D. Kammari, and G. Glazerman (Moscow, 1949).

[13] Rozenthal-Yudin, *Kratki filosofsky slovar* (3d ed. with revisions and additions: Moscow, 1951), pp. 13–14. The fourth edition, published in 1955 with additions and corrections, describes a special feature of non-antagonistic contradiction: "The characteristic feature of non-antagonistic contradictions consists in the fact that in their development they do not turn necessarily into a hostile opposition and the struggle between them does not result in conflict."

[14] *Ibid.*, p. 14.

[15] B. Kedrov, "On Forms of Leaps in the Development of Nature and Society," *Bol'shevik*, No. 15, August, 1951.

### *Claims for Mao: The "Basic" Contradiction*

It is alleged by the Chinese theorists that Mao went well beyond the Soviet *general* theory of contradictions under "socialism." That is, Mao took the general theory and applied it to the specific matter of production. In a jointly written article, three Chinese writers claim that Mao's *On the Problem of the Correct Handling of Contradictions among the People* (published June, 1957) is "a great contribution to the theory of the basic contradiction in a socialist society," the contradiction arising between the productive forces and the relations of production.[16]

The basis for this claim is Mao's statement of June, 1957, "The basic contradiction in a socialist society is still between the productive forces and the relations of production, between the superstructure and the economic base." "There is conformity as well as contradiction between the relations of production and the development of the productive forces; similarly, there is conformity as well as contradiction between the superstructure and the economic base."[17] The particular claim that this idea is Mao's contribution was made in June, 1958, on the first anniversary of the publication of Mao's above-mentioned work.

Actually, Mao seems to have added nothing original to the theory of the basic contradiction in production. Stalin had begun to elaborate on the theory in 1952. On October 2, 1952, letters written by Stalin months earlier were published under the title *Economic Problems of Socialism in the USSR.* Certain Soviet political economists apparently had written that the possibility of a contradiction between the productive forces and relations of production in Soviet society did not exist. One Yaroshenko was condemned by Stalin in this way:

[16] Hsü Li-ch'un, Ch'en Tao, and Chen Mou-i, "*On the Problem of the Correct Handling of Contradictions among the People* is a Mighty Contribution to Marxism-Leninism," *Che-hsüeh Yen-chiu*, No. 3, June 15, 1958.

[17] Mao, *On the Problem of the Correct Handling of Contradictions among the People* (New York: New Century Publishers, 1957), pp. 10–11.

> Comrade Yaroshenko is mistaken in affirming that under socialism there are no contradictions between relations of production and the productive forces of society. . . . It would be wrong to be complacent . . . and imagine that there are no contradictions between our productive forces and relations of production. Contradictions there definitely are and will be, since the development of production lags and will lag behind the development of productive forces.[18]

Stalin went on to deny, in line with Lenin's statement, that these contradictions would become antagonistic. "With a correct policy on the part of the directing agencies, these contradictions cannot turn into antagonism and the matter here cannot go so far as a conflict between relations of production and society's productive forces." Mao's general statement on contradictions — which was made in his June, 1957, article — is similar to Stalin's 1952 remark. Mao said, "Contradictions in a socialist society are . . . not antagonistic and can be solved one after the other by the socialist system itself."[19]

Theorist Ts. Stepanyan more fully expounded (in 1955) the theory of the basic contradiction under "socialism." In a definitive article, Stepanyan says, "The basic contradiction of the socialist structure is particularly manifest in the general contradiction between the productive forces and the relations of production."[20] He goes on to link the basic contradiction with the superstructure — to which the "needs of all the people" belong — and the base — to which "production of material" goods belong: "The basic contradiction under socialism is the contradiction between the limitlessly growing needs of all the people and the stage of development of the production of material and cultural goods

[18] Stalin, *Economic Problems of Socialism in the USSR* (1952), in *Current Soviet Policies*, ed. Leo Gruliow (New York: Praeger), p. 14.

[19] Mao, *On the Problem of the Correct Handling . . .*, p. 10.

[20] Ts. Stepanyan, "Contradictions in the Development of Socialist Society and the Means of Resolving Them," *Voprosy filosofii*, 1955, No. 2.

which has been achieved in each given period." Other Soviet theorists described the basic contradiction as "the contradiction between the limitlessly growing material and cultural demands of society and the stage of development of production reached in a given period, as well as the contradictions between the new productive forces and the old aspects of the relations of production." [21]

Mao's 1957 statement on the basic contradiction as a contradiction between productive forces and relations, between superstructure and base is not "a great contribution" to the theory of basic contradiction. It is merely a paraphrase of Soviet views expressed generally by Stalin in 1952 and in detail and precision by Stepanyan in 1955.[22]

### *Contradictions "among the People"*

Theorist Ai Ssu-ch'i claims that Mao's work of June, 1957, "further develops Lenin's viewpoint" on contradictions under "socialism." [23] "Comrade Mao Tse-tung . . . points out that in a socialist society the contradiction among the people is non-antagonistic." The term "people" had largely replaced the term "working class" in Mao's vocabulary, particularly in 1957, and had come to mean all those loyal to the regime regardless of class. Theorist Pang Tzu-nien says, "Chairman Mao's great contribution to the Marxist theory of state in his work *On the Problem of the Correct Handling of Contradictions among the People* is this: he drew a sharp distinction between the enemy-ourselves contradiction and the contradiction among-the-people. He also made a scientific,

[21] L. N. Kogan and E. D. Glazunov, "The Problem of Contradictions in Soviet Society," *Voprosy filosofii*, 1955, No. 6.

[22] Writing in 1954, G. E. Glazerman, too, had discussed the base-superstructure contradiction and had stated: "It is necessary to acknowledge contradictions which arise between the base and superstructure . . . under socialism" (*Bazis i nadstroika v sovetskom obshestve* [Base and Superstructure in Soviet Society] [Moscow: Publishing House of the Academy of Sciences USSR, 1954], p. 325).

[23] Ai Ssu-ch'i, "The Contradiction between Productive Forces and Relations of Production and Contradictions among the People," *Che-hsüeh Yen-chiu*, No. 3, June 15, 1958.

historical-materialist definition of the concept, 'people.'"[24] Mao apparently drew this distinction for CCP cadres in order to correct their Stalinist way of attacking as "counterrevolutionary" any minor political mistake of the intellectuals (including young students) and the remaining capitalists. (In 1956 and 1957, Mao defended the *name* of Stalin but not the political practices the Russians attribute to him.)

Because Mao included the national bourgeoisie in his "people" concept, the claim that he had made a contribution to Communist doctrine on this point appears to be, on first consideration, valid. In *On the Problem of the Correct Handling of Contradictions among the People*, Mao says, "In our country, the contradiction between the working class and the national bourgeoisie is a contradiction among the people. The class struggle waged between the two is, by and large, a class struggle within the ranks of the people."[25] Marxists-Leninists have maintained that temporary, tactical compromises with the bourgeoisie are frequently necessary in the course of the "democratic" revolution but have insisted that such compromises must be temporary because the "contradiction" between the proletariat and the bourgeoisie is basically, and in the long run, antagonistic, especially during the "socialist" revolution and construction. Mao, however, says not only that temporary compromises are necessary during the "democratic" revolution, but also that even during the "socialist" revolution an alliance can be sustained with a section of the bourgeoisie, as they are not to be counted among the enemy. We can agree with Sun Ting-kuo that "never before in history has this been written during the stage of socialist revolution."[26]

On second consideration, however, it appears that Mao owes his own theorists a heavy debt for the claim of originality. Sun

[24] Pang Tzu-nien, "Some Thoughts on Chairman Mao's Theory of Two Kinds of Contradictions Viewed from the Marxist Theory of State," *Che-hsüeh Yen-chiu*, No. 3, June 15, 1958.

[25] Mao, *On the Problem of the Correct Handling . . .*, p. 4.

[26] Sun Ting-kuo, "A Tremendous Development of the Law . . . ," p. 16.

Ting-kuo says, "Regarding the contradiction between China's bourgeoisie and the working class, Chairman Mao brilliantly expounded the view that this contradiction has an antagonistic aspect and a non-antogonistic aspect." But on this matter, Mao had merely *selected* one of four positions arrived at by various top-level Chinese Communist theorists during a conference sponsored by the Philosophical Research Office, Academy of Sciences, China. The conference, held in 1956 on October 22 and 23, bore the marks of a lengthy debate in the Soviet Union which had been sparked by Stepanyan's article: the subject was identical, but adapted to China's special conditions. Among the theorists who presented their views were Kuan Feng, Feng Ting, Ho Wei, Su Hsing, and Ai Ssu-ch'i. Discussing the "nature of the bourgeoisie–working class contradiction during China's transition period," the theorists arrived at four different positions:

> 1. That the bourgeoisie–working class contradiction during China's transition is of a dual nature, including antagonistic and non-antagonistic contradiction.
>
> 2. That this contradiction is basically non-antagonistic; but that there is an aspect in which antagonism is unavoidable. The method of peaceful transformation is basically non-antagonistic, but it includes an aspect of antagonism in solving this contradiction.
>
> 3. That the contradiction is antagonistic, but antagonistic contradiction can be solved by non-antagonistic methods.
>
> 4. That the contradiction is antagonistic and the method of solving it is also antagonistic.[27]

What is the extent of Mao's originality on the matter of the contradiction between the bourgeoisie and the working class? It is merely that he appears to have selected the second position and incorporated it into his June, 1957, work.

[27] "Statement of the Editorial Board," *Che-hsüeh Yen-chiu*, No. 4, August, 1957.

### *Mao's Liberalization*

It is on more practical matters that Mao's February, 1957, speech and the June essay (revised) based on it show real originality. In his effort to gain the lost confidence of Chinese intellectuals and to rectify bureaucratic practices of CCP cadres, Mao discarded at least one theory, one fiction. Mao explicitly rejected the Communist fiction that there could be no contradiction between the Communist party and the populace, between the "government and the masses . . . between those in position of leadership and the led." [28]

The first time this fiction came under attack by Mao was in a published dicussion of an enlarged CCP politburo meeting. On April 5, 1956, the Chinese leaders made their first comment on de-Stalinization and its shock-effect, particularly after Khrushchev's "secret speech" in February. The Chinese comment, printed in the Peking *Jen-min Jih-pao* under the title "On the Historical Experience of the Dictatorship of the Proletariat," contained the objectionable statement that "the existence of contradictions between the individual and the collective in a socialist society is nothing strange." The statement was objectionable to Moscow not because it was false, which obviously it was not, but because it was unprecedented in Communist literature. It exposed a long-standing Communist fiction as just that. It was not profound; it was elementary common sense.

Furthermore, it was objectionable to Moscow because the Chinese chose to apply it to all "socialist" countries, once again bypassing the Russians and implicitly rejecting Moscow as the only source of doctrine for Communist-led nations. Khrushchev was compelled to state publicly that Mao's thesis was not applicable to the USSR, but he was careful not to name Mao.

Theoretically, it was quite in line with de-Stalinization. Ten-

[28] Mao, *On the Problem of the Correct Handling . . .*, p. 4.

sion between the leaders and the led, and "democratic" ways of easing this tension, as well as tension between the bourgeoisie and the working class, direct policy away from dogmatic concepts of class struggle sustained under "socialism" and toward moderation. Crude methods of handling deviation must be avoided. The April 5, 1956, comment stated that a major mistake in the CCP's early years had resulted from a crude application, by dogmatists (not Mao), of Stalin's dictum that middle-of-the-road forces must be smashed. In consequence, "instead of isolating the real enemy we had isolated ourselves." The point was made that the middle-of-the-road forces which the party had erroneously attacked before Mao became its leader were the national bourgeoisie and the "democratic" parties—the groups which represent the majority of China's intellectuals. The leaders must pay attention to winning over non-Communist intellectuals as well as the masses by persuasion.

The April, 1956, comment apparently was intended in part to be viewed as another sign of the party's willingness to permit a sector of intellectual life to go on without the degree of interference which had characterized Stalin's leadership of the Soviet Union. It contained passages—such as the one on combining centralized power with "democracy"—which seemed designed to encourage the intelligentsia to believe that the regime should be viewed as authoritarian but not totalitarian. That is, it was to be viewed as a dictatorship which could not hope for *total* standardization of thought "among the people" because contradictions would continue to exist "between idealism and materialism in a socialist society and even in a Communist society . . . ; there will still be people with comparatively correct thinking and others with comparatively incorrect thinking." The fanatical view that all people will have "correct" thoughts under Communism was thus discarded by Mao in the spring of 1956.

By thus denying the perfectability of human nature which had been implicit in Marxist-Leninist doctrine on the Communist society, Mao (assuming Mao played a major role in outlining the April, 1956, comment) developed a new gloss in doctrine. This gloss and the statement that "the existence of contradictions between the individual and the collective in a socialist society is nothing strange" apparently were viewed as unorthodox by the Soviet leaders and unacceptable on the grounds mentioned above. They were omitted from *Pravda*'s April 7 reprint of the comment.

On May 2, 1956, in an unpublished speech, Mao took another step along the road to resolving contradictions "among the people" with moderation. He called on the party and the government to relax the rigid strictures under which intellectuals had been working in the arts and sciences, and epitomized the new line in an eight-character couplet—"Let all the flowers bloom, let various schools of thought contend." This "slogan" was written in the classical Chinese style partly to evoke enthusiasm among the intellectuals and partly to display Mao's facility with the history of Chinese philosophy. It was this unpublished speech which inaugurated Mao's "liberalization."

Mao's lieutenants expanded on his view of "liberalization." Propaganda chief Lu Ting-i, addressing a gathering of Communist party members, natural and social scientists, doctors, writers, and artists on May 26, set forth the CCP's new policy toward work in the sciences and the arts. Lu authorized and encouraged the expression of divergent views, noting, in Maoist language, that the arts could not advance "if there is 'only one flower in bloom'" and that China's history has shown "stagnation" in the sciences to be the result of repressed discussion. He went on to provide a shelter for intellectuals with independent—but not antiparty—ideas by stating that ideological struggle "among the people" must be "rigidly distinguished" from the struggle against the counterrevolutionaries. He stated that any attempt to solve the struggle between backward idealism and progressive materialism with "administrative orders" cannot be effective. Only through "open debates" can materialism "gradually" overcome idealism. This line was to be insisted upon by Mao in the spring of 1957 despite signs that the CCP was being criticized by the intellectuals — at first implicitly and then openly.

In further explaining Mao's liberalization, Lu seemed to suggest that scientists would not be compelled to write confessions against their *professional* convictions. They would be permitted to reply to criticisms of their ideas on academic matters without fear of being intimidated into silence by "the method of administrative order." The general principle that the minority must follow the majority must no longer be applied in non-political, scientific debates, Lu noted in his speech of May 26:

> The minority who believe in something different should be allowed to retain their own views, and the principle of making the minority yield to the majority must not be enforced. After due criticism and discussion, those who make mistakes on academic problems must not be forced to write articles to review their mistakes if they themselves are not willing. In academic circles, if a different view is brought up after a certain academic problem has been closed, such a view should still be allowed to be discussed.

Lu's conclusion is thus that all honest workers in the arts and sciences should be free from political attack by CCP fanatics. Lu proposed that on political matters, subtle appraisals rather than catch-all condemnations should be made, for it is necessary to distinguish between a political idealist who is counterrevolutionary and an idealist who is "within the ranks of the people." The latter does not attack the regime.

Lu proposed that the form of criticism of intellectuals be changed from attempting to "kill with one blow" (reserved exclusively for counterrevolutionaries) to comradely advice:

> It is common for good men to make mistakes. Nobody in the world can be completely free from mistakes. Such mistakes must be rigidly distinguished from counter-

> revolutionary statements. Criticism of such mistakes should be well-intentioned, calm, and coolheaded; reasoning should take the whole matter into consideration and criticism should proceed only from unity with a view to reaching unity.

Lu was advocating a corrective method, free from the Stalinist-Beriyaist compulsion to shoot political opponents or dishonor their names. Yet he was implicitly defending the dead Soviet dictator and criticizing Khrushchev when he called for "coolheaded" criticism, as no man can be completely free from mistakes. Implying falsely that Mao Tse-tung had *always* been a lenient confessor to misguided comrades, Lu recommended as models the mild criticism which Mao had directed against Ch'en Shao-yü and Po Ku in the early 1940's and which the CCP politburo on April 5, 1956, had directed toward "Comrade Stalin . . . who had more merits than mistakes." This form of balanced criticism was Maoist in that it was "neither overdone nor undercooked" and was designed to "benefit many people." Applied to intellectuals "who work honestly," tolerance should be basic in the party's approach, for it is "impossible" to carry out "creative work without committing mistakes."

Mao's new "liberal" attitude toward artists and scientists as well as other intellectuals was put into effect only gradually in China throughout 1956. There were indications that the policy was opposed by certain important members of the CCP leadership. Liu Shao-ch'i may have been the most important of these. In his report to the Eighth Congress of the CCP in mid-September, 1956, Liu expressed support for Mao's "hundred flowers" policy but warned of the danger that the intellectuals' bourgeois ideas would "corrupt the ranks of the proletariat." Unlike Chou En-lai in January, 1956, Liu did not encourage recruitment of intellectuals for party membership, and, unlike Lu Ting-i in May, 1956, he left no room for criticism of Communist doctrine. This relatively conservative interpretation of Mao's "liberalization" policy may have been merely a reflection of Liu Shao-ch'i's role in maintaining politically reliable party ranks and therefore merely the kind of statement a party watchdog was expected by Mao to make. In any case, "hundred flowers" received a temporary setback in the fall of 1956 during the Eighth Congress of the CCP and again in November and December following the developments in Poland and Hungary.

The developments in Eastern Europe led Mao to participate in a second major comment on de-Stalinization and its consequences. The Chinese leaders, having encouraged the Poles and Hungarians in the summer of 1956 and having, as a result, *exacerbated rather than mitigated* feelings of national independence and the desire for polycentrism (to use Togliatti's term), were compelled to reverse their course somewhat and support Moscow. In a politburo discussion, which was published in the Peking *Jen-min Jih-pao* on December 29, 1956, in an article entitled "More on the Historical Experience of the Dictatorship of the Proletariat," the Chinese leaders rejected key features of Yugoslav domestic and foreign policy and made clear to the Poles (who later stated that they had been double-crossed by Mao) that the Chinese — while supporting Polish party independence within the bloc — did not approve all features of Gomulka's liberalization.

It was in this second major politburo article that the second attack on the fiction of no tension between leaders and led under "socialism" appeared. The article stated that among the various non-antagonistic contradictions, there was the contradiction "between the government and the people in socialist countries." This is identical with the statement made by Mao in his article of June, 1957.

Whether Mao was really the author of the April 5 and December 29, 1956, statements is conjectural. As part of their effort to undercut Moscow's implicit attacks on Mao and his "personality cult," the Chinese leaders apparently intended the published version of the discussions to appear as the *collective* opinion of the politburo. Mao is not mentioned once in either of the long politburo statements, but it was implied that the CCP had made no mistakes in policy since Mao took over the effective leadership in 1935. In any case, Mao was probably the final arbiter, if not the author, of the politburo statements which contained the remarks on the leaders-led contradiction.

Prior to Mao's February, 1957, speech, his campaign to mollify and gain the confidence of non-Communist intellectuals apparently had come under attack within China. The campaign, initiated by Chou En-lai's January, 1956, speech to intellectuals and carried along by Mao himself and Lu Ting-i in May as "hundred flowers," was openly criticized by some party members as "harmful to the cause of socialism." This bold complaint earned several critics among the party's literature and art cadres a stinging rebuke administered by "culture" boss, Mao Tun:

> Criticisms that have been made of the "Hundred Flowers and Hundred Schools of Thought" line give the impression that this line can be more harmful than beneficial. It has splashed cold water in the face of intellectuals, who are inspired and animated by the new line.[29]

Mao Tun was not the only one to respond. In his February speech, Mao Tse-tung himself, reading from notes, had swept aside all party critics and opened the door for direct criticism of the CCP. Despite warnings from within the CCP, Mao's liberalization went well beyond the de-Stalinization policy instituted by other bloc leaders. According to textual extracts of the four-hour speech which appeared in the *New York Times* on June 13, 1957, and which are "absolutely authentic" in the opinion of Sidney Gruson, Mao warned members of the CCP to brace themselves for non-Communist criticism:

> Marxism-Leninism is not afraid of criticism and does not fear discussion. . . . Marxism-Leninism must come

[29] Peking *Jen-min Jih-pao,* March 18, 1957.

> out to meet criticism head on because only in this way can it be strengthened and become a really great power and not a new religion or taboo. . . . The opinions *against the policy of "Hundred Flowers"* are the result of fear of criticism, fear of losing the monopolistic position. Marx never said that he should not be criticized. To those who do not follow the teaching of Marx, I would address an old saying: "He who does not allow himself to be criticized during his life, will be criticized after his death."[30]

Mao made one of the major mistakes of his later years when he insisted in this way that the CCP open itself to verbal assaults from non-party critics.

The Soviet doctrine of "criticism and self-criticism" has been interpreted in many ways by various Communist leaders. It had been designated by A. Zhdanov as the new source of social development under "socialism." But criticism had always been of one party member by another and not of the *whole* party. No Communist leader in a position of authority prior to Mao (1957) had called for all non-Communists, for the whole intelligentsia, to engage in criticism of *the Communist party in toto*, and neither does Stepanyan in his discussion of how to use "criticism and self-criticism" to solve contradictions in a "socialist" society.

Thus, in addition to his statement that there is a conflict or contradiction between the leaders and the led even under "socialism," Mao's encouragement of criticism of *the entire CCP* from without and by the whole intelligentsia for the purpose of "party rectification" is unprecedented in Communist literature and practice. These ideas have no Soviet paternity and they represent Mao's contribution (in the face of implicit Soviet opposition as well as internal, CCP complaints) to the Communist discussion of contradictions under "socialism."

Mao's encouragement of criticism was for the specific purpose

[30] Sidney Gruson, Dispatch from Warsaw, *New York Times*, June 13, 1957 (emphasis supplied).

of preventing non-antagonistic contradictions between leaders and led from becoming antagonistic. Regarding one aspect of the practical matter of permitting criticism of the CCP from without and by the whole intelligentsia, Mao apparently emphasized in his speech the value of open disputes between Communists and non-Communists. According to the version of the original text available to Drew Middleton,[31] Mao suggested two consecutive courses. The first was to let disputes be carried on, if both sides wanted them. The second was to permit such disputes to reach their end rather than "smothering" them halfway, even if this meant permitting the disputes to go on for days until the matter was settled. In this way, non-Communist and Communist "schools of thought contended" against each other.

In 1957 there were many indications that Moscow disapproved of Mao's policy of "many schools." Among these indications was the subtle alteration of the slogan by a Soviet scholar who said that people in the USSR look with interest at the Chinese policy of permitting "many scholars" to contend.

In the June, 1957, version of his February speech, Mao reiterated his statement that Marxism can be criticized. But he added six criteria (not in his February speech) as the basis for such criticism, two of which were designed to prevent any significant political attacks on the party. "Words and actions can be judged right if they: . . . (2) are beneficial, not harmful, to socialist transformation and socialist construction, and . . . (5) tend to strengthen, not to cast off or weaken, the leadership of the Communist party."[32] Mao says that of the six criteria these two are "the most important." He then says that the criteria were put forward "in order to foster and not hinder the free discussion of various questions among the people." In making this statement in June, 1957, he was, of course, aware that free discussion would thereafter exclude any political matters. The addition of

[31] Drew Middleton, Dispatch from London, *New York Times*, May 29, 1957.
[32] Mao, *On the Problem of the Correct Handling . . .*, p. 25.

these criteria was, as a Western observer remarked at the time, as if Moses, in reviewing his works for publication, had casually inserted the Ten Commandments.

From this reversal it was only a step to the conclusion that his original concept of "Hundred Flowers" was a dismal failure. But Mao has seemed reluctant to admit this, and even today the slogan "Hundred Flowers" is retained partly to demonstrate continuity and to deny that failure.

To return to Mao's original February, 1957, speech: in attacking bureaucratic practices of CCP cadres, he makes another innovation in the statement that "small" strikes against the Communist authorities would be tolerated. In the version reported by Mr. Gruson from Warsaw, Mao says:

> Internal antagonisms should be dealt with as soon as they appear. But what to do if this is hampered by bureaucracy, which in turn leads to demonstrations and strikes? Such incidents should be considered as warning signals to sectors of the administration where bureaucracy has made its nest.
>
> In this respect, it can even be said that *small strikes are beneficial* because they point to mistakes committed. Of course, big general strikes cannot be considered in the same way because they are not fought to rectify mistakes or to satisfy rightful grievances, but are directed against the regime itself.[33]

Mao goes on to say that "persuasion" rather than reprisals or force should be used to dissuade workers from using the "method of small strikes."

The same was to hold true for strikes by students. When Tientsin University students went on strike in late 1956 to protest the extension of university courses by a year, CCP activists are said to have talked to the students "for three days and three nights," resolving the dispute by conciliation, that is, by agreeing to abol-

[33] Gruson, *loc. cit.*, June 13 (emphasis supplied).

ish the extension.[34] As Mao is said to have put it, the proper conclusion for a dispute was either that those who raised the initial argument understood they were mistaken or that *errors on the part of the authorities were exposed and corrected*.[35] Mao's concern here was with "rectifying" bureaucracy among CCP cadres in order to prevent further strikes.

It was, of course, the Polish press rather than the Soviet press which reported with approval this professed willingness of Mao to show a degree of tolerance for small strikes and resolve them by means of persuasion and conciliation. Moscow remained silent on the matter. The Poles were to learn at a later date that in June, 1957, Mao had changed his mind about these strikes.

Three of Mao's innovations — open acknowledgment that conflicts exist at times between leaders and the led in "socialist" countries, encouragement of criticism of the CCP by non-Communists and the whole intelligentsia, and toleration of small strikes and their resolution through conciliation — constituted an implicit rebuke of Soviet methods. Mao criticized Stalin for his "rule of terror and liquidation of thousands of Communists," and went on to make a more generalized statement of Soviet experience in a condescending manner:

> The Soviet Union has many experiences that can be used for the benefit of our country, especially in regard to industrial progress. But other experiences of the Soviet Union cannot be neglected and we have to consider them if only not to repeat the mistakes.[36]

Mao's statements in this vein were, of course, flattering neither to the memory of Stalin (whom he has treated strangely, at times

[34] *New York Times*, May 19, 1957.

[35] Middleton, *op. cit.* Mao retained much of this view in his revised speech of June, 1957. He stated that in order to avoid "disturbances," bureaucracy must first be stamped out. "If disturbances should occur as a result of bad work on our part, then we should guide those involved in such distubances on the correct path" and take a lesson in order to "improve our work" (*On the Problem of the Correct Handling* . . . , p. 28).

[36] Gruson, *loc. cit.*, June 13.

implying praise and at times condemnation) nor to the post-Stalin Soviet leadership. Furthermore, they did nothing to discourage feelings of nationalism among the restive anti-Stalinists in the bloc who, like Mao, wanted to avoid Soviet "mistakes." There appears to be little real difference between these statements and anti-Stalinist statements on Soviet "mistakes" made by Gomulka in 1956 and 1957. The fact that Mao, too, in 1956 and 1957 accepted Moscow's criticism of Stalin, with only the minor reservation that it not to be too negative, is a matter he now tries to conceal.

### *Mao's "Realism"*

During liberalization and party "rectification" in 1957, Mao apparently was anxious to prove to the Communist bloc and neutrals that in China a moderate attitude could be adopted by the CCP toward non-Communists without the drastic repercussions of a "Hungary." He was in a cocky mood. In his February speech, Mao played the role of teacher, and probably thought himself a good one, much better than his contemporaries in other Communist parties. In discussing the kinds of contradictions which might drive a wedge between the "masses and the leaders," Mao says:

> The leaders must show great farsightedness in noticing and solving these contradictions by the proper methods and in the right time. Those leaders who will not take notice of these contradictions or who will not be able to solve them by a proper method are threatened by serious political danger. And this may happen because not only do they not keep up with the course of history, but also because the high positions they hold may incline them to subjectivity and cause them to be blind to reality.[37]

[37] Gruson, Dispatch from Warsaw, *New York Times*, June 16, 1957 (continues dispatch of June 13).

Mao seems to have designed this Socratic homily partly as a warning to CCP cadres during party "rectification" and partly as an indirect means of saying to other Communist leaders in the bloc that he, Mao, is not one (like Stalin) to be "blind to reality."

Mao believed that he was being realistic in acknowledging the "leaders-led" contradiction and permitting, even encouraging, open criticism of the party. In the Gruson version of his February speech, he states two reasons for continuing his "Hundred Flowers" policy. First, know your enemy:

> There need be no fear that the policy of "Hundred Flowers" will yield poisoned fruit. Sometimes it is necessary even to have this poisoned fruit to know what it is we are fighting against. For this reason, too, it has been decided to publish the full works of Chiang Kai-shek and even a volume of some of the Voice of America broadcasts. It is not enough to attack reactionaries. We must know exactly what the reactionaries want and what they represent.[38]

When, during the question and answer session, an incredulous listener asked if it were "really necessary" to publish Chiang's works and VOA broadcasts, Mao gave a second reason for "Hundred Flowers," toughen your forces:

> The new generation, which did not fight face to face with imperialism and reactionaries, must know why we are calling on them to continue that fight. And another reason. We cannot breed flowers in a hothouse. Such flowers will be neither beautiful or healthy. We must strengthen and harden them if their fruits are to be lasting.[39]

Was Mao more realistic than his incredulous and apprehensive questioner? Inasmuch as "Hundred Flowers" was a fiasco, providing intellectuals with a means of undermining the authority

[38] Gruson, *loc. cit.*, June 13.
[39] *Ibid.*

of the CCP and even of Mao himself, it would seem that—from a Communist point of view—the questioner was right and Mao was wrong: "Hundred Flowers," as implemented between late February and early June, 1957, was a mistake.

The decisive test for Mao's realism or lack of it, however, would not be his decision in 1956 *to begin* a free criticism policy,[40] but whether he would persist in it if it were clearly a failure. Apparently out of conceit and obstinacy, he did indeed insist, for a time, that the policy be sustained and made even more liberal despite signs of danger to CCP prestige. For Mao's name had been directly associated with "Hundred Flowers" and he and his policy were admired in some parts of the bloc and the free world. To halt the "Hundred Flowers" was to admit personal failure. Stalin was not know for admission of personal failure and neither is Mao.

Nevertheless, it was only a pretense of "Hundred Flowers" which was sustained after June, 1957. When it was suggested to Chou En-lai—who had established the "soft" line on liberalization with Mao—by a foreign student that the CCP's action in calling a halt to free criticism in June, 1957, contradicted Mao's idea of "Hundred Flowers," Chou snapped that it was not a contradiction at all: "Hundred Flowers" continues—but why should enemies of "socialism" be permitted to speak?

The image of Mao which emerges from these developments in 1957 is that of a leader who bends theory to fit his view of what is needed on the practical level. Beyond doubt, his view of what is needed on the practical level is sometimes obscured and distorted

[40] This does not deny that Mao, like several leaders in the bloc, overestimated the degree of popular support the regime had at the time. Mao's decision to push ahead with "liberalization" apparently was based on his estimate that the populace in general and the intellectuals in particular supported the CCP. In his original February speech, he says: "The CCP now has 12,000,000 members. This is a percentage lower than that of many other countries, but it is not the figures that count. The Hungarian party had a percentage much higher, but the people refused to follow it; the party disintegrated in two days" (Gruson, *loc. cit.*, June 16).

(partly by conceit). Nonetheless, Mao in 1957 gave theory second place to practical policy.

Mao was not really serious about the *theoretical* concept of non-antagonism in contradiction. For example, he manipulated this concept in a rather flippant way. In the Gruson version of his February speech, he says:

> . . . it is possible that the enemy-nation type of contradiction may evolve into a non-antagonistic type of contradiction. For instance, this would happen if Chiang Kai-shek would return Taiwan to People's China. In that case, it would become a purely internal matter of People's China and the differences would be of a non-antagonisitc type.[41]

Thus, for reasons of state, Mao removes the idea of non-antagonism from the theoretical level, showing how it can be twisted and reduced to a tool of policy, and a very convenient tool indeed, since it is he who decides what is non-antagonistic and what is not.

The Mao of 1957 attempted to storm the fortress of originality once again as he had attempted in previous years, and he did not try half-heartedly. In his February, 1957, speech, Mao leaves the great names of Communism in his wake:

> These problems [of contradictions in "socialist" society] are new in Marxism-Leninism. Marx and Engels did not know about these problems for obvious reasons. Lenin mentioned them but did not enlarge upon them because during his lifetime, as a result of foreign intervention, it was difficult to speak about internal problems only.
>
> As for Stalin, his opinions can be considered only with disapproval. The experience of the Soviet Union in this respect shows that Stalin made the mistake of substituting internal differences for external antagonism, which resulted in a rule of terror and the liquidation of thousands of Communists.[42]

[41] Gruson, *loc. cit.*, June 16.
[42] Gruson, *loc. cit.*, June 13.

It is in this way that Mao cleared his own path to originality. And when, following the speech, his eulogists searched every sentence for an unique idea, it appeared that even Lenin was by contrast a novice on the matter of contradictions under "socialism." Thus in March, 1957, Ou-yang Yu-ching says that Lenin "had spoken of the disappearance of antagonism and the continued existence of contradiction. But no one has, with Chairman Mao's clarity, set forth the concept that we should acknowledge the existence for a long time of contradictions among the people."[43]

### *Mao's Positions Discarded*

That Mao went too far for a Communist (and that he is determined not to go so far again) in his liberalization policy of 1956–57 is indicated by the fact that three of his four innovations are not discussed by Chinese writers today. That is, of the four (leader-led contradiction, non-Communist criticism of the CCP, toleration of small strikes, and the non-antagonistic contradiction between the national bourgeoisie and the working class) only the last one remains as an acceptable matter for discussion. The revived "Hundred Flowers" of 1961 is not the "Hundred Flowers" of 1957. "Debate" is permitted only on academic subjects. The discussion of political subjects which is fostered at the "meetings of immortals" (*shen-hsien hui*) is just that—it is *fostered*, guided, and controlled in order to prevent the "negative" criticisms of 1957 from reappearing.[44]

In his June, 1957, retreat from experimenting with liberalization, Mao also went too far, in the view of at least one kind of

[43] Ou-yang Yu-ching, "Several Thoughts on Hearing Chairman Mao's Report," Peking *Jen-min Jih-pao*, March 19, 1957.

[44] For a good discussion of the revived "Hundred Flowers" policy, see Dennis J. Doolin, "The Revival of the 'Hundred Flowers' Campaign: 1961," *China Quarterly*, No. 8, October–December, 1961. For an analysis of the original 1956–57 campaign and for the relevant documentary materials from Chinese Communist publications, see Roderick MacFarquhar, *The Hundred Flowers Campaign and the Chinese Intellectuals* (New York: Praeger, 1960).

Communist. Mao came remarkably close to giving a public demonstration of the validity of Trotsky's analysis of the nature *of bureaucratic-power rule* in the Soviet Union. In his *The Revolution Betrayed* (1937), Trotsky had argued that the Bol'shevik revolution of 1917 overthrew the power of all classes—other than that of the new Bol'shevik bureaucracy—but failed to attain real "socialism" as Marx and Engels understood it. Therefore, said Trotsky, the Soviet bureaucracy was a unique type of class-rule:

> Caesarism arose upon the basis of a slave society shaken by inward strife. Bonapartism is one of the political weapons of the capitalist regime in its critical period. Stalinism is a variety of the same system, but upon the basis of a workers' state torn by the *antagonism between an organized and armed Soviet aristocracy and the unarmed toiling masses.*[45]

Now in his work *On the Problem of the Correct Handling of Contradictions Among the People*, Mao indicates which forces maintained the stability of the mainland regime during the Hungarian revolution and its effect in China and, implicitly, during the free criticism period of "Hundred Flowers." The "armed" Chinese aristocracy, to borrow from Trotsky, was the main force:

> Of course, the consolidation of our state is not primarily due to the suppression of counter-revolution. It is due primarily to the fact that we have a Communist Party and a Liberation Army steeled in decades of revolutionary struggle, as well as a working people that has been similarly steeled. Our party and our armed forces are rooted in the masses; they have been tempered in the flames of a protracted revolution; they are strong and they can fight.[46]

In the passage immediately preceding this one, Mao says that the "incident" in Hungary "caused some of our intellectuals *to lose*

[45] Leon Trotsky, *The Revolution Betrayed* (Garden City, N.Y.: Doubleday, 1937), p. 278 (emphasis supplied).

[46] Mao, *On the Problem of the Correct Handling . . .*, p. 13.

*their balance a bit* but there were no *squalls* in our country" (emphasis supplied). Despite the metaphoric language, this is a statement of the effectiveness of CCP control. At the same time, it is a comment on the degree to which intellectuals are tyrannized in China.

Mao's blunder lay in his belief that the intellectuals had been generally won over to Communist views by 1956 and that by "thought reform" man's mind could be changed. It was a blunder, perhaps natural in his position of despot isolated from many aspects of daily life in China, of mistaking obedience for love.

To sum up, Lenin maintained that "contradictions" would still exist in a "socialist" society, but that these would not be "antagonistic." Chinese theorists acknowledge this as Lenin's position, but point out that he did not develop this thought. Stalin's discussions of the concept, and developments of it by Soviet theorists after 1935, are also minimized by Peking. Chinese theorists allege that Mao applied the general theory of "contradictions" to the specific matter of production, developing the theory of a contradiction between productive forces and relations of production. Actually, Mao's pronouncements on this question made in 1957, do not differ from Stalin's, made in 1952. Neither Stalin nor Mao did anything more than assert that contradictions of this kind "cannot" be antagonistic—an assertion hardly worthy of being called a contribution to theory. Mao's only novel remark is that the contradiction between the national bourgeoisie and the workers can be solved without antagonism.

Mao's principal title to originality on "contradictions" is in respect to the more *practical political matters* on which Chinese writers enter no claim for him. That is, Mao in 1957 explicitly rejected the Communist fiction that there cannot be conflicts between the leaders and the led in a "socialist" society. Mao's encouragement in 1957 of criticism of the CCP from outside the party and by the whole intelligentsia was also unprecedented, as was his stated toleration of "small" strikes. Moscow, recognizing that these pragmatic political innovations constituted a rebuke to Soviet methods at the time, disapproved of all three of them. These departures from doctrine and Soviet practice proved embarrassing to Mao and are no longer openly discussed in China.

Mao made several bad miscalculations during "liberalization." First, in the summer and fall of 1956, he encouraged the Poles and Hungarians in their defiance of the Soviet leaders, contributing to rather than detracting from the swirl of polycentrism stemming from Khrushchev's de-Stalinization. When, therefore, Mao in November and December of 1956 turned temporarily to give some support to Khrushchev's effort to prevent further deterioration of Soviet authority in Eastern Europe, he was correcting his own mistake almost as much as Khrushchev's. Second, from the spring of 1956 to the summer of 1957, he had initiated and then persisted in a "liberalization" campaign in China which resulted in a loss of CCP prestige. He was warned; he could have halted the campaign before it got out of hand. Yet, in early 1957, he *insisted* on continuing it in an even more radical way, blinded by his own idea of "free" discussion and by personal vanity. In this sense, he was a victim of a fantasy—his own—and if during the "Hundred Flowers" period he looked at the real world, he saw it through a glass darkly.

# 6

# The "Transition to Communism": "People's Communes"

For a short period in 1958, Mao, then sixty-four years old, envisaged the advent of Communism in his lifetime. In mid-1958, after the Russians themselves had discussed various aspects of the final transition but could not decide how far off it was,[1] Mao apparently directed his writers to claim that the final transition was clearly at hand in China. One writer stated that the transition to full state ownership would be "completed in 3 or 4 years in some areas, while other areas might require 5 or 6 years, or a bit more."[2]

To look back at developments in China in 1958, it seems to

[1] The theoretical and practical problems connected with the "transition to Communism" were discussed June 23–26, 1958, at a conference held in Moscow by the Department of Social Sciences of the Academy of Sciences of the USSR. K. V. Astrovityanov and M. B. Mitin seem to have had different views on how far off full Communism was in the Soviet Union, the former being inclined to see it closer at hand than the latter. Cf. K. V. Ostrovityanov, "Theoretical Problems of Building Communism and the Tasks of the Social Sciences," *Pravda*, June 27, 1958, and M. B. Mitin, "The Role of Marxist-Leninist Ideology in the Building of Communism," *Pravda*, July 4, 1958.

[2] Ho Ch'ien, "Communism Is Not a Mystery," *Hsüeh-hsi*, September 10, 1958. When, in August, 1958, the people's commune program was set fully in motion, the Chinese deliberately blurred the distinction between the stages of "socialism" and Communism. A great deal of CCP discussion on this point was little more than an exercise in semantics, a word game in which it was possible to "advance toward Communism" before entering the formal stage of direct "transition to Communism."

have been Mao's intention to hurdle the big material-technical obstacle separating China from the "transition to Communism" by stressing the super-collectivism, the more primitive view of Communism, delineated in the classics of Marxism-Leninism. Mao's plan was to downgrade the importance of the productive forces—that is, a highly *industrialized* economy—as the main precondition for Communism by calling for the establishment of new relations of production—that is, a highly *collectivized* economy.

The organizational form which would enable China to make the transition to super-collectivism was the "people's commune" with its "buds of Communism" in (1) the public mess halls and (2) the partial wage–partial free supply system for providing basic living necessities. What China lacked in highly advanced industry would be provided by near-primitive "indigenous" industry and, more importantly, by the superior collective organization as well as the psychological attributes of a highly developed political consciousness in the Chinese people. Unlike the Russian, the Chinese, Mao apparently believed, had attained the goal of accepting the "spirit" of Communism: "I am for all, and all are for me." [3]

Unlike many utopians of the eighteenth and nineteenth centuries, however, Mao is a Communist of the Marxist-Leninist faith, which means that he tried to redefine utopia in terms of reality. Moreover, as a Chinese, he has a highly developed time-sense, which has made him think of China's superiority over all other countries in two dimensions: historically and futuristically. With this sense, combined with a strong feeling of his own importance in Communist history, it was for Mao only a small step from extending China's superiority beyond the confines sought for it by the Soviet leaders to attaining full Communism before the Soviet Union. Thus Mao's view of this historical enterprise points up the

[3] Peking *Kung-jen Jih-pao*, October 14, 1958.

duality of his thinking. On the utopian level, Mao in mid-1958 apparently was completely convinced that the mentality of most Chinese on the mainland showed sufficient intensity of "socialist" consciousness to enable them to leap beyond the selfish motives which so many philosophers throughout the centuries have attributed to all men. On the realistic level, Mao believed that if they were not quite ready to make this leap by themselves, their consciousness could be rigorously "organized" by the regime's cadres.

By substituting highly "conscious" and regimented manpower in the "people's communes" for tractors and other modern agricultural machinery, Mao attempted to move to a higher level of collectivized relations of production before China had attained highly developed productive forces.

In defending Mao's plan against Chinese and Soviet critics in November, 1959, theorist Ch'en Cheng-liang first stated that "right opportunists" complain that China has few tractors and a backward agricultural technology and therefore "lacks a material base" and fully developed productive forces for pressing on to the super-collectivism of people's communes. He then conceded that the "level of China's agricultural productive forces is still low at present," but insisted: "It does not follow from this that we can begin revolutionary activity only when the productive forces have reached a very high level and material conditions are fully prepared."[4] Ch'en went on to stress the "decisive" importance of relations of production — people's communes — over the productive forces. He asserted that the people's communes show the "superiority" of the relations over the forces, and the role they play in influencing the forces. To the question, Why were people's communes established? Ch'en replied:

[4] Ch'en Cheng-liang, "The People's Commune Is a Necessary Product of China's Political and Economic Development," *Hsin Chien-she* (New Construction), November 7, 1959.

> Upon discovering that the higher agricultural cooperatives did not meet the demand for development of productive forces, the party and Chairman Mao led the peasants to improve further the relations of production [by forming people's communes]. . . . The party and Chairman Mao discovered this form of social organization to develop China's productive forces.

In their criticism of Mao's view on people's communes, Soviet theorists centered their attention on the matter of the material-technical backwardness of China's economy. They implied that Mao's view was a departure from the "real" — but not Stalin's — economic laws of "socialism" and Communism, and insisted that higher levels of collectivization in the relations of production must await the construction of an advanced industrial economy. According to Soviet theorists, the drive toward a qualitatively new degree in the development of the material-technical basis of the economy had been downgraded by Stalin, and Mao (by implication) followed along in this "error."

In his *Economic Problems of Socialism in the USSR* of 1952, Stalin had placed his emphasis on the relations of production and condemned the hapless economist Yaroshenko for overrating the role of the productive forces. Regarding new relations of production, Stalin laid it down that they are

> the *chief and decisive* force which in fact determines the further and, moreover, mighty development of productive forces, and without which the productive forces are doomed to stagnate. . . . the role of new relations of production is that of the main driving power for the further development of the productive forces.[5]

When, therefore, Mao stressed the relations of production in the economic base — that is, stressed the people's communes — as the

[5] Stalin, *Economic Problems of Socialism in the USSR*, p. 13 (emphasis supplied).

source providing the decisive motive power for China's transition to Communism, he used an emphasis similar to Stalin's.

That it is Stalin's emphasis of 1952 on the relations of production (as well as Mao's) which Khrushchev apparently has directed his writers to attack is indicated by, among other things, the Soviet discussion of the economic "laws of transition to Communism" in the spring of 1962.[6] Stalin's alleged rejection of the idea that in order to build Communism there must be fundamental changes in the productive forces had already been extensively attacked in 1961. One Russian theorist in that year criticized Stalin for using the expediency of "administrative and organizational matters connected with circulation and distribution" in his *Economic Problems* to solve the most complicated problems involved in the transition to Communism, characterizing Stalin's path as "utopian and harmful." He pointed to Stalin's failure to emphasize production:

> It is not accidental that the absence of a program for increasing agricultural production up to a level necessary for a transition to Communism is combined in *Economic Problems* with an unjustifiable *running ahead* in the sphere of distribution and social relations. . . .
>
> The [new] Program of the CPSU organically combines measures for the development of the productive forces in the countryside which provide for an abundance of agricultural products with measures for transforming socialist social relationships into Communist ones. *Here, the production tasks are viewed as the basis for solving the social tasks. . . .*
>
> In *Economic Problems* . . . problems involved in building communism . . . are viewed *without considering the determining role of production.* Their solution does not involve fundamental changes in the productive forces, technology, labor productivity, and the

[6] A. Pashkov, "The Economic Laws of the Building of Communism," *Kommunist*, No. 4, March 15, 1962.

> qualitative advances linked with this in the very character of social labor — in a word, *Economic Problems* avoids the main link which is the creation of the corresponding material and technical base.[7]

We do not fully accept the allegation of Stalin's critics that he had underrated in theory the role of the productive forces all along. He did so primarily in his last work, *Economic Problems,* the one work which has provided Khrushchev and his writers with a club to pillory Stalin (and, by implication, Mao). The point is that with the precedent of *Economic Problems* before him, there was really no original thinking involved in Mao's stress on the relations of production.

There is no indication that Mao in 1958 was concerned with the philosophical aspects of production. That is, he did not discuss "historical materialism" as hinged to the productive forces (which would have led him back to "mechanism") or to the relations of production (which would have led him away from historical materialism). He seems merely to have singled out one point in the Stalinist corpus of writing — the relations of production — and stressed it in a practical context. By isolating, as Stalin had in 1952, the economic relations rather than forces, he was describing a more primitive version of Communism than were Khrushchev's theorists. But in the final analysis, all talk about whether the productive forces should have the key role in determining relations of production became superfluous, as it was Mao who really determined these relations in China.

## *The Communist Aspect of "People's Communes"*

Chinese theorists discussing Mao's people's communes in 1958 pointed to several features, designated "buds of Communism" — Lenin's phrase from *A Great Beginning* (June, 1919) — which

[7] L. Gatovskiy, "The Scientific Basis for Building the Economy of Communism," *Kommunist,* No. 17, mid-November, 1961 (emphasis supplied).

were to put China ahead of the Soviet Union on the road to Communism. These were as follows:

> (1) the twofold system of "free supply" (distribution "according to need") and of wages (distribution still "according to work");
> (2) the public mess halls, nurseries, kindergartens, and rural "housing estates";
> (3) ownership by "all the people" — that is, the state — in rural areas;
> (4) integration of *hsien* (township) government with the commune;
> (5) establishment of a commune militia; and
> (6) elimination of the difference between town and country, worker and peasant, and mental and manual labor.

As precedents for most of these concepts, Chinese theorists in 1958 cited many classical texts, including *Lectures at Elberfeld* (Engels, 1845), *Principles of Communism* (Engels, 1847), *Communist Manifesto* (Marx and Engels, 1847–48), *Anti-Dühring* (Engels, 1875), *Critique of the Gotha Program* (Marx, 1875), *Preface to Civil Wars in France* (Engels, 1891), *Report on the Rural Poor* (Lenin, 1903), *State and Revolution* (Lenin, 1917), *A Good Beginning* (Lenin, 1919), *Anarchism or Socialism?* (Stalin, 1906), *Dizzy with Success* (Stalin, 1930), and *Economic Problems of Socialism in the USSR* (Stalin, 1952). The list is much longer, but the above sample suggests the nature and extent of the scripture upon which the Chinese have drawn. Never before had the Chinese Communists felt compelled to establish the orthodoxy of one of Mao's innovations with so formidable an appeal to the classics. The Chinese apparently wanted to have it both ways for Mao: his commune concept is *within* the orthodox mainstream and yet it is novel; it draws on the classics and yet goes beyond them. Mao, they said, had wedded classical thought to contemporary fact in China. Actually, Mao and his lieutenants were almost certainly aware that a simpleminded — or unsophisticated

—fundamentalist case would build for them a strong position from which to fend off Soviet criticism of the commune program and of the claims for Mao.

In line with Engels' precedent, the Chinese also drew upon the ideas of the utopians of the sixteenth, eighteenth and nineteenth centuries.[8] The "utopian socialists" whose ideas they used included Thomas More, Morelly, Babeuf, Saint Simon, Fourier, and Owen —men who, according to Engels, were victims of fantasies but whose works "give us delight for their stupendously grand thoughts and germs of thought that everywhere break out through their fantastic covering."[9] "Stupendously grand thoughts"—or a single such thought—was the ingredient Mao used in 1958 to promote his view of the commune for China. He apparently tried to imitate the utopians' style and their complete dedication to a powerful idea. To paraphrase Engels, "socialism" was for all of them the expression of absolute truth, reason, and justice, and need only be discovered in order to conquer the world through its own power. It was with *the power of ideas* that Mao hoped to go ahead of the Soviet Union—utopian thoughts made realistic. These included utopian (or irrational) thoughts on ways to make man and soil more productive.

Thus Mao has made it easy, for anyone who cared, to trace the "Communist" aspects of his people's commune back either to the great names of Marxist thought or to the "utopian socialists," or both.[10] His case is simply that his views are closer to classical

[8] *On Communist Communes,* compiled in book form by the Basic Department of Marxism-Leninism of the Chinese People's University, Part 3 (Peking, July, 1958). The compilers caution their Chinese readers to be wary of these materials on the "utopian socialists," as the introductions to these classics were written by men "who were not necessarily progressive."

[9] Engels, *The Development of Socialism from Utopian to Scientific* (1876) (New York: International Publishers, 1945), p. 10.

[10] Marx and Engels seem to have derived some of their ideas on Communism from French revolutionaries of the eighteenth century. The first impulse, or the first definite notion of Communism as the economic ideal of human society, seems, in turn, to have been derived by the French revolutionary Gracchus Babeuf from a study of the work of an obscure author, about whom little is known.

doctrine than Khrushchev's and for this reason, among others, unassailable. That is, his unique view of what the classical commune should be is firmly rooted in accepted tradition.

### *The Claim for Mao*

What, then, is the Chinese Communist claim for Mao's creativeness and what is its validity? To begin with, Mao's chief eulogist, Ch'en Po-ta, writing in July, 1958, as the "people's commune" movement was getting underway, claimed that "Comrade Mao Tse-tung's thinking on the commune — which combines aspects of industry, agriculture, commerce, education, and the military — is a conclusion drawn from the experience of actual life." That is, the "conclusion" was reached by Mao independent of but not at variance with the views of the utopian and the "scientific socialists." It was, as Ch'en put it, conceived under Mao's own theoretical banner — the banner of the "creative development" of Marxism-Leninism in China. Ch'en's remarks were pervaded by this stress on the independence of Mao's new "conclusion" and on the warrant given for striking out boldly with original ideas: Marx, Engels, and Lenin "could not provide each country and nation with a detailed plan" and held that Marxist theory "should be enriched and developed uninterruptedly." Lenin in 1919 set new tasks and problems for Communists of the "East" to solve in the conditions of their native land. In China, Ch'en asserted, it was Mao himself who solved these problems "courageously and with extraordinary brilliance." [11]

---

His name was Morelly, and his work was published about 1755. See Ernest Belfort Bax, *The Last Episode of the French Revolution — Being a History of Gracchus Babeuf and the Conspiracy of the Equals* (Boston, 1911), pp. 77–135.

For a brief discussion of Soviet experience with rural communes and for an analysis of the Sino-Soviet dispute regarding Mao's people's communes, see Donald S. Zagoria, *The Sino-Soviet Conflict — 1956–1961* (Princeton, N.J.: Princeton University Press, 1962), Part 2.

[11] Ch'en Po-ta, "Under the Banner of Comrade Mao Tse-tung," *Hung Ch'i*, No. 4, July 16, 1958.

The next step in advancing the claim for Mao's originality was to pinpoint the precise feature of the "people's commune" which makes it novel. To do this, theorist Fan Hung in April, 1959, first conceded that Marx, Engels, Lenin, and Stalin had all made contributions to the theory of the commune.[12] In his *Principles of Communism*, for which the *Communist Manifesto* was substituted, Engels had predicted that the "citizens' commune"—similar to Mao's term, "people's commune"—would be the basic social unit of the future society of full Communism. Engels also outlined the plan for community housing and "collective living." Fan asserted that Marx concurred in Engels' views. As for Lenin and Stalin, they concentrated their attention on the "agricultural commune" as the social unit for Communism. Fan finally singled out the problem of *how* the collective ownership system is transformed into the system of "all people" (i.e., state) ownership as the realm in which Mao made his contribution.

Marx and Engels, Fan declared, had envisaged a utopian leap into "all-people" ownership without a prolonged transition from collective ownership. Lenin was not faced with the problem, "because he died before the kolkhozy had been established." As for Stalin, his prescription set forth in *Economic Problems* called for an advance to a system of "product exchange," but this, Fan insisted, "will not directly change the system of collective ownership." Mao's "new contribution," however, permitted a change to "all-people" ownership because his commune was a gigantic amalgam of heretofore collectively owned and operated socio-economic organizations of China. The point of originality was Mao's idea of *integrating and combining* industry, agriculture, commerce, education, and military affairs and the *consolidation* of township government into the administrative structure of a "people's commune." All organizations in the countryside moved

[12] Fan Hung, *Marx, Engels, Lenin, and Stalin on the Theory of Communism* (Peking, April, 1959), pp. 42–51.

simultaneously toward "all-people" ownership facilitated by the enormous scope of the integrating process.

We agree with Fan Hung that Mao's concept is novel. Although it has one or several features in common with Engels' citizens' commune, the nineteenth-century Russian peasant commune, the twentieth-century Soviet agricultural commune, and Khrushchev's agrogorads, in its entirety and as a gigantic amalgam of functions, Mao's "people's commune" is a unique socioeconomic-political-military unit. It had wider military competence than Engels' citizens' commune—at least in the early, utopian phase of the fall of 1958—and wider industrial and commercial competence than its Russian and Soviet Russian antecedents.

### *"Uninterrupted Revolution"*

In October, 1958, writer Ch'ih Liao-chou raised yet another claim for Mao's originality. Mao, he asserted, did not confine the theory of "uninterrupted revolution" to the rapid transition from bourgeois to "socialist" revolution, but also applied it to the *post-revolutionary* building of "socialism" and Communism:

> In accordance with the dialectical law of the development of things in which contradictions constantly arise and are constantly solved, Chairman Mao did not restrict the application of this Marxist-Leninist theory of uninterrupted revolution to the one point of democratic revolution changing into socialist revolution but . . . fully extended the application of this theory in order to guide the complete revolutionary movement of our country, including the new democracy revolution, socialist revolution, social construction and the transition from socialism to Communism.[13]

According to Ch'ih, the objects of this "uninterrupted revolution" in China were the relations of production "which are lagging

[13] Ch'ih Liao-chou, "Disseminate the Ideology of Communism," *Hsüeh-hsi*, No. 19, October 10, 1958.

behind the development of the productive forces and therefore interfering with the development of the productive forces." That is, the agricultural producers' cooperatives were retarding agricultual production, and a new, higher form of collectivism—the people's commune—would provide the best way to organize relations of production under the circumstances. There was no need to wait for mechanization before moving on to higher forms of collectivism, as regimented manpower—"the greatest labor army in the world"—could be substituted for agricultural machinery. The import of all this was that Mao allegedly was the first to carry the idea of "uninterrupted revolution" to the period following the conquest of state power.

Precisely at what point in the concept of "uninterrupted revolution" did Mao make an original contribution, if at all? To begin with, confusion exists about just what idea Mao is said to have developed further, "permanent revolution" or "uninterrupted revolution." Both have a history in the Communist movement.

"Permanent revolution" was, according to Bertram D. Wolfe,[14] a concept first set forth by the Russian revolutionary Parvus in the introduction to Trotsky's pamphlet *Before the Ninth of January* (1905). The theory in effect rejects the idea of a pause between the bourgeois revolution—when the capitalists consolidate their power after the overthrow of monarchy—and the "socialist" revolution. Trotsky used "permanent revolution" to mean that the proletariat begins by making a bourgeois revolution and continues it "in permanence" until it becomes a completely proletarian revolution. Trotsky, convinced that the proletariat was already on the scene and organized, felt they need not wait for the bourgeoisie to make their bourgeois revolution; he would have the proletariat make it for them. This would combine the bourgeois and the proletarian revolutions into a single process,

[14] Bertram D. Wolfe, *Three Who Made a Revolution* (New York: Dial, 1948), pp. 289 ff.

*dominated throughout by the proletariat.* Wolfe points out that in 1905 Lenin characterized this idea as an "absurd, semi-anarchist view" but that by 1917 he reversed his position and accepted it.

In addition to telescoping the bourgeois and the "socialist" revolutions, Trotsky used "permanent revolution" to insist that the proletarian revolution must not be confined to one country but must be extended to other countries. For in his original statement on this matter, Marx had laid it down in his *Address to the Communist League* (1850) that in contrast to the bourgeoisie, the proletariat makes the revolution "permanent" until it has conquered state power in all major countries.

Wolfe notes that in an effort to conceal the Trotsky-Parvus origin of the phrase, the Soviets under Stalin (and today) substitute the words "continuous revolution" for it. The term "continuous" seems to be used interchangeably with "uninterrupted" by the Russians and the Chinese. The Russians, however, have not used the term *together with* the word "revolution" to indicate internal social or political transformations, but Mao has so employed it.

An important Soviet economic textbook says: "Socialist economy develops uninterruptedly along an ascending curve and at a rapid rate, on the basis of proportions laid down by the socialist state in conformity with the requirements of the law of planned development of the national economy."[15] The word "revolution" does not appear. This passage, however, does point to the need to press along hard with the business of developing the national economy, and when his eulogists attribute creativity to Mao on this point, perhaps what they mean is that he called on the Chinese worker and peasant to press along *much harder and faster* than his Russian brother. If this is indeed part of the claim for Mao, it can hardly be assigned a place among his contributions to theory

[15] *Political Economy* (London, 1957), p. 560.

and practice. Lenin, in the 1920's (when he spoke of a "great leap" in production), and Stalin, in the 1930's, had pushed the peasants and workers with similar vigor.

Regarding the use of the word "revolution" where the Russians do not employ it, this too is not a contribution to theory or practice, but rather to verbal usage. In this sense, "uninterrupted revolution" is an artificial expedient that has more to do with the art of writing and expression than revolutionary changes.

In more practical matters, if Mao intended the unique aspect of his "uninterrupted revolution" idea to be the transformation of the social and political *simultaneously* with the economic instiutions of China, his argument would fall away under the precedent of drastic sociopolitical-economic changes in the Soviet Union under Lenin and Stalin.

Some claims for Mao on the idea of "uninterrupted revolution" concern primarily the matter of tempo. Thus writer Su Hsing in February, 1960, stated that Mao's ideas on economics ("uninterrupted leap forward," "walking on two legs," "taking the whole country to be a chessboard," "exerting energy reaching to the sky," etc.), "advance, in theory and practice, the theory of the high-speed development of the national economy."[16] The point of emphasis here seems to be unprecedented "high-speed' industrialization. But, as noted earlier, regarding this matter, Stalin had set a precedent requiring a rather grueling workpace. Actually, with the exception of the World War II period, Stalin's industrialization programs were more "uninterrupted" and rapid than Mao's. From December, 1958, on into 1964, China's industrialization has not only been "interrupted" but virtually sidetracked as his "high-speed" construction and production, bad planning, self-deceptive

[16] Su Hsing, "Study Comrade Mao Tse-tung's Ideology of the High-Speed Construction of Socialism," Peking *Jen-min Jih-pao*, February 25, 1960. The idea of "taking the whole country to be a chessboard," usually associated with the inactive politburo member, Ch'en Yün, is explicitly attributed by Su Hsing to Mao himself.

handling of statistics, and generally irrational (utopian) economic measures resulted in economic standstill.

When, in December, 1958, the Chinese leader shifted his emphasis away from the high-speed concept of "uninterrupted revolution," his defenders in the CCP stated that Mao had not been rash, and had not advocated "uninterrupted revolution" alone but also the theory of developing the revolution "by stages." Mao, they defensively insisted, had warned against "falling into the utopian dream of skipping the socialist stage and jumping over into the Communist stage."[17] But to concede this was to imply that Mao's "uninterrupted revolution" was managed no better than Stalin's, and in 1958 probably worse.

Where, then, is the unique aspect of Mao's "uninterrupted revolution"? It is, according to Philip Bridgham, the undertaking to establish progressively higher levels of collective relations of production *in advance of* industrialization and mechanization. Even Stalin, in the late 1920's, could boast of a large number of tractors before collectivization was undertaken in the Soviet Union, although in 1952 he placed theoretical emphasis on the primary importance of relations of production. Mao, however, could boast only of his vast labor army as the substitute for tractors and other agricultural machinery.

Thus "uninterrupted revolution" as applied to agricultural cooperativization and collectivization is the novel aspect of Mao's idea. It is in his statement on the cooperativization of agriculture in 1955 that we first find a uniquely Maoist concept. This was, as Mao put it in *On the Question of Agricultural Cooperativization* of 1955, as follows: "In the field of agriculture, under the conditions prevailing in China . . . we must develop cooperativization first, and only thereafter can we utilize machinery." This is a

[17] Shu T'ung, "Apply the Theoretical Weapon of Uninterrupted Revolution and Promote a Constant Leap Forward in Agricultural Production," Peking *Jen-min Jih-pao,* February 6, 1960. Shu, who was at that time writing as first secretary of the Shantung CCP Provincial Committee, has been replaced.

clear-cut departure from Lenin (as well as Stalin), whose view was that there must be agricultural mechanization *before* cooperativization can take place. It was a further departure when, in 1958, Mao called for an even higher level—collectivization—into "people's communes" before a significant number of tractors and other mechanized agricultural equipment had been produced. Both represented distillations from experience.

We agree, therefore, with the claim made by writer P'eng Chi-yün in the Peking *Jen-min Jih-pao* of January 5, 1962, that Mao's *On the Question of Agricultural Cooperativization* "further developed the Marxist-Leninist theory of agricultural collectivization." Another writer extended the scope of this claim by stating that Mao showed "originality in handling Lenin's cooperative plan" from the period of combining mutual-aid teams into the commune era.[18] This, too, seems to be a valid assertion.

### *Mao's Miscalculation*

Within five months after the commune program was given impetus by the CCP, it was apparent that the utopian aspects of it as enumerated above would have to be abandoned. The Chinese used various devices to camouflage the nature and extent of the policy reversal in December, 1958, and cushion its impact on party cadres and the people at large. Immediately following the sixth Plenum of the eighth CCP Central Committee which ended on December 10, 1958, at Wuhan, the CCP initiated a concerted effort to dissociate the party's leadership in general and Mao in particular from the more radical and unsuccessful features of the original commune program. A December 21 Peking *Jen-min Jih-pao* editorial denied that the commune had resulted "from utopian concepts or the commands of a few people," suggesting that such charges originated at the Central Committee's sixth Plenum earlier

[18] Wang Ch'ien, "The Transformation of Agriculture from Mutual-Aid Teams to the People's Communes," Taiyuan *Shansi Jih-pao*, October 4, 1959.

in the month. Liu Shao-ch'i admitted in a major published article nearly one year later (on October 1, 1959) that there had been "controversy between different views within our party on . . . the people's communes" and cited views — presumably expressed at the sixth Plenum at Wuhan — of party cadres that the communes were "set up 'much too soon,' were 'in a mess,' and 'outstripped the level of socialist development and level of people's political consciousness.'"

The commune distribution system — "according to need" — was a marked failure by the fall of 1958. It was destined to fail because it was based on a fundamental misconception of human nature, to wit, the view that psychological and spiritual incentives could be substituted for material incentives as the principal stimulus for production. Liu Shao-ch'i had to deny that this equalitarian idea had "encouraged idlers." As for Mao's expectation that the commune distribution system would control peasant consumption more effectively and therefore promote investment and economic growth, Chou En-lai was compelled to defend him in October, 1959, against the charge of critics that this control was tantamount to "keeping a horse running while giving it no feed." Thus, by the fall of 1959, many editorials and speeches had in effect exposed the emptiness of the original ideological pretension of Mao to have discovered a new, more advanced distribution system leading to Communism.

With these admissions, however, the Chinese leaders combined an intensive and repeated assertion that the communes had been the "spontaneous" creation of China's masses rather than of just a few leaders, or of even one leader. This developed into a line which was sustained throughout 1959 and 1960. A particularly remarkable defensive statement was made in November, 1959, by writer Ch'en Cheng-liang in a vehement reply to Soviet and Chinese Communist critics — that is "right opportunists" — who had questioned the voluntary nature of commune development:

> . . . in the winter of 1957 and the spring of 1958 many areas *voluntarily* merged small cooperatives into larger cooperatives so as to cope with production . . . and it was in this process that a few localities of Honan and some in other regions held aloft the brilliant banner of people's communes for the first time in China. The party warmly welcomed and supported this great *creation by the masses*. . . .
>
> The party's August 1958 resolution on communes gave a concentrated expression to *the will of hundreds of millions of people*. . . .
>
> Right opportunists find no "objective demand" for the commune movement . . . but they neglect the revolutionary *enthusiasm of more than 500 million peasants*, thus committing a basic political error. . . . The commune movement is a mass movement . . . of peasants who *demand* formation of communes. . . . Thus, contrary to views of right opportunists, the movement cannot "go beyond" their "consciousness." The movement is precisely an *expression of the consciousness of the Chinese peasants*.[19]

Ch'en continued on in this way at great length and with increasing vehemence and redundancy: the commune movement was "spontaneous and voluntary," the peasants "demanded" it, and all the party did was to give "expression to their will." The fiction of spontaneity became a major device for concealing Mao's miscalculation of the Chinese peasant's "Communist consciousness." When, therefore, Mao's chief Western eulogist, Edgar Snow, spoke to various Chinese including leaders of the CCP in the fall of 1960 during his trip to the mainland, he seems to have been impressed by the view that the commune program was a "more or less spontaneous development."[20] But this view is contradicted even by writer Ch'en Cheng-liang—if not by the knowledge

[19] Ch'en Cheng-liang, "The People's Commune . . ." (emphasis supplied).

[20] Edgar Snow, *The Other Side of the River* (New York: Random House, 1961–62), p. 431.

of how a Communist dictatorship operates *from above* — who stated that the commune movement "is a great creation by the party and Chairman Mao" and "the party and Chairman Mao discovered this form of social organization to develop the productive forces of our country."[21] Thus the Chinese Communist eulogists apparently have been directed to sustain the claim that the commune is Mao's "discovery" but, in doing so, to deny he had imposed his will on the Chinese people.

No amount of claims by his various eulogists can conceal the fact that in addition to other mistakes in concrete economic policy, Mao had overestimated the degree of "Communist consciousness" of the Chinese peasant in 1958. His view of what he and the CCP could do with the Chinese economy and people was marked by a kind of ideological hysteria, which his eulogists even today attempt to conceal by insisting that Mao always investigates, works primarily from concerte facts, and never permits romantic ("subjective") ideas to force his thinking. In the "great leap forward" of industry and agriculture as well as in the "people's commune," Mao saw a shortcut for millions of Chinese, the CCP, and himself to full Communism. Mao's view was that there would be an abundance of food and clothing for all Chinese under full Communism but that *until* that time arrived, the highly indoctrinated Chinese people would accept a low standard of living. His chief enemy, Khrushchev, slightly distorted Mao's view to mean that even *after* full Communism the people would have little to eat. In his report on *The Present Stage of Communist Construction and the Party's Tasks in Improving the Management of Agriculture* (March 5, 1962), Khrushchev by implication attacked Mao's view as tantamount to foodless Communism:

> The preaching of equality in the spirit of the first Christian communities with their low standard of living and asceticism is alien to scientific Communism. Com-

[21] Ch'en Cheng-liang, "The People's Commune. . . ."

> munism cannot be depicted as a table laid with empty plates and occupied by highly conscious and completely equal people. To invite people to such Communism is tantamount to inviting people to eat soup with a fork. This would be a caricature of Communism.

Mao provided Khrushchev with an easy target by rejecting the empiricism of the CCP's economists. He apparently has been sobered by the failures of 1958–59, but how long this will continue to be true will depend on whether Mao makes fewer demands on economics and the nature of the Chinese man and more on his own self-control.

To sum up, Chinese theorists acknowledge that Mao's view of the classical commune owes a debt to "utopian socialists" and Marx, Engels, and Lenin, but they insist that his "people's commune" is a further development of the classical concept. Specifically, the "people's commune" is said to be unique because it shows a new *way*, or action program, for advancing from collective to "all-people" (state) ownership and because it has wider competence in political, social, economic, and military fields than any previous commune concept. This claim seems to be valid. The attendant claim that Mao's idea of the "uninterrupted revolution" as appplied to post-revolutionary policies is an original contribution is spurious in most respects. Its only unique aspect is the warrant it provides for establishing progressively higher levels of collective relations in production *in advance of* industrialization and mechanization. The establishment of cooperatives in 1955 and of communes in 1958 were clear-cut departures from Lenin's "cooperative plan," in which he had envisaged collectivization only after thousands of tractors were available for use in the countryside. These departures and the techniques and methods associated with them constitute Mao's contribution to the program of rural collectivization for Communist-led regimes.

# Conclusion

Socrates said that he was wiser than his contemporaries because he alone knew that he knew nothing. This rhetorical device expressed a thought which was not to be taken too literally; it was simply intended to warn men against assuming they knew more than they actually knew. But this stricture against immodesty has long been buried by the eulogists of Communist leaders. Even Khrushchev, who has condemned Stalin for presuming personal omniscience, encourages Russians to create paeans of praise to his own wisdom. He has not, however, gone so far as Mao. The claims made for Mao's genius, vision, and infallibility are the most numerous and pretentious made for any living national leader. The Chinese Communists would have men believe in the validity of these claims, but, as we have tried to demonstrate, many are spurious. While rejecting his pretensions to great theoretical ability and insight, we acknowledge as novel certain formulations on practical matters.

We have shown that what is novel pertains primarily to the pragmatic policies Mao devised for attaining power and consolidating that power. To enumerate, the departures from "classical" doctrine are: describing anew the process of qualitative change in things, formulating the strategy for revolution as being protracted guerrilla warfare waged from self-sustaining rural base areas, including the small capitalists in the post-revolutionary political structure, devising the detailed method for "buying out" small capitalists, postulating a "non-antagonistic contradiction" between worker and capitalist, openly rejecting the myth that no conflicts between leaders and led exist under a Communist regime, encouraging non-Communists to criticize the Communist party, professing toleration of small strikes, organizing people's communes as a new socioeconomic formation, and collectivizing agriculture in advance of rural mechanization. With the exception of Mao's view of qualitative change, these "contributions" are departures from traditional doctrine and Soviet views on *practical matters*. We conclude, therefore, that the "thought of Mao Tse-tung" appears in the final analysis to draw its uniqueness from revisions, improvements, or even complete abandonment of various aspects of the foundation tenets and Soviet practices. And the view of Mao as an intellectual, whose erudition in philosophy surpasses that of any living Communist, is more picturesque than true.

### *Theory and Practice: An Ambiguous Dichotomy*

To say that he is a poor philosopher is not to scoff at his achievement, but to see it in a better light. Mao Tse-tung has attained his highest distinction as a Communist revolutionary leader. He fought a long guerrilla war brilliantly and made an enormous nationalistic peasant revolution work well. He has been extremely adaptable in this undertaking, revising or even abandoning the directives of the Comintern under Stalin when these did not square with the reality he was confronting. He formulated a new operational strategy, roughly within the framework of Lenin's general concept of establishing peasant soviets in backward countries. But he has attained no real distinction as a great theory-maker unless "theory" is taken to mean political stratagems rather than basic abstract principles. Thus he has not changed such basic concepts as production, accumulation, surplus value, exploitation, and economic determinism; he has merely repeated Lenin's emphasis on political control in discussing these concepts. He has provided no fundamentally new interpretation of any other basic principle in Marxist-Leninist theory but rather a gloss on some, particularly on the matter of rural revolution. The degree of allegiance Mao has displayed to the doctrines of Marx and Lenin has varied at different times, although he seems to have been more conversant with the views of the latter and of Stalin. He has either insisted on a rigorous fidelity to the original context of a particular tenet or has deliberately distorted or ignored the context, his primary guideline having been his needs of the moment.

Many of Mao's innovations in fact seem have been additions to rather than complete reinterpretations of theory. To be specific:

1. With respect to class struggle, he has not changed or rejected what Lenin said on the matter of using the bourgeoisie in backward countries during revolution. Rather than set forth a reinterpretation, he has used his writers to *add another group* — patriotic aristocrats, princes, and kings — to the class forces working for revolution. This tactical expansion of the united front has not been used by Mao to change, under the guise of enriching the basic theory of the bourgeoisie-against-proletariat struggle or Lenin's view that the Communist party is the representative or vanguard of the proletariat.

2. With respect to the dictatorship of the proletariat, Mao has not changed Lenin's view of the important concept, but has *added* the national bourgeoisie to the group of classes retaining political rights. The national bourgeoisie continues to be a suspect class and capitalists' property and minds are to be converted into state property and the "collective" mind.

3. Regarding the future Communist society, he has not changed Marx's view of distribution, town-country harmony, common ownership, and elimination of exploitation, but has *added* the concept that "contradiction" among men and between

various ideologies will continue to exist. His idea of "people's communes" does not reject and is not a reinterpretation of Engels' concept of "citizens' communes," but *adds* to the extent of its competence.

Mao has retreated from other innovations. These are:

1. He has drawn back from his aberration of 1958 regarding a rapid advance to the Communist society and super-collectivization before the national economy has been developed fully and industrialized.

2. He has retreated from the idea of a contradiction between leaders and led under Communist rule.

3. He has not reiterated his willingness, professed in 1957, to tolerate small strikes.

4. He will no longer permit, as he did in 1957, criticism of the CCP by non-Communists.

Whether Mao's most fully articulated and most important idea — namely, rural guerrilla revolution — constitutes a basic reinterpretation of theory is a difficult question to answer in simple terms. Although Mao assigned the peasants a somewhat greater role in revolution than had Lenin, he has not changed the basic tenet that even a peasant revolution must be led by the proletariat — that is, the Communist party. He has, however, developed a view of rural guerrilla warfare which had never before appeared in Communist literature on the peasants as a revolutionary force. That is, it had never been discussed despite Marx's statements on peasant armies and Lenin's comments on peasant revolution and peasant soviets. Vietnamese, Burmese, and Malayan Communists and the Cuban and Algerian guerrillas have drawn on Mao's ideas rather than on the "classical" texts for prosecuting their rural warfare. Mao's brilliant works on rural self-sustaining bases and protracted guerrilla warfare seem to be the "classics" of Maoism that will endure, becoming perhaps the Chinese contribution to the "classical" doctrine of Marxism-Leninism. Although other Chinese leaders have been more competent on purely military matters, Mao has not been surpassed as the systematizer of the political and military doctrine of protracted guerrilla conflict by any other leader of his time. Thus his eulogists insist that he made a new "theory" of revolution for all Communists.

Up to this point we have employed, in the interest of clarity, a rigorous distinction between theory and practice. Theory has been used to mean the abstract principles integrating a body of facts. In fairness to Mao, however, we must now turn to use "theory" as we have seen the Soviet Communists use it in discussing Lenin or Stalin. That is, *a "theory" is a statement or an idea meant to inform practice directly.* This reduces the dichotomy of Mao the theorist and Mao the practical man, compelling us to say that his changes in practice may well "feed back" and eventually stimulate permanent changes in accepted doctrine. Whether these changes will indeed become the permanent, orthodox, or "classical" truth will depend largely on the willingness of future CPSU leaders to view them as such. The present Soviet leadership continues to deny Mao *any* originality as a Communist theorist and ridicules *all* claims for him.

With respect to the degree of influence Mao's stratagems will have on various parties in the international movement other than the CPSU, this will in turn depend primarily on at least three factors:

1. The degree of anti-Chinese or anti-Soviet sentiment in these parties.

2. The local tactical situation. A pro-Soviet party in Latin America, for example, may still find it expedient to use some of Mao's rural guerrilla warfare tactics despite its loyalty to the CPSU, and a pro-Chinese party in southeast Asia may still find it expedient to take Khrushchev's "parliamentary road."

3. The local leadership situation. A national Communist leader may insist on his own reading of the "classics" and reject both Mao and the European leaders as final authorities.

To sum up the foregoing analysis, the "thought of Mao Tse-tung" may be viewed as the Marxist-Leninist legacy, plus certain new guidelines for rural revolution (and construction of the economy), minus certain conclusions found to be obsolete or incompatible with Mao's view of his own and China's interests. This definition is close in substance to Liu Shao-ch'i's as set forth in his *On the Party* (1945), but, as John K. Fairbank has noted, there is also a deep current of ethnocentrism underlying Maoism which provides it with a distinctive Chinese cultural nature. A newly emergent feature is Mao's view that the only "true" Communists are those in various parties who support him in his dispute with Khrushchev. This view appeared explicitly in CCP materials for the first time in 1963. It carried two implications: (1) the "thought of Mao Tse-tung" contains concepts which perpetuate Marxism-Leninism faithfully while the "revisionism" of Khrushchev has become illegitimate as doctrine, and (2) the "center of gravity" of the world Communist movement has shifted to the nations of the East, with China as the vanguard.

## *Mao's Political Style*

There appears to be a unique element in Mao's way of building a totalitarian political party. In the early period—that is, when Mao studied the works of foreign Communists in the 1930's and began to "bolshevize" the CCP in the 1940's—his texts were primarily those of Stalin. He began, however, in the early 1940's to infuse into the CCP a "style of work" which differed somewhat from that of the CPSU. Mao's organization became tighter than Stalin's had even been as the Chinese leader and his lieutenants developed indoctrination procedures which welded the party members to the CCP's regulations and cause in a remarkably firm mental commitment. The Russian Communist was indeed subjected to political indoctrination, but the Chinese Communist was subjected to it much more intensively, learning many things by rote and in closely controlled "struggle" groups. We agree with Robert J. Lifton on the following point: the requirement that the Chinese Communist identify himself with the party and its cause is more concrete and explicit than it was for the Russian. The man who played the biggest role in helping Mao build this highly disciplined party machine is his chief lieutenant, Liu Shao-ch'i, a gray, colorless man who nevertheless has the authority, prestige, and party position to take over the leadership when Mao retires or dies.

Maoist cleansing of the party ranks—the Chinese call it "party rectification"—has played a decisive role in maintaining an intense spirit of militancy and loyalty in the CCP. Certain Far Eastern parties are now trying to emulate this militancy. Mao has been successful because, in controlling the mental environment of party conscripts, he has been able to simplify moral problems (which should not be simplified), undermine elements of cultural heritage (many of which were worth retaining), and clear the vision for the sight of an absolute ideal (the achievement of which always was dubious and, in any case, gives a warrant for terror). There are today very few—only a handful—of defectors from the CCP primarily because Mao's way of instilling loyalty and responsiveness to the party is the most effective ever devised by any leader in the entire history of the world Communist movement. The Confucian strain in Maoism appears only as an aid used in CCP organization and indoctrination procedures. Applied Confucianism does not go beyond the matter of self-cultivation, self-examination, and study by rote. When, therefore, the master party-builder, Liu Shao-ch'i, cites Confucius and Mencius in his important work, *How To Be a Good Communist* (1939), he does so only for the purpose of instilling certain indoctrination methods and study techniques.

On the matter of handling political opponents within his party, Mao has proved to be more like Stalin than Lenin. He shows no real tolerance for active dissenters from his policies. He purges them.

While there conceivably is a real difference between Mao's

purge of Kao Kang and Jao Shu-shih in 1955 and Stalin's purges in the 1930's, certain similarities are striking. First, important party men *other than Mao*—Liu Shao-ch'i and Teng Hsiao-p'ing—conducted the proceedings against Kao and Jao; this is suggested by the available evidence. Various men other than Stalin personally carried out the purge trials of the 1930's in the Soviet Union. Second, Mao and his lieutenants attempted to *pre-date* the crimes of the accused in order to prove an early and continuous history of conspiratorial activity although, in fact, the plot probably had shorter historical roots. Regarding this technique, the prosecutors used by Stalin had shown Mao the way, as they had centered their attention on proving conspiracy early in the party careers of many of the men on trial. Third, Mao and his lieutenants attempted to show that the crimes of the accused were precisely concordant with the desires of the party's major enemy—"imperialism"—and that the accused had become *agents* of this enemy. Stalin's men had shown the way on this matter, too. Fourth, Kao, Jao, and the seven men who fell with them in 1955 have *not reappeared*. Kao, the Chinese say, expressed his "ultimate betrayal of the party by committing suicide" and Jao and the others presumably are in prison or dead.

If there is any real difference between this morbid operation and Stalin's purges, it does not lie in the degree of toleration shown the accused, but primarily in the fact that the CPSU conducted *public* show trials in the 1930's while the CCP maintained secrecy of proceedings. A purge which leads to the imprisonment or death of party leaders is no less bloody just because it is conducted behind a closed door.

Unlike Stalin, however, Mao has not pursued all dissenters from his policies with morbid vindictiveness. Chang Kuo-t'ao, a CCP leader who disagreed with Mao's tactics and deserted from Mao's organization to set up his own in the 1930's, is still permitted to live (in his refuge in Hong Kong); Trotsky was murdered (in his refuge in Mexico). Another early rival of Mao's,

Li Li-san, is still alive and has a relatively minor job in the CCP on the mainland. The Chinese Communists probably hope that the continued physical existence of these two men will "prove" that Mao is more tolerant of major opponents than Stalin was. But their continued existence proves only that Mao has shown restraint toward *two* dissenters. As for other major dissenters, in addition to the southwest Kiangsi leaders who were purged by Mao's supporters during the "Fut'ien Incident" of December, 1930, and the seven men who fell with Kao and Jao in 1955, Marshal P'eng Te-Huai, General Huang K'o-ch'eng, and central committee member Hung Hsüeh-chih are three major victims of the 1959 purge who have disappeared and are now probably under arrest. Moreover, politburo alternate, Chang Wen-t'ien, has also faded from the scene since mid-1961, apparently because he opposed the anti-Soviet views of Mao and his lieutenants.

The difference between Mao and Stalin on the matter of political tolerance emerges as one of degree of morbidity. Mao apparently prefers to appear as a compassionate rival while Stalin preferred to appear as a merciless one. That is, both men have physically destroyed party opponents, but Mao has made a greater effort to deny or conceal many of these acts of destruction.

Since Khrushchev's revelations in 1956 of Stalin's brutal handling of CPSU opponents, Mao has tried hard to dispel the impression that he handled former comrades in much the same way. Thus the Kao-Jao purge in March 1955 was the last Stalin-type operation of its kind; that is, it was the last extensive denunciation of party opponents among the CCP leadership. Subsequently, Mao has had his opponents removed *without fanfare*, as he would have outsiders believe that he is more lenient than Stalin was and than Khrushchev now is. He has implied that unlike the CPSU, the CCP has applied his "lenient" policy to major dissenters — that is, "treating the illness in order to save the patient." This is Mao's metaphorical way of describing the use of psychological terror to attain political obedience. While CCP documents frequently cite the above-mentioned phrase in connection with cleansing the ranks, the crucial first half of the treatment is rarely underscored. This half was formulated by Mao in *Oppose the Party "Eight-Legged Essay"* (1942) as follows: "The *first* method is to administer a powerful shock to the patients; yell at them, 'You're sick!' so that they are frightened and break out all over into a sweat. *Then* we tell them to take the treatment" (emphasis supplied). Mao's party spokesmen claim that because this method of cleansing the party ranks calls for thought-education rather than disciplinary punishment, he has further developed the Communist method of building a combat party. Mao's thought-education technique is indeed unique, comprising a new way to terrorize dissenters effectively and providing a "second chance" for those who would repent. It is decidedly not true, however, that Mao has rejected disciplinary punishment of his major opponents in the CCP.

In addition to his actions, Mao's expressed view of politics makes it clear that he rejects the liberalism of the Western democracies without reservation. His understanding of this liberalism is fragmentary and superficial. As a young man in normal college at Changsha from 1912 to 1918, Mao had "somewhat vague passions about 'nineteenth-century democracy,' Utopianism and old-fashioned liberalism," according to his statement to Edgar Snow. When he came under the influence of Ch'en Tu-hsiu and Li Ta-chao, however, these vague ideas of democracy were rejected. In *On the Correct Handling of Contradictions among the People* of June, 1957, Mao indicates that this rejection is permanent:

> Those who demand freedom and democracy in the abstract regard democracy as an end and not a means. Democracy sometimes seems to be an end, but it is in fact only a means. . . . Both democracy and freedom are relative, not absolute, and they come into being and develop under specific historical circumstances.

Democracy, for the Chinese leader, is clearly not a final goal. Regarding the matter of end and means, Arthur Koestler in *The Yogi and the Commissar* (1944) offers a perceptive analysis of the Communist mind which has *subordinated the means* to the end, and notes that the result is a slope-pattern which starts with the healer's knife and ends with the bloody Moscow purges. The fatal mechanism of this slope, Koestler says, was already known to Pascal: "Man is neither angel nor brute, and his misery is that he who would act the angel acts the brute." Now in the February, 1957, version of his speech on contradictions, Mao defended the killing of 800,000 regime opponents from 1949 to 1954 on the grounds that they were "enemies of the people." Even if the figure is accurate—although, in fact, it almost certainly had been pared down—the toll in human lives was heavy. Yet this is the most liberal speech that Mao has made since coming to power. It is a measure, therefore, of his revolutionary callousness and political intolerance that, even during the liberalization period, Mao insisted that democracy and freedom are "relative, not absolute" and that democracy is not an end—the position of a reactionary.

As for his tolerance of individual differences among men, Mao rejects all personal individuality and sharply attacks the Confucian and Western liberal ethic in his *Oppose Liberalism* of 1937. As for his tolerance of non-Communist political critics and opponents, he rejects any "benevolence" in handling them in his *On the People's Democratic Dictatorship* of 1949, arguing in effect that his dictatorship would nevertheless be a good tyranny.

### *Mao's Strategic View*

As for his view of the world beyond China, the militancy with which Mao approaches international questions is a reflection of his civil war experiences when his armies fought those of the Japanese and the KMT. Trotsky, to a considerable degree, and Lenin and Stalin, to successively lesser degrees, recognized the importance of revolutionary wars in colonial and semicolonial areas. Mao, however, has raised armed national conflict in the form of peasant insurrection to an unprecedentedly high level of priority. As a result of his experience in civil war, he has come to a strong conviction that a rural-based Communist army will place Communists in power with greater guarantees of permanence than any other kind of seizure of power. Mao clearly views himself as the "theorist" of revolution in underdeveloped countries; he has written very little about revolution in the Western industrial countries, confining himself on this matter to the statement that the October 1917 Revolution in Russia can serve as the example for revolution *in the West.* But it is an almost exclusive emphasis in Maoist materials published today on the mainland that Western influence *in underdeveloped countries* will be rolled back through protracted guerrilla fighting. For example, replying to Ambassador Adlai E. Stevenson's United Nation's speech in late December, 1961, in which reference was made to the Maoist stress on revolutionary protracted warfare, the Peking *Jen-min Jih-pao* authoritative writer, "Observer," stated on December 10, 1961:

> To put it frankly, all oppressed nations and peoples will sooner or later rise in revolution. . . . This is why Chinese pamphlets introducing guerrilla warfare have such wide circulation in Africa, Latin America, and Asia, and are looked upon as precious things, even after they are worn and have come apart and the print has become elligible through use . . . . the revolutionary theories, strategies, and tactics, summed up by the Chinese people in revolutionary practice and expressed in Comrade Mao Tse-tung's writings in a nutshell, are carrying more and more weight with the peoples of various countries. . . .

"In a nutshell," the enduring parts of Mao's works discuss revolution only as armed, rural-based revolution. Mao clearly believes that the classic-type revolution for the major Western countries, including Russia, is the short-lived coup in the cities, and that the classic-type revolution for all underdeveloped countries is the protracted conflict in the countryside similar to the revolution he led in China.

Yet another direct result of his experiences in China's civil war is Mao's policy to despise the United States as the main enemy. Mao is not talking about the present decade alone, but about the rest of the twentieth century as well. He is directing the CCP to make irreversible the hatred that not only this but the next several generations of Chinese should have for the United States. The United States, his propagandists say, owes his regime a "blood debt" on the matter of Taiwan. Of the few words Mao permitted Edgar Snow to quote from a long interview held in October, 1960, the following were included in his remarks on the United States: "Taiwan is China's affair. We will insist on this."[1] That is, the United States must withdraw from the defense of Taiwan and leave the Nationalists to the mercies of Peking's armed forces; there can be *no other way* to moderate the tensions between Washington and Peking.

Mao and his lieutenants apparently also feel that the minds of men in other countries can be turned against the United States to Peking's advantage. This belief was reflected in Premier Chou En-lai's statements to Edgar Snow in November, 1960, when he described the United States as the "common enemy." Chou's logic was that in order to force the United States to withdraw from the defense of Taiwan, the international struggle must be intensified elsewhere, not moderated:

> Looking at the development of the overall [i.e., strategic] situation, even if the US does not withdraw from the Taiwan region and no breakthrough occurs there,

[1] *Look*, January 31, 1961, p. 88.

> breakthroughs will occur elsewhere. . . . As to where the breakthrough occurs first, this depends on the development of the [anti-American] struggle.[2]

In view of this strategic estimate, Mao's formulation that the American "paper tiger" should be despised "strategically" is not at all adventurist. Because the Chinese leader does not expect an early rollback of American forces in the Taiwan Strait area, he and his lieutenants have fallen back on a policy which entails insignificant risks, namely, the strategy of encouraging breakthroughs (major United States defeats) *elsewhere.* When, therefore, Chinese Communists writers in *Hung Ch'i* in October, 1960, rejected the view of "some people" (the Soviet leaders) who hold that "it is incompatible to slight the enemy strategically and to take full account of him tactically at the same time," their meaning was simply that this formulation is not adventurist, inasmuch as the risk is a controlled one in the decisive tactical half of the statement. This cautious aspect of the "paper tiger" idea is an extension of Mao's earlier thinking on how to handle much stronger forces — the Japanese and KMT armies. In his lectures given in Yenan in the spring of 1938 (now known as *On Protracted War*), Mao laid it down that the CCP's policy for "decisive engagements" should be "to fight resolutely a decisive engagement in every campaign or battle when victory is certain; to avoid a decisive engagement in every campaign or battle when victory is uncertain; and to avoid absolutely a strategic decisive engagement which stakes the destiny of the nation." In extension of this latter point, Mao stated, "Even a gambler needs money to gamble with, and if he stakes all he has on a single throw of the dice and loses it through bad luck, he will not be able to gamble again. . . ." Mao clearly believes that many "great revolutionary wars" will result in a diminution of American influence

[2] *Ibid.*, p. 98.

in underdeveloped areas, and he is encouraging other peoples to fight them. But as for any war that Peking might feel compelled to fight, it is unlikely that he would "stake the destiny of the nation."

## *The Cult of Mao*

Mao's pride in his views on protracted war, like his pride in other personal views, has contributed to his craving for adulation. He has encouraged and elevated adulation of his own person to a level as mentally deadening and morally outrageous as any previous idol-worship has ever been. There is no significant difference between Mao's cult and Stalin's. The young people of China are urged to revere him as a demigod who can make no mistake in policy, as the following passage, appearing in the journal *Chung-kuo Ch'ing-nien*, January, 1963, indicates:

> As everybody knows, Chairman Mao at all times stands higher and sees farther than anyone else. . . . The way he looks at problems must be like standing on top of a skyscraper, looking out and down at the streets and highways below. Each path, each turn, each curve comes into his view. How is it possible for him to lose direction?

This passage exposes the hypocrisy of Peking's September, 1963, claim that "we are against dishonest and excessive eulogy of individuals and exaggeration of their role." We wonder if the more intellectual, reasonable, and sophisticated minds in the CCP are still able to respect the man who encourages the creation of such a fatuous image. These men would deny Mao the perfection attributed to him, realizing (with Kant) that man is at best a crooked stick; but they and non-Communist intellectuals must remain a silent minority. As for most Chinese, the image may well be acceptable because of the will to illusion—that is, the will to entertain certain beliefs regardless of their truth.

In depicting Mao as a leader-prophet, his propagandists have gone so far as to attribute implicitly a magical and an almost religious quality to his writings and to the man himself.

Regarding the magical quality of Mao's writings, the Chinese have gone beyond the practice of Stalin's eulogists, who praised their leader's works as "brilliant," to state that Mao's philosophical essays contain insights which can be applied to solve many *technical* problems. When workers at a Shanghai factory were confronted with serious trouble in fitting a steam engine into the hull of a fishing boat, they solved the problem by studying Mao's *On Practice* and *On Contradiction*, "applying the principle of concentrating on the main contradiction."[3] The Chinese have made even more ridiculous claims for Mao's philosophical works: for example, they have showed the way to solve technical problems in the use of lathes and in the manufacture of clothing. The Russians never went quite so far in advancing claims for Stalin and his works.

Regarding the quasi-religious quality of Mao's person, this image was developed with greater extravagance in 1963 and 1964 than ever before. Lei Feng, the martyred model soldier and CCP member, is said to have written in his diary that "the blood given by the party and Chairman Mao has penetrated every single cell of my body"[4] and that

> Yesterday I had a dream. I dreamt of seeing Chairman Mao. Like a compassionate father, he stroked my head. With a smile, he spoke to me: "Do a good job in study; be forever loyal to the party, loyal to the people!" My joy was overwhelming; I tried to speak but could not.[5]

Although the Russians at one time had worked hard to depict Stalin as a man of supernatural genius and virtue, the Chinese apparently have been more scandalous in their effort virtually to deify Mao. In 1949, the Chinese declared themselves against the

[3] Peking *Kung-jen Jih-pao*, October 8, 1963.
[4] *Chung-kuo Ch'ing-nien Pao*, March, 1963.
[5] Peking *Jen-min Jih-pao*, February 7, 1963.

celebration of the birthdays of their leaders and, in 1956, against the deification of their leaders. Nevertheless, they have in many other ways raised Mao's image to that level usually reserved for the divine or the prophet.

This image of Mao as leader-prophet will probably be used by his successor to maintain authority and prestige for the CCP in the world Communist movement. He now serves as the Chinese symbol in the CCP's dealings with other parties. The man most likely to take over Mao's dominant position when he retires or dies, Liu Shao-ch'i, apparently knows as well as any man the distinction between the pretense and the true character of Mao's omniscience. Liu probably will be obliged to abide publicly by this fiction once Mao, who was seventy on December 26, 1963, is gone. But the cult of Mao is now so ubiquitous in the CCP that Liu will probably be compelled to play down its more extreme, near-charismatic aspects in order to bolster his own authority and build an image of himself as an independent and creative thinker. He has already started the process in a small way, as his name is increasingly equated with Mao's in Chinese journals as a source of insight and inspiration. Liu's *How to be a Good Communist* was praised in February, 1964 in terms previously reserved for Mao's works alone: "an outstanding contribution to the Marxist-Leninist theory of party building"; [6] he is thus credited with having developed doctrine independently, as the theory referred to is classical doctrine rather than the "thought of Mao Tse-tung." The CCP is now re-writing party history in order to establish Liu as a major policy-maker in the party's earlier period.

The "thought of Mao Tse-tung" pervades the minds of most Chinese on the mainland more completely than other revisions

[6] Chao Han, "Forever Maintain the Revolutionary Spirit of the Proletariat — On Re-reading *'How to be a Good Communist,'" Hung Ch'i,* February 4, 1964. Liu apparently has increased his prestige among certain Asian Communists. For example, the North Vietnamese party in May, and the Indonesian party in September, 1963, praised Liu's works as valuable documents for their own party members.

of Marx ever did in any Communist-led nation. The Chinese Communist leaders view this situation as one of their unique advantages over the Soviet Union and the Western democracies, as total submersion in Mao's concepts and ideals is held to have the advantage of producing a great degree of social coherence and revolutionary militancy. And so it does. Yet there are major disadvantages in demanding acceptance of this near-fanatical set of beliefs. First, the demand arouses permanent hostility in those who do not share this fanaticism, and internal and external dissenters are constantly driven to respond with hatred rather than with forbearance. Second, in raising to the level of an absolute law the demand that adherents keep the Maoist political faith, those men in China who would establish important policies almost entirely on the principles of reason have been reduced to silence on many occasions. Thus the more fanatically loyal Maoists have been given free rein to tamper with the future of the nation.

Mao probably will advance his effort against the United States by using an opportunistic mixture of revolutionary militancy and revisionist flexibility. That Mao will not be constrained by doctrinal considerations when he sees an opportunity to make an advance is indicated by his handling of France's initiative. Mao responded by moving toward the French in late 1963 with considerable speed, leaving his doctrinal position on imperialism, which had been rigid in the wake of the advance, to be adjusted only in January, 1964. A loose dialectical formula was finally devised (in Peking *Jen-min Jih-pao*, January 21, 1964) on the "dual character" of leaders in capitalist countries, who allegedly want to free themselves from United States "control": "They therefore have something in common with the socialist countries. . . ." This concept — i.e., that imperialist leaders can co-operate with Communist-led countries — is a more formal and radical revision of doctrine than Khrushchev's description of some of these men as "sober-minded"; it is of a piece with a similar Maoist revision (made in Peking *Ta Kung Pao,* January 28, 1964): "part of the big entrepreneurs" in Japan can be included in the anti–United States united front. In this and other opportunistic ways, Mao will attempt to establish the view set forth in the January 21, 1964, editorial, namely, that "there is not a single country or people in the world today which is not subjected to . . . United States imperialism." Thus his foreign policy will remain centered on the United States in a no-compromise, hostile struggle, and he, Chou En-lai, and Chen Yi have made it clear in 1964 that an American withdrawal from Taiwan is *an unalterable precondition* for any possible reduction of Peking-Washington tensions.

# Index


Abd-el-Krim, 67
Acton, H. B., 22
Ai Ssu-ch'i, 11–12, 14–20, 146, 148
Aristotle, 98
Astrovityanov, K. V., 168

Babeuf, G., 175
Bakdash, K., 102
Bax, E. B., 176
Bridgham, P., 182
Brzezinski, Z. K., 133
Bukharin, N. I., 45, 48, 107

Carew Hunt, R. N., 2
Carlson, E. F., 58
Chang Ju-hsin, 31–32, 37, 39–40, 87–88
Chang Kuo-t'ao, 195
Chang, T. C., 43
Chang T'ai-lei, 33
Chang Wen-t'ien, 196
Chao Han, 204
Chen Mou-i, 144
Chen Tsan-wei, 92
Ch'en Cheng-liang, 170, 184–86
Ch'en Kung-po, 33, 42
Ch'en Po-ta, 18, 32, 34, 37, 51, 53–54, 176
Ch'en Shao-yü, 153
Ch'en Tao, 144
Ch'en Tu-hsiu, 29, 38, 197
Ch'en Yün, 116, 181
Chi Yün, 90
Chiang Kai-shek, 7, 46, 59, 116, 161, 163
Ch'ih Liao-chou, 178
Chou En-lai, 57, 63, 135–36, 153, 155, 162, 184, 200
Chu Chien-nung, 49
Chu Kuang-chien, 120–21
Chu Te, 57–59, 73, 91
Confucius, 194

Dimitrov, G. M., 94–95
Doolin, D. J., 164

Engels, F., 1–4, 8, 11–14, 16, 20–21, 26, 30, 34–35, 47, 50, 81–82, 106, 109–12, 114, 125, 127, 136–37, 163, 165, 174–78, 187, 191

Fairbank, J. K., 193
Fan Hung, 177–78
Fang Lin, 26
Faure, E., 135
Feng Ting, 148
Feng Yu-lan, 13
Fourier, F., 175

Gatovskiy, L., 173
Glazerman, G. E., 143, 146
Glazunov, E. D., 146
Gomulka, W., 133, 160
Gorky, M., 12
Gruson, S., 155, 158, 160–63

Hegel, G. W. F., 16, 140
Hilferding, R., 105
Hinkle, L. E., 131
Ho Chi-fang, 65, 68
Ho Ch'ien, 168
Ho Kan-chih, 38, 75
Ho Wei, 148
Hook, S., 106
Hsiao Chou, 24
Hsü Li-ch'un, 144
Hu Ch'iao-mu, 25, 29, 55, 59, 97
Hu Feng, 18
Hu Sheng, 17
Hu Tsung-nan, 60
Hua Kang, 43
Huang K'o-ch'eng, 196
Hung Hsüeh-chih, 196

Jao Shu-shih, 195–96

Kaganovich, L., 124
Kammari, M. D., 143
Kan Nai-kuang, 45
Kant, I., 202
Kao Kang, 195–96
Kautsky, K., 41
Kedrov, B., 20, 143
Kerensky, A., 85
Khrushchev, N. S., 4–5, 64–65, 67–69, 85, 98–101, 103, 132–33, 136–37, 149, 153, 167, 172–73, 176, 178, 186, 188, 192–93, 196
Koestler, A., 198
Kogan, L. N., 146
Konstantinov, F. V., 87, 143
Kuan Feng, 148
Kuan Meng-chüeh, 55
Kuan Ta-tung, 114
Kugelmann, L., 83
Kuo Hua-jo, 55

Lei Feng, 203
Lenin, V. I., 2–4, 8–21, 26–29, 30–31, 34–36, 38–43, 46–47, 50–52, 54–56, 65, 71–74, 76–79, 81–88, 90–93, 98, 101, 106–7, 109–12, 114, 125, 127, 134–38, 140–43, 145, 163–64, 166, 173–74, 176–77, 180–81, 183, 187, 189–92, 194, 198
Li Kuang-yu, 132
Li Li-san, 196
Li Mien, 77
Li Ta, 8–9, 20, 49–51
Li Ta-chao, 197
Li Wei-han, 117–18, 129–30, 132
Lifton, R. J., 193
Lin Piao, 57, 61
Liu P'ing-lin, 77, 81
Liu Shao-ch'i, 91, 128–29, 136, 153–54, 184, 193–95, 204
Lu Ting-i, 18, 151–53, 155

MacFarquhar, R., 164
Mach, E., 10
Mao Tse-tung: and agricultural collectivization, 114–15, 170, 182–83, 187, 189; on appearance and essence, 13; on class struggle, 190; on Communist dictatorship, 75–98, 102–4, 124, 190, 198; and Confucianism, 194; on contradiction, 14–22, 139–41, 144–57, 160–61, 163–67, 189–91; critics of in CCP, 65, 155–56, 170, 183–84; cult of, 5, 133, 154, 188, 202–4; and falsified dates, 22–27; on general line, 117; on guerrilla warfare, 54–59, 72–73, 188, 191–92, 199; international strategy of, 198–202; on knowing-process, 9–11; and liberalism, 197–

98; and national bourgeoisie, 17–20, 33–34, 50–52, 59, 74–75, 79–87, 95, 97, 102–3, 107–9, 111-16, 126–38, 147–48, 150, 164, 166, 189–90; and New Democracy, 79–80, 89, 93–94, 96, 105, 115–16, 118–21; on paper tiger, 59–71, 73, 201; as party-builder, 193–94; as peasant organizer, 30, 38–40, 44–50, 189; as philosopher, 7–8, 13, 21–22, 27–28, 163, 173, 189; place in Communist hagiography, 4, 9, 191; rejection of "ism," 6; and revisions of texts, 37–38, 48–49, 72–73, 79, 94, 157–58; on revolution, 39, 44–64, 88; "road" of, 54, 71–72, 91; on rural bases, 53–54, 71–73, 78, 188, 191, 199; Soviet treatment of, 5, 8, 14–15, 31, 55–56, 65, 67, 73, 86–88, 93, 100–102, 123, 133–35, 137, 151, 156–57, 159–60, 163, 171–73, 184, 186–87, 192, 201; on theory of truth, 11–13; treatment of opponents, 153, 194–98; treatment of Stalin, 139, 147, 153, 159–61, 163; and "true" Communists, 193; on uninterrupted revolution, 178–82; 187; as worker organizer, 30, 42
Mao Tun, 155
Martynov, A., 93
Marx, K., 1–4, 8, 13–14, 21, 23–24, 30, 34, 40, 50, 75–76, 82–83, 90, 106, 109–10, 112, 114, 125, 127, 134–38, 140–41, 156, 163, 165, 174–77, 180, 187, 190–91, 205
Mencius, 194
Meng Hsien-chang, 118–19
Middleton, D., 157, 159
Mikoyan, A., 98, 133, 137
Mitin, M. B., 56, 168
Mo Ti, 13
Mo Wen-hua, 55
Molotov, V., 99
More, T., 175
Morelly, 175–76
Moses, 158
Myat Htoo, 91
Nagy, I., 133
Nasir, G. A., 102
Nkrumah, 102

Ou-yang Yu-ching, 164
Owen, R., 175

Pang Tzu-nien, 146–47
Parvus, 179–80
Pascal, B., 198
Pashkov, A., 172
Pavlov, I. P., 129
P'eng Chi-yün, 183
P'eng Pai, 42–45, 48, 52, 73
P'eng Shu-chih, 37
P'eng Te-huai, 57–59, 73, 196
Pien Chang, 141
Plekhanov, G., 4, 41, 83
Plyshevskiy, I., 56
Po I-po, 132
Po Ku, 153
Pospelov, P., 96

Radek, K., 51, 84–86, 95
Roy, M. N., 36
Rozenthal, M., 20–21, 142–43
Russell, B., 98

Saint Simon, C. H. de, 175
Schwartz, B. I., 48, 54, 93–94
Sergivev, A. V., 100
Shao Li-tzu, 46
Shapiro, L., 104
Sharp, S. L., 93
Shen Chih-yüan, 20, 22
Sheng Shih-ts'ai, 26
Shepilov, D. T., 100
Shu T'ung, 182

Shu Wei-kuang, 127
Shub, D., 74
Shumiatsky, B., 33
Skilling, H. G., 93
Snow, E., 27, 56–57, 185, 197, 200
Sobolev, A., 56, 92–93, 131
Socrates, 188
Stalin, J. V., 2–5, 8, 13–15, 19, 21, 23–24, 30–34, 37–39, 45–47, 50–52, 55–56, 65, 67, 73, 75–78, 81–82, 84, 87–88, 90–93, 95–99, 104–6, 112, 115–17, 122, 136–37, 139, 141–47, 150, 159–63, 166, 171–74, 177, 180–81, 183, 188–90, 192–96, 198, 202–3
Stepanyan, Ts., 20, 145–46, 148, 156
Stevenson, A. E., 69, 199
Strauss, L., 13
Strong, A. L., 60
Su Hsing, 148, 181
Sukarno, 102
Sun Ting-kuo, 141, 147–48
Sun Tu, 70
Sun Yat-sen, 7, 36, 116

T'an P'ing-shan, 45–46
T'ao Chu, 134
Teng Hsiao-p'ing, 195
Teng Li-ch'un, 67
Teng T'o, 30
Ti Chao-pai, 98
Tito, J. B., 97, 134
Togliatti, P., 154
Toure, S., 102
Trainin, I. P., 96
Trotsky, L., 4, 35, 76, 78, 82, 165, 179–80, 195, 198
Tu P'ing, 66
Tu Shou-su, 77, 81
Tu Sung-shou, 44
Tung Pi-wu, 29, 33

Voitinsky, G., 33

Wang Chuan-shan, 13
Wang Ch'ien, 183
Wang Ch'ung, 13
Wang Tzu-yeh, 31
Whiting, A. S., 36
Wilbur, C. M., 33
Wittfogel, K. A., 4, 40, 47–48, 120
Wolfe, B. D., 3, 40, 104, 179–80
Wolff, H. G., 131
Wu Chiang, 67, 97
Wu Ch'uan-che, 108–9, 125–27

Yao P'eng-chang, 118, 121
Yaroshenko, 144–45, 171
Yefimov, G., 123
Yu Kuang-yüan, 17, 98
Yudin, P., 15, 20–21, 96, 142–43

Zagoria, D. S., 176
Zhdanov, A. A., 20, 142–43, 156
Zhukov, Ye., 91–92
Zinoviev, G., 84–86, 95, 107